BASIC TEXTS IN COUNSELLING AND PSYCHOTHERAPY

Series Editor: Stephen Frosh

This series introduces readers to the theory and practice of counselling and psychotherapy across a wide range of topic areas. The books will appeal to anyone wishing to use counselling and psychotherapeutic skills and are particularly relevant to workers in health, education, social work and related settings. The books in this series are unusual in being rooted in psychodynamic and systemic ideas, yet being written at an accessible, readable and introductory level. Each text offers theoretical background and guidance for practice, with creative use of clinical examples.

Published

Jenny Altschuler
WORKING WITH CHRONIC ILLNESS

Bill Barnes, Sheila Ernst and Keith Hyde
AN INTRODUCTION TO GROUPWORK

Stephen Briggs
WORKING WITH ADOLESCENTS

Alex Coren
SHORT-TERM PSYCHOTHERAPY

Emilia Dowling and Gill Gorell Barnes
WORKING WITH CHILDREN AND PARENTS THROUGH SEPARATION AND DIVORCE

Loretta Franklin
AN INTRODUCTION TO WORKPLACE COUNSELLING

Gill Gorell Barnes
FAMILY THERAPY IN CHANGING TIMES 2nd ed.

Fran Hedges
AN INTRODUCTION TO SYSTEMIC THERAPY WITH INDIVIDUALS

Sally Hodges
COUNSELLING ADULTS WITH LEARNING DISABILITIES

Ravi Rana
COUNSELLING STUDENTS

Tricia Scott
INTEGRATIVE PSYCHOTHERAPY IN HEALTH CARE

Geraldine Shipton
WORKING WITH EATING DISORDERS

Laurence Spurling
AN INTRODUCTION TO PSYCHODYNAMIC COUNSELLING

Paul Terry
COUNSELLING THE ELDERLY AND THEIR CARERS

Steven Walker
CULTURALLY COMPETENT THERAPY

Jan Wiener and Mannie Sher
COUNSELLING AND PSYCHOTHERAPY IN PRIMARY HEALTH CARE

Shula Wilson
DISABILITY, COUNSELLING AND PSYCHOTHERAPY

Invitation to authors

The Series Editor welcomes proposals for new books within the Basic Texts in Counselling and Psychotherapy series. These should be sent to Stephen Frosh at the School of Psychology, Birkbeck College, Malet Street, London, WCIE 7HX (email s.frosh@bbk.ac.uk).

Basic Texts in Counselling and Psychotherapy
Series Standing Order ISBN 0–333–69330–2
(*outside North America only*)

You can receive future titles in this series as they are published by placing a standing order. Please contact your bookseller or, in the case of difficulty, write to us at the address below with your name and address, the title of the series and the ISBN quoted above.

Customer Services Department, Macmillan Distribution Ltd.
Houndmills, Basingstoke, Hampshire RG21 6XS, England

CULTURALLY COMPETENT THERAPY

WORKING WITH CHILDREN AND YOUNG PEOPLE

STEVEN WALKER

First published 2005 by
PALGRAVE MACMILLAN
Houndmills, Basingstoke, Hampshire RG21 6XS and
175 Fifth Avenue, New York, N.Y. 10010
Companies and representatives throughout the world

PALGRAVE MACMILLAN is the global academic imprint of the Palgrave Macmillan division of St. Martin's Press, LLC and of Palgrave Macmillan Ltd. Macmillan® is a registered trademark in the United States, United Kingdom and other countries. Palgrave is a registered trademark in the European Union and other countries.

ISBN-13: 978–1–4039–3308–9
ISBN-10: 1–4039–3308–1

This book is printed on paper suitable for recycling and made from fully managed and sustained forest sources.

A catalogue record for this book is available from the British Library.

A catalog record for this book is available from the Library of Congress.

10   9   8   7   6   5   4   3   2   1
14   13   12   11   10   09   08   07   06   05

Printed in China

To Nina Farhi

CONTENTS

Introduction	**1**
Overview of the book	4
Terminology	5
1 Cultural Competence	**7**
Introduction	7
Conceptualising culture	10
Ethnicity and culture	12
Developmental resources	14
Diversity and difference	20
Globalisation and identity	21
Culturally competent practice	23
Case illustration	27
Commentary	27
Summary	30
2 Similarities and Differences	**32**
Introduction	32
Sociological perspectives	35
Identity formation	36
Generational influences	39
The culture of self-esteem	41
Preventive practice	42
Systemic and psychodynamic theories	44
Family therapy practices	45
Systemic and psychodynamic work	46
Contemporary developments	50
Summary	53
3 Integrating Theory, Skills and Values	**55**
Introduction	55
Integrating and complementing	57
Synthesising and blending	60

Establishing the therapeutic relationship 64
Empowering by relinquishing 66
Attachment and loss 68
The symbolism of eating disorders 71
Summary 73

4 **Socially Inclusive Practice** **76**
Introduction 76
Social exclusion 78
Social policy context 80
Therapy and cultural development 83
Socially excluded groups 85
Cultural dislocation 89
Elements of socially inclusive practice 91
Summary 94

5 **Assessment and Intervention** **96**
Introduction 96
Perceptions of child and adolescent
  problems 99
Assessment as process 102
Integrated intervention 105
Early intervention 106
Postmodernism, culture and therapy 108
Bonding and attachment 109
Integrating systemic and attachment
  theories 111
A culturally competent theoretical
  model 115
Summary 117

6 **Religion and Spirituality** **119**
Introduction 119
Religion and belief 121
Culture and spirituality 125
Child development 127
Psychology, religion and spirituality 130
The inner world of the child 132
Therapy and cultural belief 134
Summary 137

7 Fairy Stories, Myths and Legends   **139**
  Introduction   139
  Towards deeper cultural meaning   142
  Narrative therapeutic ideas   144
  Links between dreams/fantasies and legends   147
  Thematic analysis of myths and legends   149
  Engaging children and young people   151
  Movies, television and fairy tales   153
  Summary   155

8 Evaluating Practice and the Evidence Base   **157**
  Introduction   157
  Safeguarding children's culture   159
  The research evidence   161
  Children in families   164
  A children's rights perspective   165
  Including children and young people   169
  Ethical considerations   170
  Change and the evidence base   173
  The broader cultural view   174
  Summary   176

Bibliography   178

Index   210

INTRODUCTION

UNICEF has described worldwide progress towards improving the welfare of children and young people since the 1991 World Summit for Children as poor. Huge challenges exist in many South American, African and Asian countries to improve diagnosis and identification of troubled children, while in the industrialised countries of North America and Europe unprecedented levels of child and adolescent mental health problems are being reported (Lidchi 2003, Walker 2003b). Islamophobia, anti-Semitism, ethnic cleansing, genocide and increasing human rights abuses characterised the end of the 20th and beginning of the 21st century. Appalling and distressing imagery of the ability of humankind to violate and destroy each other in acts of uncontrolled rage or planned systematic torture and mass murder has become imprinted on our collective consciousness. What must children and young people make of the world around them and the behaviour of adults towards each other? What overt or covert messages are they picking up about the value of human life and about how to relate to other people? And what meaning do children and young people attach to behaviour rooted in a lack of respect for others' culture?

This is the global backdrop to the central purpose of this book which is to explore and understand how, by employing cultural competence in our therapeutic practice, we can reach out to children and young people from any religious, ethnic or social background and engage them in work that makes sense and is relevant to them personally. In so doing we may play no small part in contributing to the essential task of restoring fundamental societal values of respect, acceptance and concern for every citizen. If we demonstrate confidence and a willingness to acknowledge the importance of cultural differences and how they impact on a troubled young person's self-concept, then we are making a positive statement both socially and therapeutically. This book cannot, in the space available, address the historical, political and economic contexts that have brought us to this stage in the evolution of humanity, essential as they are to embed the text in the intellectual topography. Instead it will start from where we are and offer a scholarly resource combined with practical guidance for counsellors and psychotherapists and all those working in caring contexts with children and young people, seeking to improve and extend their therapeutic repertoire and manoeuvrability.

The last 20 years has witnessed the gradual relaxation of barriers previously preventing the movement of people within an enlarging European Union and increasing levels of global trans-national migration together with the exponential increase in air travel between continents. Combined with mass movements of refugees and asylum seekers either fleeing from persecution or poverty, countries are experiencing rapid sociological changes affecting the cultural and ethnic constitution of previously homogeneous societies. The notion of multicultural societies is not new and laws have been passed to protect ethnic minority communities against prejudice and discrimination for many years. Yet the outcomes for black children and young people are still always lower than for comparable white children and young people, whether we examine the data on exam results, occupational status, income levels or the negative numbers in juvenile justice, state accommodation and lone parenthood.

How can this be after years of equal opportunities policies, racism-awareness training, anti-racist training, positive discrimination and the gradual inclusion in therapeutic training of the subject of race and culture? Why are we all so hesitant, wary, cagey and downright scared about issues of 'race' and culture? What is it about these subjects that have the capacity to freeze us, leave us tongue-tied and afraid of saying or doing the wrong thing? The answer is not simple but it deserves an authentic attempt to find out and in so doing throw some light into the shadows where our fears and fantasies about working with difference roam. The literature on cultural competence in the helping professions is beginning to grow and this text contributes to the aim of providing an opportunity for those working in counselling or therapeutic contexts to reflect on their practice and think through some of the complexities attached to the subject.

Not many years ago, the term 'global village' was coined to describe how the world was shrinking metaphorically, through technological developments and the speed of mass communications resulting in the bringing together of different peoples and cultures. The optimists felt that this would enable greater understanding and sharing of values and mutual respect and tolerance. The pessimists felt that the closer we got, the differences between peoples would be magnified and result in conflict based on fear and rejection of alternative beliefs and customs. Economic disparity would then cause envy and anger, leading to discontent and hostility between peoples. History teaches us that nationalism – the political expression of a country's culture – can easily translate into expansionism, leading to imperialism and colonialism with dire long-term consequences after short-term benefits have been exhausted.

Until relatively recently you would have been hard pushed to find culture mentioned in therapeutic textbooks other than being included in a chapter on ethnicity or anti-discriminatory practice. Even then these chapters seemed to be at worst tokenistic or at best a belated attempt to provide some help to practitioners seeking knowledge and skills in working with a diverse community of clients whose needs had been traditionally neglected. Anti-racist texts especially in the more progressive social work, nursing and psychology fields were not uncommon in the 1970s and 1980s but their often hectoring tone and limited therapeutic utility left many feeling berated, criticised, emotionally bruised and intellectually unsatisfied.

The concept of cultural competence is a small tentative step to try to take away the anxiety and fear from exploring different ways of engaging children and adolescents, many of whom (from whatever background) would find it hard to access help for their psychological problems. Cultural competence is probably a provisional paradigm whose usefulness will no doubt rightly be exhausted as society continues to develop and mature. But it feels appropriate for now as a staging post along the road of self-discovery and improvements in theoretical and practical therapeutic concepts that are necessary to respond to the changing socio-cultural landscape. As we as a human race evolve, so must our therapeutic techniques and methods and models of practice so that no person is neglected, overlooked or denied access to the help of another human being because they are different.

This book aims to define a culturally competent practice by drawing upon psychodynamic and systemic theories in a unified way, rather than in the conventional, separate way. By illuminating the synergies between the two as they are applied in practice, this will help construct a culturally competent framework into a coherent practical basic text for modern students or qualified staff seeking to advance their skills in counselling or psychotherapy. In addition, sociological material is used to provide an important and often overlooked element impacting on the prospects for successful therapeutic engagement. Thus by demonstrating how seemingly different paradigms can be employed in a synchronised pursuit of improved process and outcomes, the book will mirror the capacity for practitioners to feel more at ease in working with cultural difference.

This book aims to fill a gap in the available literature that fails to fully address the needs of the changing demographic and ethnic tapestry of contemporary multicultural societies. The book will develop the dated concepts of anti-racist and anti-discriminatory practices that were necessary to challenge Western ethnocentric practices embodied in the classical psychodynamic and systemic textbooks, but which have often succeeded in paralysing practitioners and raised anxieties about potentially harmful practices. Cultural competence therefore moves into a different intellectual and emotional realm from the either/ or, punishment/guilt paradigm affecting therapeutic work with children and young people. This book seeks to liberate and empower practitioners seeking to meet the needs of all the troubled children and young people who come to them for help.

Overview of the book

This book will equip staff with the necessary skills and understanding to harness the unique cultural characteristics of individuals, families and groups in making effective assessments, care plans and interventions for troubled children and young people. The book will examine the concept of cultural competence through the prism of traditional and *avant-garde* therapeutic relationships. It will enable those in training or practice to explore a crucial practice resource in work with children and young people and the contribution of participatory practice to this experience. The chapters will offer theoretical and practical guidance for psychodynamic and systemic approaches, and assist practitioners in considering creative ways in which these might be used in working with individuals, families and groups in all communities.

Overall the book will guide staff through the full process from initial assessment, identification and analysis of risk, to the development, management and evaluation of intervention. It will empower practitioners to plan for non-stigmatising interventions rooted in psychodynamic principles and systemic practice. The book is organised exclusively for the needs of staff requiring clear, concise practice guidance in working with children and young people. Theoretical content will be balanced with consistent learning outcomes geared to competent qualifying levels for those embarking upon counselling, psychotherapy or family therapy accreditation. Beginning with an introduction to the basic concept of cultural competence and the variety of ways culture can be defined and reflected upon in therapeutic work and the theoretical foundations of psychodynamic and systemic theories, the book moves through a progression of descriptions of modern methods and models and how to integrate them as a means to offering culturally acceptable help. The crucial area of socially inclusive practice is critically examined and it aims to illustrate the culturally competent applicability of this way of working with dis-empowered and traditionally neglected service user groups.

Family assessment is illuminated with up-to-the-minute guidance and support for those in front-line stressful situations or those in secondary therapeutic intervention. Family support is described and discussed as an illustration of realistic and achievable ways of using a combination of psychodynamic and systemic skills and concepts in fieldwork contexts. Religion and spirituality are examined as essential components of many children and young people's cultural identity. These subjects are only recently getting the attention they deserve in the systemic and psychodynamic literature. The chapter on myths, fairy tales and legends assesses the relevance of these fantastic narrative tales to counselling and psychotherapy, which are often obscured by mainstream cultural hegemonic literature. The book concludes with an exploration of the concept of evidence-based practice with an analysis of the effectiveness and efficiency of contemporary inter-ventions. The importance of evaluating professional practice in this therapeutic area by harnessing the capacities and cultural strengths of the families and groups in which children and young people live will offer the reflective practitioner more resources to draw upon.

Terminology

The terminology in this book has been kept as accessible as possible within the confines of the editorial guidelines and the series' intended audience. It is necessary, however, to explain how certain terms have been used in order to at least offer the reader some context to under-stand their use. 'Culture' is used in places where it is specifically defined but elsewhere it is used in the sense of the organisation of experience shared by members of a community, including their standards for perceiving, predicting, judging and acting. 'Black' is used in the contemporary accepted sense of meaning that group of people who by virtue of their non-white skin colour are treated in a discriminatory way and who experience racism at the personal and institutional level in their everyday lives. 'Race' as a term is declining in use due to its origins in meaningless anthropological classifications by early imperialists seeking to legitimise their exploitation of indigenous land and wealth. It is a social construction but one which is still found in statutes, policy material and in common parlance.

'Therapy' is used in the generic sense to mean – in this text – counselling, psychotherapy or systemic practice that seeks to attend to the internal unconscious conflicts at the root of many psychological problems experienced by children and young people in the context of environmental influences and the interaction between the internal and external world of clients. Thus the term 'therapist' is used to describe those with formal registration and/or those using therapeutic concepts in professional training or work contexts such as social work, nursing, counselling, youth work and psychology.

'Ethnicity' is subject to much definitional debate in the literature but for clarity and brevity the term is used throughout this text to mean the orientation it provides to individuals by delineating norms, values, interactional modalities, rituals, meanings and collective events (Sluzki 1979). 'Family' is also a term around which there is some debate as it is both a descriptor and a socially prescribed term loaded with symbolism. In this book the term 'family' is used to embrace the widest ethnic and cultural interpretation that includes same-sex partnerships, single parent, step family, kinship groups, heterosexual partnerships and marriage, extended family groupings and friendship groups or community-living arrangements.

1

CULTURAL COMPETENCE

The men of culture are the true apostles of equality.
— Sohrab and Rustum

Introduction

The importance of counsellors and psychotherapists developing a culturally competent practice for working with children and young people cannot be overstated. If we are to truly reach them therapeutically and create the crucial relationship within which they can begin to understand themselves better then we need to work hard at knowing them fully. This means adapting and developing our methods and models of practice to fit the child – not the other way round. It means resisting offering a *monotherapeutic* experience to every child or young person regardless of their unique characteristics. In so doing we can engage them and enable their needs to permeate our working practices more comprehensively. It means ensuring that we do not make generalisable assumptions about a child or young person's home life, customs or beliefs from a cursory question or relying solely on information about religion, ethnic origin or family background (Parekh 2000, Hartley 2003, Kehily and Swann 2003).

Children and young people are developing psychologically in an external world in which information, and the power it has to influence and shape their beliefs and feelings have never been greater. Control and manipulation of that information is being concentrated in a few hands themselves closely identified with a narrow ideological doctrine that legitimates certain forms of behaviour, attitude and culture. Western developed countries led by America dominate the production, marketing and distribution of products representing brand names and iconic images aimed at maximising profit in the global marketplace (Hall 1993). Children and young people are viewed as consumers and in this context the nature of their indigenous culture is seen as another part of their identity to be moulded in order to maintain cultural conformity. Young people's desperate need to fit in, be included and be the same as other children is exploited relentlessly by corporations propagating certain values that reinforce the consumerist culture of the early 21st century.

Children and young people face considerable challenges in maintaining their cultural integrity in the face of institutional racism, homophobia, economic activity or migration patterns. The consequences may lead to significant emotional and psychological problems expressed, for example, by high rates of school exclusion among African-Caribbean children (Otikikpi 1999), suicide and para-suicide of gay and lesbian young people (Trotter 2000) or unemployment among Bangladeshi youth (Jones 1996). The cultural assets of minority children regularly go unrecognised, denied or devalued within the wider community (Newman 2002). It is crucial therefore that support offered by counsellors or psychotherapists includes opportunities to celebrate their heritage and creates links with other members of their cultural or social group. Children from migrant cultures are especially vulnerable to feelings of inferiority resulting in frustration, anxiety and poor school attainment (Spencer 1996). In the USA the promotion of resilience in black communities is an important strategy aimed at developing cultural confidence and enhancing problem-solving capacities (Reynolds 1998).

'Culture' is a word that appears in everyday discourse – so much so that as with much common parlance it ceases to require any great effort at understanding what it means. We all seem to know what we are talking about when we mention 'culture'. Yet the variety of definitions and interpretations of the word allow it an elasticity that is more a hindrance to clarity than a help. The increasing need to improve our therapeutic work with children and young people requires us to examine their changing cultural environment for evidence of how we might harness new ways of understanding them and their troubles. At a general level, culture is associated with high art, refinement, superior taste and so on, or there is popular culture which is associated with the masses, low taste, tabloid media and TV soap operas.

We can also acknowledge that there is a 'therapy culture' – that is, something associated with Western methods of responding to individual human psychological difficulties. Depending on the context, it can be used as a term of criticism implying that the problems of society are caused by the culture of therapy which posits people as victims and weak-willed (Masson 1988, Furedi 2003). Or it can be used in a benign sense illustrative of how advanced societies are becoming in attending to the stresses and pressures of modern life. What is certain is that those of us seeking to help troubled children and adolescents need to develop our understanding of how cultural influences affect, maintain and ultimately provide solutions to the psychological difficulties of young people.

'Culture' in the anthropological sense has come to mean the way of life followed by a people. This concept developed as the history of Western expansionism and colonialism encountered manifestations of difference around the world. These encounters prompted a reaction at several levels of consciousness. Politically there was a need to justify the appropriation of native land and resources, economically the imperial explorers required raw materials to service industrialisation, but *psychologically* there was a fear of difference that had to be rationalised – hence the early attempts at racial categorisation and efforts to construct order from diversity and chaos in human lifeways. 'Culture' can also be defined in opposition to nature – the product and achievement of human beings representing a rising-above of their natural instincts. In this sense human nature is typically understood as the opposite of culture. 'Culture' can also mean the difference between humans and animals – the capacity to use language and complex communication to symbolise that which is not present (Jenkins 2002).

Thus the bearers of a culture are understood to be a collectivity of individuals such as a society or community. However, the cultural patterns that shape the behaviour of children and young people in groups should not be confused with the structure of institutions or social systems, even though there is a link between them. We can think of culture in one sense as the organisation of experience shared by members of a community, including their standards for perceiving, predicting, judging and acting. This means that culture includes all socially standardised ways of seeing and thinking about the world; of understanding relationships among people, things and events; of establishing preferences and purposes; and of carrying out actions and pursuing goals (Valentine 1976, Haralambos 1988, Jenkins 2002). As the history of the past three centuries demonstrates, the impact of Western imperialism has reproduced its economic and political structures worldwide, resulting in the development of industrial societies in former agrarian countries that have disrupted cultural patterns.

Inequalities in the distribution of wealth among these newly developing countries have created expectations and increasing demands for fairer trade relationships. Globalisation combined with instant international communications has brought the consequences of these unequal relationships and the needs of poor nations closer to our attention than ever before. Thus, developed nations are confronted with a variety of cultures with a common experience of exploitation and a need to reconcile conflicting feelings, guilt, confusion. and responses. There is still a requirement for systematic knowledge about groups or categories of humanity who are more mobile and are attracted to Western lifestyles of wealth, materialism and welfare. In the early part of this 21st century the recent history of ethnic conflicts, population changes and poverty has prompted the emigration of refugee and asylum seekers towards the West.

The more privileged and comfortable strata of Western societies, as well as new urban communities in former agricultural economies, are facing the reality of desperately poor people who feel more and more marginalised and neglected. Resentment is a feature of the reaction of wealthier nations to inflows of dependent people and the realisation among refugees that they are not universally welcome. There is a need therefore to render knowledge about difference and cultural diversity coherent in order to inform public attitudes and social policy, as well as enhance therapeutic practice. One way of doing this is to attribute a culture or sub-culture to a broad variety of social categories. Hence we encounter relatively meaningless terms such as the 'culture of poverty', 'youth culture', 'pop culture', 'black culture' or 'drug culture'. There is even a 'refugee culture' that apparently explains the motivation of families from troubled or impoverished regions to take incredible risks to seek refuge and safety.

Conceptualising culture

Cultural competence can initially be understood in the context of a desire to improve our practice in order to meet the needs of the growing multicultural and ethnically diverse society developing around us. It assumes that historical and orthodox assumptions about human growth and behaviour have served their purpose in meeting the needs of troubled children and young people in particular circumstances and at particular points in time. Now in the early stages of the 21st century changes are required to address and respond to the psychological and emotional problems of a modern generation of families and offspring who cannot be easily fitted into existing theoretical paradigms. There is increasing evidence for the need to refine and develop our methods and models of assessment and intervention so that they are more relevant and accessible to children and young people from a much wider range of backgrounds than was the case in the not-too-distant past (Madge 2001).

This is not to say that children and young people in the majority ethnic communities do not require improved methods of help and support. They are being socialised and exposed to a quite different society than former generations. The pace of life, enhanced stressors, individualism and consumerism are blamed for producing heightened states of arousal and stimulation. Evidence has begun to emerge of genetic changes, the development of new illnesses and of course a range of new risk factors to their mental health – especially the availability of cheap psychoactive drugs and greater access to alcohol. Depictions of family life, for example, in children's literature has changed dramatically in the past 40 years from misleading idyllic paternalistic havens of safety and security to the grim reality of poverty, child abuse, divorce, mentally ill parents and personal and institutional racism (Tucker and Gamble 2001).

'Ethnicity' requires some clarification as another term that can be used in a variety of contexts but without much thought as to its meaning. Its use alongside the term 'culture' causes confusion especially when the two become almost synonymous. This is because there is no easy definition, but we at least need to know the complexities of the use of the term 'ethnicity' because it perhaps reflects something deeper and more ambivalent about the way we internally manage difference and otherness. Part of the problem lies in mixing up birthplace with ethnic identity. A white person born in Africa and a black person born in Britain can be defined by their ethnic grouping and place of birth. Further confusion has historically prevailed due to the way the official census data have been collated. In the UK, the methods of data collection since 1951 upto 1981 have altered from just recording the country of birth and the birthplace of parents, when there was no question on ethnicity. In 1991 a question on ethnicity offered a range of categories and in 2001 there were further changes to account for citizens with dual or mixed heritage.

The term 'race' is now generally accepted to be redundant as a meaningful scientific category; however, *the idea of race* as a general descriptor of assumed national, cultural or physical difference persists in society (Amin et al. 1997). The concept is embraced at the policy level with legislation such as the Race Relations Act in the UK and institutions such as the Commission for Racial Equality. Legislation such as the 1989 Children Act, the 2005 Children Act and Children's National Service Framework, which contextualise work with children and young people, expects practitioners to take account of a child's religious persuasion, racial origin, and cultural and linguistic background, without adequate guidance as to what is meant by 'race' or 'culture'. The issue becomes more complex when we consider census data that show the increase in numbers of children from dual and mixed heritage backgrounds and consider the particularly complex set of problems they can encounter.

Ethnicity and culture

The linkage between race, ethnic identity and inequality has been repeatedly established in terms of its effect on wealth, status and power. These socio-economic and other environmental variables are recognised as risk factors for the development of child and adolescent mental health problems. The data show that black and other ethnic minority young people and adults charged with anti-social behaviour are more likely to receive punitive or custodial disposals in the criminal justice system rather than community options geared to a better understanding of their causality. High levels of psychological problems are reported from male and female black populations within young-offender institutions. Socially constructed notions of racial difference thus remain a potent basis for identity – our sense of sameness and difference (Bilton et al. 2002). This has led to frequent criticisms of discriminatory and stereotyping attitudes by the legal system.

Earlier scientific work in the 19th and 20th centuries had attempted to conceptualise race and classify people in different countries according to their supposedly inherent superiority or inferiority. Similar comparisons were made on the basis of gender and class, which permitted the tolerance of inequalities based on innate biological differences. A eugenics movement was inspired by these findings whose aim was to improve the genetic stock of the human race by eradicating people with less than perfect genetic dispositions. In the latter part of the 20th century advances in genetic research were able to dismiss these earlier notions of racial hierarchies, classifications and the supposed link between biology and behaviour (Kohn 1995).

However, vestiges of these outdated concepts still survive at the popular level as people try to understand where they fit into an ever-shrinking world where much more is known about other countries, customs and culture. Cheap air travel, faster communication and the creation of refugee and asylum seekers from troubled areas are bringing images, experiences and feelings to our collective consciousness. Skin colour, language and religion are still interpreted as signifiers of more profound differences in abilities and outlook, as well as being used to justify discriminatory practices or outright racism. For some people the notion of white superiority is barely below the

surface especially in the context of a colonial history and latter immigration. Table 1.1 provides an example of the incredible cultural
diversity in the United Kingdom that belies populist notions of an
Anglo-Saxon monoculture. This is a clear example of an economically
successful country that benefits from immigration while perpetuating
xenophobia and racist hysteria reflected in popular media. It is

Table 1.1 People born outside Great Britain and resident here, by countries
of birth, 1991

Countries of birth	No. resident in Britain	% of Britain's population
Northern Ireland	245,000	0.45
Irish Republic	592,000	1.08
Germany	216,000	0.39
Italy	91,000	0.17
France	53,000	0.10
Other ECs	133,900	0.24
Scandinavia & EFTA	58,300	0.11
E. Europe & former USSR	142,900	0.26
Cyprus	78,000	0.14
Rest of Near & Middle East	58,300	0.11
Aust, NZ, & Canada	177,400	0.32
New Commonwealth	1,688,400	3.08
Jamaica	142,000	0.26
Rest of Caribbean	122,600	0.22
India	409,000	0.75
Pakistan	234,000	0.43
Bangladesh	105,000	0.19
Rest of South Asia	39,500	0.07
Southeast Asia	150,400	0.27
East Africa	220,600	0.40
West & Southern Africa	110,700	0.20
Rest of the World	566,200	1.03
Asia	231,000	0.42
North Africa	44,600	0.08
South Africa	68,000	0.12
Rest of Africa	34,300	0.06
USA	143,000	0.26
Rest of Americas	42,000	0.08
Total born outside GB	3,991,000	7.27

Source: Owen 1992–1995.

therefore important to understand the specific manifestations of cultural differences in every country rather than try to prescribe a universal explanatory theory. We need therefore to find an explanation for racial inequalities that can attend to the social construction as well as the individual internal construction of difference and the link with cultural competent practice.

Developmental resources

In considering the various ways in which children's mental health is understood, it is useful to consider some of the orthodox theoretical and research-based evidence on human growth and development as part of the standard repertoire of guidance available. Counsellors and therapists are expected to have a sound grounding in these subjects to help inform all aspects of their work with a range of child and adolescent age groups. The theories are vast and to do them justice would require more space than this text permits. Some of the classic authors and contemporary literature need to be critically reviewed as part of a professional and theoretical discourse that is notable for its lack of culturally competent concepts. They illustrate the way conventional child development is conceptualised offering a normative model of childhood that assumes a *universalist* application when it should be used as a limiting starting point requiring adaptation and amendment as you begin the process of engagement with your client.

A good starting point is in a sense where some of the theories end. Wherever the emphasis is placed on the spectrum of the nature-versus-nurture debate and any explanation for human behaviour in the literature, you need to be clear where *you place yourself* as a practitioner – not for the purpose of trying to prove a theory right or to convince yourself of the correct explanation for the behaviour of a child or young person, but to make more explicit your own personal bias. This is not a weakness, but a strength. A practitioner knowing where they stand and understanding there are other perceptions and beliefs about a child's development, and adopting an inquisitive, culturally flexible stance will be acting more in the child's best interests – rather than trying to defend the indefensible or answer the unanswerable.

Recent advances in genetic research and refinement of developmental instruments for assessing children and young people's emotional and behavioural health have concluded that to regard nature and nurture as separate and independent is an oversimplification. A more helpful answer to what shapes children and adolescent's mental health is *both* nature and the environment, or rather, the *interplay* between the two. Thus it is crucial to incorporate an understanding of culture and the way it can both shape your perception of a child and young person's psychological difficulties and affect that young person's perception of themselves. The multidisciplinary complexion of many staff groups working with child and adolescent mental health problems and the structural/ organisational changes towards more inter-agency and inter-professional working mean that a variety of counsellors and psychotherapists will be familiar with the orthodox developmental theorists. These suffice as a baseline starting point from which to modify and improve upon so that they maintain their relevance in a rapidly changing multicultural society.

Whether the ideas of Freud, Klein, Piaget, Eriksen, Skinner, Bowlby and others help or hinder the process of your work, the important point is that they permit the adoption of some intellectual rigour to the way your work is organised (Mills and Duck 2000, Beckett 2002). This can provide a framework within which the selection of assessment and intervention methods and models can take place. Crucially, it will enable a more systematic process to proceed in a recognisable direction or provide a knowledge base to discuss ideas put forward by other staff. This will be helpful in supervision, case conferences, legal proceedings or report-writing contexts. Sometimes it is helpful to acknowledge that there is no clear-cut explanation, or there are multiple interpretations for a child's emotional and behavioural problems that are concerning others.

Staff with a systemic or psychodynamic perspective can especially utilise theoretical concepts from social policy and sociology to add to their framework of explanation. This distinguishes their contribution from most other agency staff in child mental health work. The combination can be powerful, adding weight to professional arguments and provide authority for interpretations. They can also be burdensome and confusing and should therefore always be used cautiously. They enable a social model of mental health to be acknowledged alongside others and therefore more readily advance a culturally competent practice. The choice is again vast in the area of sociology alone. Marx, Durkheim, Mills, Parsons, Popper, Habermas and others offer a rich and diverse knowledge base (O'Donnell 2002). The important point is that the chosen theoretical preference can be identified and acknowledged, and a plan can proceed consistently within that premise.

The importance of reflective practice whilst undertaking culturally competent work with children and adolescents cannot be emphasised enough. In the process of using measures of human growth and development, it is crucial. This is because children and young people are constantly changing, as are their circumstances. Your assessment could be out of date within weeks, reliant on too few factors or based on inaccurate referral information. This requires a high level of concentration and alertness to changes that will be unique and unpredictable, as well as changes that appear to conform to a predictable developmental transition. Such changes may have nothing to do with your intervention and some may have everything to do with it. The key is in appreciating that developmental issues are significant and require you to have a good grasp of them (Thompson and Thompson 2002).

Human growth and development theoretical resources should be seen as part of a wide spectrum of potential, rather than deterministic, interactive causative factors in the genesis of child and adolescent mental health problems. Some social psychologists criticise the emphasis in child development theories on normative concepts and suggest enhancing the judging, measuring approach towards one that embodies context, culture and competencies (Woodhead 1998). An illustration of developmental measures is shown in Table 1.2 and should be adapted to every individual situation encountered and always be considered against the white, Eurocentric perceptions they embodied when first constructed. A more recent view of personality development lists five factors that combine elements of the older more classic ways of understanding a child or adolescent together with notions of peer acceptability and adult perceptions. Its simplicity and integrated structure offer a useful addition to other conventional schemas (Hampson 1995, Jones and Jones 1999):

Extroversion includes traits such as extroverted/introverted, talkative/ quiet and bold/timid.
Agreeableness based on characteristics such as agreeable/disagreeable, kind/unkind and selfish/unselfish.
Conscientiousness reflects traits such as organised/disorganised, hardworking/lazy, reliable/unreliable, thorough/careless and practical/ impractical.
Neuroticism based on traits such as stable/unstable, calm/angry, relaxed/tense and unemotional/emotional.
Openness to experience includes the concept of intelligence, together with level of sophistication, creativity, curiosity and cognitive style in problem-solving situations.

Table 1.2   Summary of developmental concepts

Theory	Age				
	1	2–3	4–5	6–11	12–18
Eriksen's psychosocial stages of development	The infant requires consistent and stable care in order to develop feelings of security. Begins to trust the environment but can also develop suspicion and insecurity. Deprivation at this stage can lead to emotional detachment throughout life and difficulties forming relationships.	The child begins to explore and seeks some independence from parents/carers. A sense of autonomy develops but improved self-esteem can combine with feelings of shame and self-doubt. Failure to integrate this stage may lead to difficulties in social integration.	The child needs to explore the wider environment and plan new activities. Begins to initiate activities but fears punishment and guilt as a consequence. Successful integration results in a confident person, but problems can produce deep insecurities.	The older child begins to acquire knowledge and skills to adapt to surroundings. Develops sense of achievement, but marred by possible feelings of inferiority and failure if efforts are denigrated.	The individual enters the stage of personal and vocational identity formation. Self-perception is heightened, but there is potential for conflict, confusion, and strong emotions.
Freud's psychosexual stages of development	The oral stage, during which the infant obtains its principle source of comfort from sucking the breast milk of the mother, and the gratification from the nutrition.	The anal stage, when the anus and defecation are the major sources of sensual pleasure. The child is preoccupied with body control with	The phallic stage – the penis as the focus of attention is the characteristic of this psychosexual stage. In boys the Oedipus complex and in girls	The latency stage, which is characterised by calm after the storm of the powerful	The genital stage whereby the individual becomes interested in opposite-sex partners as a substitute for the

Table 1.2 (Continued)

Theory	Age				
	1	2–3	4–5	6–11	12–18
		parental/carer encouragement. Obsessional behaviour and over-control later in childhood could indicate a problematic development in this stage.	the Electra complex are generated in desires to have a sexual relationship with the opposite-sex parent. The root of anxieties and neuroses can be found here if transition to the next stage is impeded.	emotions preceding it.	opposite-sex parent, and as a way of resolving the tensions inherent in the Oedipal and Electra complexes.
Bowlby's attachment theory	This stage is characterised by pre-attachment undiscriminating social responsiveness. The baby is interested in voices and faces and enjoys social interaction.	The infant begins to develop discriminating social responses and experiments with attachments to different people. Familiar people elicit more response than strangers.	Attachment to main carer is prominent, with the child showing separation anxiety when carer is absent. The child actively initiates responses from the carer.	The main carer's absences become longer, but the child develops a reciprocal attachment relationship.	The child and developing young person begins to understand the carer's needs from a secure emotional base.

| *Piaget's stages of cognitive development* | The sensory motor stage, characterised by infants exploring their physicality and modifying reflexes until they can experiment with objects and build a mental picture of things around them. | The pre-operational stage, when the child acquires language, makes pictures and participates in imaginative play. The child tends to be self-centred and fixed in her/his thinking, believing they are responsible for external events. | The concrete operations stage, when a child can understand and apply more abstract tasks such as sorting or measuring. | This stage is characterised by less egocentric thinking and more relational thinking – differentiating between things. The complexity of the external world is beginning to be appreciated. | The stage of formal operations characterised by the use of rules and problem-solving skills. The child moves into adolescence with increasing capacity to think abstractly and reflect on tasks in a deductive, logical way. |

Diversity and difference

Culture defines accepted ways of behaving for members of a particular society. But such definitions vary from society to society leading to misunderstanding and a failure to engage therapeutically in a helping relationship. Klineberg (1971) offered an example of just such a misunderstanding. Amongst the Sioux Indians of South Dakota, it is regarded as incorrect to answer a question in the presence of others who do not know the answer. Such behaviour would be regarded as boastful and arrogant and an attempt to shame others. In addition the Sioux regard it as wrong to answer a question unless they are absolutely sure of the correct answer. A white American teacher in a classroom of Sioux children and unaware of their culture might easily interpret their behaviour as a reflection of ignorance or hostility. In a therapeutic context we can imagine our reaction to exploratory questions which resulted in a silent response with consequent interpretations of resistance, with further attention being paid to that area. An understanding of the role of certainty and respect on the other hand could open up creative possibilities for engagement.

Culture is not static – it is an organic living entity with an external and internal presence. Any attempt to define it or them is bound to be provisional because people – and more especially children and young people – are developing rapidly at many levels of physicality and consciousness. They do so in an equally fast-changing and bewildering societal context that sets the scene for our understanding of culture. It is possible, however, to select some common characteristics that can help us think about the concept of culture in a more useful way that enables us to focus our therapeutic efforts to the best advantage of children and young people (Jenkins 2002):

- Culture is definitely human; it is the characteristic way that humans do things, rooted in our capacity for complex communication and reflexive relationships.
- It carries within it implications of controlled development and change. Culture is the medium within which human individuals grow and become competent.
- Culture is also a matter of differentiating human collectivities, and their characteristic patterns of behaviour, one from another.

It is important to understand the different ways in which child and adolescent development is conceptualised by diverse communities. In Western industrialised countries there is a more clearly defined division between childhood and adolescence compared with developing countries. The change is less pronounced and shorter in countries where the tradition of further and higher education is less and there is greater sharing of domestic or agricultural labour between adults and younger family members. There is an assumption in Western industrialised countries that adolescence has been stretched so that it covers a much greater time span than in previous generations. This is cited as a cause of much problematic behaviour and psychological problems in contemporary young people. There is also evidence of the earlier onset of puberty in the more affluent societies, and delays in the onset of menarche have been reported in girls who are exceptionally physically active (Beckett 2002). On the other hand children from non-Western countries or whose parents were raised there will have expectations and experiences based on a very different time span. Parents may have been married at the age of 12 or 13 years and perhaps have served as soldiers in civil wars, or been responsible for the care of several younger siblings.

Globalisation and identity

The term 'globalisation' has begun to feature in the literature reflecting profound shifts in the economic and social patterns of relationships between the richer industrialised countries and the poorer developing countries. It involves closer international economic integration prompted by the needs of capitalism, but also has demographic, social, cultural and psychological dimensions (Midgley 2001, Pieterse 2004). Consistent with the link between the social context of child and adolescent mental health problems, it is therefore important to consider the global context in terms of the challenges for building culturally competent practice.

Critics of globalisation argue that its impact is to maintain unequal power relationships between the richer and poorer countries so that patterns of wealth and consumer consumption in Europe and North America can be sustained. This involves the exploitation of labour and other resources in poorer countries, thereby preventing them from achieving a diverse and equitable economic and social structure within which health and social welfare programmes can develop. The consequences of globalisation are being noticed in the way traditional social care systems are taking on the characteristics of business ethics and commercialism (Dominelli 1999, Mishra 1999). One of the side effects of this process is the standardisation and conformity required for consumer consumption patterns in order to maximise profit. The consequence is the steady and inexorable erosion of traditional markers of indigenous cultural identity combined with the elevation of global branding.

This critique of the latest phase of capitalist development echoes earlier concerns about the impact on economic growth and subsequent erosion of traditional government policies of full employment and social welfare (Corrigan and Leonard 1978, Bailey and Brake 1980). A failure to fully develop social welfare services, or to have them subjected to the gyrations of speculative global financial markets, invariably corrodes the quality and the depth of services designed to reach children and families in personal and culturally appropriate ways. This means that services are pared to the minimum, oriented towards crisis intervention and designed in the narrowest terms to conform with inflexible eligibility criteria that limits access. These features are inconsistent with culturally competent practice that aims to spread accessibility, improve acceptability and enrich our creative potential to respond to a diverse society.

The paradox of globalisation is that as new varieties of cultural expression are encountered and celebrated there is an underlying impulse to impose a sameness by the powerful Western nations on the developing nations. Thus at a supra-national level there is a parallel process occurring – the individual rejection of difference by the powerful countries with the technology and military capacity to influence the majority powerless countries. This must both steer and reinforce the latent fear of the other inside individuals who then feel they have permission to reject black and ethnic minority families. This contradiction is further illuminated by government policies against racism and yet resorting to draconian measures to control the immigration of refugees and asylum seekers.

The globalisation of culture produces deeply contradictory states for individuals and groups, with consequences for the development of an integrated sense of self. Hence we observe the way black youth are regarded as predisposed to violence and disorder, which is interpreted by the police as evidence of anti-social predisposition, resulting in per-secutory oppression and aggressive reactions. On the other hand, black athleticism and success in international sport produces a celebra-tory image masking denigratory undertones (Briggs 2002). White youth can be seen and heard imitating black youth culture in terms of dress and accent, while African-Caribbean youngsters, for example, learn the patois of their grandparents, celebrate Rastafarianism wear-ing dreadlocks, which some regard as a hostile anti-establishment stance. Young Asian women are torn between the aspirations of their white peers for sexual independence and socialisation and the expectations of some parents for social restrictions and arranged marriage.

Culturally competent practice

Dilemmas in trends towards cultural competence have been highlighted by reference to the practice of forced/arranged marriages and dowry, genital mutilation of children and harsh physical punishments condoned by some societies (Midgley 2001). These practices can be used to counter the argument for respecting ethnic and cultural diversity and support the notion of universal values as the basis for competent practice. Ethnic rivalries and the pride in national identity on which they are based also sit uneasily with culturally competent aspirations of international collaboration and mutual understanding.

However, rather than seek answers to these difficult issues in an introspective way, this emphasises the need for therapists and their professional representatives to reach out to the international community with service users to continue to debate, discuss and strive for ways to discover solutions. In the area of child and adolescent mental health we need to understand the impact such practices and the beliefs on which they are based are having on the mental health and emotional development of those adults promoting them and the children and young people experiencing them.

Cultural competence has been defined as developing the skills in assessing the cultural climate of an organisation and being able to practise in a strategic manner within it. It has also been broadened to include any context in which workers practise in order to permit effective direct work at many levels (Baldwin 2000, Fook 2002). Whether at the strategic organisational level or the direct interpersonal level we can actively resist those pressures to conformity and routinised practice that, in often discreet and inconspicuous ways, can undermine efforts to practise in culturally competent ways. The requirements of social justice demand vigilance and creativity in order to contribute towards an emancipatory practice that can liberate both workers and service users from prescribed practice orthodoxies. Such practice is the antithesis of stereotyped, one-dimensional thinking and is characterised by

- a commitment to standing alongside oppressed and impoverished populations;
- the importance of dialogic relations between workers and service users;

- orientation towards the transformation of processes and structures that perpetuate domination and exploitation (Leonard 1994).

These characteristics are in harmony with culturally competent practice. They do not imply that therapists should reject statutory practice for the voluntary sector, childcare for community work or psychodynamic theories for advocacy. These simplistic oppositional devices do not help us manage the complexities and dilemmas in seeking different practice orientations (Healy 2002). The possibilities for creative practice within organisational constraints are there. They may be limited and subjected to pressures of time, but in the personal relationship with service users and particularly children and adolescents with mental health problems, the rewards are unquantifiable for both worker and client. Even introducing a small change in practice can have a much larger disproportionate and beneficial impact.

There is growing interest in the development of multidisciplinary and inter-professional working in order to maximise the effectiveness of interventions to meet the diverse needs of multicultural societies and service users (Magrab et al. 1997, Oberhuemer 1998, Tucker et al. 1999). The characteristics of such work apply in a framework familiar to health and social care staff working therapeutically. It begins with assessment, then proceeds through decision-making, planning, moni-toring, evaluation and finally to closure. It is argued that this common framework offers the optimum model for encouraging reflective practice to be at the core of contemporary work (Taylor and White 2000, Walker 2003a). Reflective practice offers the opportunity to shift beyond functional analysis to making active links between the value base, policy-making process, and the variety of interventions conducted.

Combining reflective practice with culturally competent practice, we have the opportunity to make a major contribution towards responding to the social policy aspiration of inclusion and anti-oppressive practice. In so doing we can facilitate closer co-operation between professionals coming into contact with vulnerable families on a shared agenda of challenging institutional and personal discrimination (Eber et al. 1996, VanDenBerg and Grealish 1996, Sutton 2000). Drawing together the elements of practice that can contribute towards a model of culturally competent care means it is possible to define cultural competence as a set of knowledge-based and interpersonal skills that allow individuals to understand, appre-ciate and work with families of cultures other than their own. Five components have been identified comprising culturally competent care (Kim 1995):

- awareness and acceptance of cultural differences;
- capacity for cultural self-awareness;
- understanding the dynamics of difference;
- developing basic knowledge about the family's culture;
- adapting practice skills to fit the cultural context of the child and family.

These are consistent with other work which critique the historical development of cross-cultural services and offer a model of service organisation and development designed to meet the needs of black and ethnic minority families (Dominelli 1988, Moffic and Kinzie 1996, Bhugra 1999, Bhugra and Bahl 1999). Culture has been defined as the sets of shared cultural perspectives, meanings, and adaptive behaviours derived from simultaneous membership and participation in a multiplicity of contexts such as geographical, religion, ethnicity, language, race, nationality and ideology. It has also been described as the knowledge, values, perceptions and practices that are shared among the members of a given society and passed on from one generation to the next (Leighton 1981). Four particular theories have been identified in modern systemic practice, for example, that attempt to harmonise systemic theory with cultural competence (Falicov 1995):

Ethnic focused – this stresses that families differ, but assumes that the diversity is primarily due to ethnicity. It focuses on the commonality of thoughts, behaviour, feelings, customs and rituals that are perceived as belonging to a particular ethnic group.
Universalist – this asserts that families are more alike than they are different. Hence, universalist norms are thought to apply to all families.
Particularist – this believes that all families are more different than they are alike. No generalisations are possible, each family is unique.
Multidimensional – this goes beyond the one-dimensional definition of culture as ethnicity, and aims at a more comprehensive and complex definition of culture that embraces other contextual variables.

An attempt to elaborate a theoretical framework for multicultural counselling and therapy suggests that an overarching theory needs to be employed that permits different theoretical models to be applied and integrated. The synthesis between systemic and psychodynamic practice offers a more comprehensive way of achieving this. In this way, both client and worker identities can be embedded in multiple levels of life experiences with the aim of enabling greater account being taken of the client's experience in relation to their context. The power differentials between worker and children and adolescents are recognised as playing an important role in the therapeutic relationship. Clients are helped in developing a greater awareness of themselves in relation to their different contexts resulting in therapy that is contextual in orientation and can, for example, draw upon traditional healing practices (Sue et al. 1996).

Ethnocentric and particularly Eurocentric explanations of emotional and psychosocial development are not inclusive enough to understand the development of diverse ethnic minority groups. Failure to understand the cultural background of families can lead to unhelpful assessments, non-compliance, poor use of services and alienation of the individual or family from the welfare system. By using an anti-discriminatory, empowerment model of practice we are ideally placed to work with other professionals in multidisciplinary contexts to enable the whole team to maintain a focus on culturally competent practice. For example, the increased demand for help from parents and children themselves suffering the effects of mental health problems has prompted policy initiatives to invest in and reconfigure child and adolescent mental health service provision in more acceptable and accessible ways.

The aim is to make them more accessible and acceptable to all cultures by improving multi-agency working (Davis et al. 1997, House of Commons 1997, Mental Health Foundation 1999). However, in order to be effective all staff need to address the different belief systems and explanatory thinking behind psychological symptoms. Skills and values are required to articulate these concepts in such teams. Challenging crude stereotypes, questioning implicit racism and simply ensuring that other staff stop and think about their assumptions can help. Combining with respectful consideration of indigenous healing practices within diverse populations can optimise helping strategies. The traditional methods and models of therapeutic practice have failed to take full account of cultural factors but contemporary literature is attempting to catch up. The following areas offer guidance to enhance your communication skills (Whiting 1999):

- Families may have different styles of communicating fear, grief, anxiety, concern and disagreement.
- Emphasis should be placed on listening with the goal of understanding the family's perspective.
- Care should be taken to explain to the family the agency culture.
- Steps should be taken to recognise and resolve conflicts which occur between the cultural preferences, understandings and practices recommended by professionals.
- Communication is enhanced if you can demonstrate sensitivity towards the family's cultural values.
- Appreciating the family's cultural understanding of the problem will help build a trusting relationship.

Case illustration

A family of Iraqi asylum seekers fled the country before the recent American and British invasion in 2003. The father Mohammad had worked in a civil service position in a government agency connected to the petroleum industry. He had been accused of passing information to the UN regarding breaches of the sanctions imposed on the use of oil revenues. Mohammad claims he was tortured and had death threats made against his wife and three children. The children are all under ten years of age and his wife Saleha is a nursery teacher. Some of the children speak very little English. The family have been dispersed to a market town in a northern county where there are very few Iraqis, or any families from Middle Eastern countries. The local Housing Department have referred the family to your office, following reports of racist attacks on the run-down council estate where they have been housed in emergency accommodation. A teacher has called your team three times in the past fortnight expressing concern about one of the children who is wetting and soiling in class, provoking bullying and humiliating behaviour from other children.

Commentary

Using a systemic perspective your first task is to make a map of all the people, agencies and services connected to this family. You will find it helpful to then make contact with as many as you can within a realistic timescale to start to plan your response. This information-gathering exercise will enable you to begin to evaluate the different agendas and perceptions of other staff working with or concerned with the family. Your priority is to establish meaningful contact with the family and gain factual evidence of racist incidents for possible criminal prosecution against the perpetrators, as well as offering a caring, sympathetic relationship. Bear in mind that the family are likely to be highly suspicious of your motives and will require a lot of genuine evidence that they should trust you. Their naturally defensive behaviour may come across as hostile/uncommunicative and you need to deal with this in a non-confrontational manner.

A translator/interpreter should accompany you, having been fully briefed beforehand about your task and the different roles each of you holds, to assess their suitability for this particular task. Do not assume that every interpreter is the same, and try to evaluate their beliefs/attitudes and whether there may be ethnic or religious differences between them and the family. For a variety of reasons they might be inappropriate for this task despite having the right language skills. Strict translation of words and terms will be unhelpful, therefore time needs to be spent on the interpretation of the interpretation. Right from the start you can better engage with the family by

- enabling everyone to have their say;
- circular questioning to enable expression of feelings;
- reinforcing the integrity of the family system;
- noting patterns of communication and structure.

Having established a helping relationship, a systemic perspective enables you to locate the family system within a wider system of agencies, resources and a local environment that is generally hostile. Your networking skills can mobilise the statutory agencies to provide what is required to attend to the immediate areas of concern and clarify roles and responsibilities. A case conference or network meeting can put this on a formal basis with an action checklist for future reference to monitor the plan. One option may be to plan some family sessions together with a colleague from another agency such as Health or Education. This could combine assessment and intervention work to ascertain medium-term needs whilst using therapeutic skills to help the family establish their equilibrium. The key is to enable them to re-establish *their* particular coping mechanisms and ways of dealing with stress, rather than trying to impose an artificial solution. Maintaining a systems-wide perspective can help you evaluate the factors and elements building up to form a contemporary picture of their context. Working with them as a family and demonstrating simple things like reliability and consistency will provide them with an emotional anchor – a secure-enough base to begin to manage themselves in due course. What the above tells us is that the subjects of culture, race and ethnicity are evolving all the time, as society changes and develops according to demographic changes, advances in social science research and the personal internal psychic changes happening as a result of external modifications to the environment, and vice versa. We can observe that previous assumptions about superiority, normality and behaviour among different peoples have been discarded. Thus we need to hold in mind a provisional understanding of what are at present acceptable as terms and descriptions to describe the diversity of populations. These may not be suitable in the changing landscapes of the future (Alibhai-Brown 1999).

Restricted conceptualisations of culture as a set body of information – something to be learned in order to better understand a child or young person – offer a static model for engaging with all troubled children. It is more useful to think of culture as a process for generating frameworks of perception, a value system and a set of perspectives. Knowledge about culture is not something external – to be found, memorised and then utilised. Cultural competence is therefore best understood as engaging in the process of transaction where we encounter difference and try to evolve our meaning-making skills (Tseng 2002).

Holliday (1999) takes up this notion by trying to distinguish between large culture and small culture, in which he emphasises the need to move beyond the orthodox definition of culture as related to ethnicity, national and international characteristics. Small culture is also distinct from subculture, which is normally taken to mean something within and subservient to large culture. Small culture in Holliday's meaning is a way of understanding many cultures in all types of social grouping which may or may not have significant ethnic, national or international qualities. Thus the apparent patterns and characteristics of cultures reveal on closer inspection the variations and variability within and between cultures in reciprocal patterns of influence.

A prescribed, normative and superficial notion of large cultural difference leads to an exaggeration of those differences, resulting in the psychological concept of 'other' reduced to a simplistic, easily digestible or exotic or degrading stereotype (Holliday 1999). An example from ethnographic research in Southall, West London, revealed that people there had a sophisticated understanding of culture and community. When asked what was meant by culture it became clear that a person could speak and act as a member of a Muslim community in one context, in another take sides against other Muslims as a member of the Pakistani community, and in a third, count himself part of the Punjabi community that excluded other Muslims but included Hindus, Sikhs and even Christians (Baumann 1996). Thus a more enlightened concept of culture accepts it is a dynamic, ongoing group process which operates in changing circumstances to enable group members to make sense of and operate meaningfully within those circumstances. For counsellors and psychotherapists it offers a way of illuminating the full inter-cultural complexity of our world.

Summary

Children and young people face considerable challenges in maintaining their cultural integrity in the face of institutional racism, homophobia, economic activity or migration patterns. The consequences may lead to significant emotional and psychological problems.

The cultural assets of minority children regularly go unrecognised, denied or devalued within the wider community. Children from migrant cultures are especially vulnerable to feelings of inferiority, resulting in frustration, anxiety and poor school attainment.

Cultural competence can initially be understood in the context of a desire to improve our practice in order to meet the needs of the growing multicultural and ethnically diverse society developing around us. Historical and orthodox assumptions about child development need to change to address and respond to the psychological and emotional problems of a modern generation of families.

Staff with a systemic or psychodynamic perspective can especially utilise theoretical concepts from social policy and sociology to add to their framework of explanation. They enable a social model of mental health to be acknowledged alongside others and therefore more readily advance a culturally competent practice.

Culture is not static; it is an organic living entity with an external and internal presence. Any attempt to define it or them is bound to be provisional because children and young people are developing rapidly at many levels of physicality and consciousness. They do so in an equally fast-changing and bewildering societal context that sets the scene for our understanding of culture.

Critics of globalisation argue that its impact is to maintain unequal power relationships between the richer and poorer countries so that patterns of wealth and consumer consumption in Europe and North America can be sustained. The consequence is the steady and inexorable erosion of traditional markers of indigenous cultural identity combined with the elevation of global branding.

Combining reflective practice with culturally competent practice, we have the opportunity to make a major contribution towards the social policy aspiration of inclusion and anti-oppressive practice. It is possible to define cultural competence as a set of knowledge-based and interpersonal skills that allow individuals to understand, appreciate and work with families of cultures other than their own.

Ethnocentric and particularly Eurocentric explanations of emotional and psychosocial development are not inclusive enough to understand the development of diverse ethnic minority groups. Failure to understand the cultural background of families can lead to unhelpful assessments, non-compliance, poor use of services and alienation of the individual or family from the welfare system.

2

SIMILARITIES AND DIFFERENCES

We – are we not formed, as notes of music are,
For one another, though dissimilar?
                                    – Percy Bysshe Shelley

Introduction

Counsellors and psychotherapists using a systemic and/or a psycho-dynamic approach to their work need to reflect on their use and understandings of the theoretical base from which their practice emanates in terms of cultural competence. Where did it originate from? What was the background of the person/people advancing such theories? What assumptions underpin the approach about notions of identity, beliefs and meanings? One way to begin this process is to consider the similarities and differences in both approaches as a reflection of the culture of each. In this sense, culture means the assumptions and commonly agreed characteristics, skills and tech-niques associated with work that can be identified as belonging to a prescribed form. The problem we encounter in embarking upon such a task is that within each approach, as they are examined more closely, there begin to emerge subtle and some not-so-subtle practice differences according to a number of variables such as

- location of work
- individual interpretation of the approach
- context of referral
- age of child or young person
- experience and skill of the therapist
- quality of supervision
- engagement of the client.

By acknowledging the variety of ways each of or a combination of these approaches are implemented you can begin to appreciate the challenge of trying to categorise something about which a great deal has been written, taught and experienced. In terms of cultural competence, counsellors and therapists have not usually been exposed to knowledge and learning resources that address in a comprehensive way the concept of culturally competent practice. In attempting to construct practices that can be applied universally and therefore be readily identifiable, taught and regulated, these and all other therapeutic approaches have tended to avoid the messy complexity, uncertainty and seemingly overwhelming task of ensuring that the approaches can and should be accessible to any and every child or adolescent.

As we have noted, child development theories offer both an opportunity and a challenge when trying to understand what is troubling a child or young person in the context of their age and perceived developmental stage (Winnicot 1971, Bollas 1991, Waddell 1998). Combined with assessment of parenting capacity and the influence of wider environmental factors, a multidimensional model offers an appropriate and ostensibly holistic tool for determining the aetiology, treatment and prognosis of the problem presented. Systemic and psychodynamic approaches used by counsellors and psychotherapists have both similarities and differences in their understanding and employment of such information. However, with careful examination it is possible to discern more similarities than differences, especially in the context of modern developments in the practice of family therapy and individual psychotherapy with children and young people. Both theoretical models have demonstrated a flexibility and ability to evolve and change over time, thus reflecting their essential reflexive nature and potential for culturally competent practice.

The strongest evidence for prediction of mental health problems in the developmental progress of children and adolescents across cultures is that of general family stress (Bagley and Mallick 2000). Looked at more closely, this includes the effects of physical, sexual and emotional abuse in the context of a climate of persistent negative family interactions. These findings are supported by other studies (Bagley and Young 1998, Kashani and Allan 1998, Vincent and Jouriles 2000) which seek to illuminate and distinguish the particular factors influencing those children likely to develop mental health problems. The factors include risks and resilience, thus a young person might be vulnerable to psychological problems but these are mitigated by unique or culturally generalised protective factors. Counsellors and psychotherapists seeking to intervene effectively have to carefully consider the various ways potential mental health problems are thought about, understood and communicated in every family, in every culture.

A number of studies compared levels of stress in adolescents and family functioning across different national boundaries including Canada, United States, Britain, Malaysia, India, Hong Kong and the Philippines (Bochner 1994, Bagley and Mallick 1995, Martin et al. 1995, Gibson-Cline 1996, Watkins and Gerong 1997). A meta-analysis of these studies found that the underlying causes of personal distress could be relatively similar between cultures (Bagley and Mallick 2000). Family dysfunction as perceived by the adolescent will therefore, with other perceived stressors, be a statistically significant predictor of various kinds of problem behaviours and emotional states in all ethnic groups. The conclusion is that there is possibly a measurable, culturally universal, aspect of the relations of adolescents to family and other stress in terms of emotional and behavioural problems, and impaired self-esteem. A causal pattern from stress to mental health problems cannot be demonstrated beyond reasonable doubt but it offers some evidence of important characteristics to consider when using a systemic or psychodynamic approach.

There is a fine balance between normalising behaviour attributed to various causal factors, and moving too quickly to subscribe to a formal psychiatric diagnosis or even formulating a hypothesis to be tested, inappropriately. Each way of conceptualising the presenting problem has implications for the short- and long-term outcomes of assessment and intervention. A failure to recognise and acknowledge significant mental health problems could be just as damaging to the young person and others involved with them, as could seeking to explain their behaviour with a definitive psychiatric diagnosis. In terms of cultural competence this issue becomes crucial because different children will be affected in different ways by such a label.

For some refugee and asylum-seeking young people, for example, it could be a relief to have an explanation for feelings and behaviour that they find hard to make sense of, whereas for others it could exacerbate feelings of blame, guilt and self-loathing. The enduring social stigma of mental health problems, combined with institutionally racist practices, provides an overall context for these feelings to be repressed, displaced or acted out. Child abuse is now recognised as a problem of significant proportions in most cultures and the emotional and psychological consequences are well documented in the literature (Doyle 1997, Brandon et al. 1998, Trevithick 2000). Yet, despite compelling evidence, practitioners still persist in ascribing other explanations for the behaviour or emotional state of minority ethnic individuals and families (Hill 1999). Even within cultures there are marked differences based on gender. A recent study of Australian children, for example, who had been sexually abused found that boys were more likely to be in contact with public mental health services than girls. Abused boys and girls were more likely to receive a diagnosis of conduct disorder or personality disorder.

Sociological perspectives

In addition to assessing the relevance of the orthodox developmental theories for a culturally competent understanding of child and adolescent development, there are other, less prominent but as important resources for counsellors and psychotherapists to draw upon to help inform therapeutic practice in this area. Sociology may be suffering from less emphasis in government policy and occupational standards guidance but it still offers a valuable conceptual tool to enable a rounded, holistic process of therapeutic assessment and intervention. Sociological explanations for child and adolescent mental health problems can be located in a macro understanding of the way childhood itself is considered and constructed by adults (James and Prout 1990):

- Childhood is a social construction. It is neither a natural nor a universal feature of human groups but appears as a specific structural and cultural component of many societies.
- Childhood is a variable of social analysis. Comparative and cross-cultural analysis reveals a variety of childhoods rather than a single or universal phenomenon.
- Children's social relationships and cultures require study in their own right, independent of the perspective and concern of adults.
- Children are and must be seen as active in the construction and determination of their own lives, the lives of those around them and of the societies in which they live.

An examination of the experience of childhood around the world today shows how greatly varied it is, and how it has changed throughout history. Contemporary children in some countries are working from the age of eight and are independent from the age of 14, whereas in other countries some do not leave home or begin work until they are 21 (Hendrick 1997, Alderson 2000, Bilton et al. 2002). The conventional developmental norms show how adults construct childhood and therefore how to measure children's progress and detect mental health problems. They are, however, set down as solid absolutes and are based on notions of adults' fears about risk and lack of confidence in children, and rooted in adults' own childhood experiences. These theories have had positive effects but they have also restricted the field of vision required to fully engage with and understand children and adolescents from the diversity of cultures in a multi-ethnic society.

Early childhood studies are beginning to challenge the orthodoxy in child development theories so that children are seen as accomplishing, living, competent persons rather than not yet quite fully formed people who are learning to become adults (Early Childhood Education Forum 1998). The idea that the stages have to be accomplished sequentially ignores the different pace at which different children change according to external and other influences. Adults simply need to reflect on themselves to see that adults of the same developmental age can be at very different stages of emotional maturity, skill and capacity. We therefore need to use concepts of development and orthodox definitions of child and adolescent mental health problems cautiously and sceptically. An appreciation of how these concepts are constructs reflecting historical and cultural dominant values, and how they reinforce the power relationships between adults and children is required.

In order to engage with these ideas, practitioners need to demonstrate and incorporate in routine practice an element of intellectual modesty. This can be difficult when workloads are increasing and demands on time are enormous, or there appears to be a risky situation to deal with. It is also hard to admit to not knowing or being confused or uncertain – these are not what managers, the public, parents and policy makers expect. Yet they may be a realistic and more accurate picture than presenting a neat, coherent explanation for a child's behaviour in a short timescale. The competitive power dynamics in inter-agency meetings or high-pressured conferences cannot tolerate ambiguity – they demand clarity, brevity and certainty. However, hasty judgements made to protect embarrassment or personal vulnerability can have long-term consequences for the children and young people with whom you work.

Identity formation

An ecological systemic theory of the psychosocial development of ethnic minority children and young people views development as a complex product of individual and contextual influences (Spencer 1999). It is relatively easy to understand the impact of societal, media and government policy influences on the emerging self-awareness of ethnic minority children confronted by crude stereotypes. What is harder to appreciate is the subtle processes underway in younger children as they transit particular developmental stages while trying to develop a sense of individual identity based on the significance attached to group membership (Frosh 1991). If we accept that the root of much psychopathology lies in disturbed or distorted developmental transitions then we must consider more carefully the *additional* burdens placed on ethnic minority children faced with more complexities to navigate.

The significance attached to particular ethnic group membership will itself of course be mediated by familial influences, genetic pre-disposition and temperament/personality characteristics unique to the individual. Thus in attempting to understand the experiences of children and young people we enter the paradox of trying to hold a singular concept of ethnic identity simultaneously with a *multiple* concept of individuation. Rather than accepting a systemic formulation of interactional influence or a linear psychodynamic formulation of personality development, we require a more sophisticated blend of the two. Given that the developing child's earliest social relationship with the environment is with the primary caregiver, the quality of this relationship will determine to a large extent the child's subsequent approach to relating to the external world. In addition to the inborn genetic and physical ability to organise experience, it will rely on the presence of others to provide certain experiences to develop adaptive capacities and strengths.

The developing child therefore builds mental representations from an early age, made up of external experiences and the internal experiences of thoughts, imagining, memories and dreams. Accessible memory is thought to begin at around 3 years although what actually gets represented may not be historically accurate because experiences have to be interpreted. These mental representations contribute to the organisation of present behaviour when presented with new situations as well as act as guidelines when we can identify situations which appear similar (Hughes 1999). Previous experience therefore leads to the development of expectations of ourselves and others in certain settings where we not only tend to expect particular responses from others but also try to elicit them. This can explain the persistence of habitual ways of relating and the power of resistance to change, which can be understood both as unconscious motivation and as systemic circularity.

If we accept that the role of the primary caregiver is fundamental then it is reasonable to assume that their relationship with the external world based on their early experiences provides a chain of experiences linked to the earliest relationship between ethnic minority peoples and majority cultures. History demonstrates the distorted, prejudiced and discriminatory values enshrined in the treatment of ethnic minority people bought and sold as human cargo for slave traders on the back of scientifically flawed theories of race and human nature. The effects of these ideas and the values of white supremacy have tended to be understood in terms of economic and social disadvantage – the external symptoms that are more easily recognised, quantified and addressed. Indicators of poverty, unemployment and educational attainment can be used to illustrate the effects as well as provide a tangible focus for efforts to mitigate them.

However, what is more difficult are the *psychological* effects of generational experiences of immigrant families subjected to overt hostility, discrimination and disregard. What are the accumulated internal interpretations of generations being treated as sub-human, worthless and a threat to 'normal' society? The responses and ways of adapting to life in a racist society are obviously as varied as the unique characteristics of individuals and families. However, we can go some way to better understand the impact by accepting certain common experiences as possible options. These can provide us with clues about how to organise our work along more culturally competent lines.

The psychodynamic flight-or-fight response can serve as a useful starting point, offering as it does a framework within which to measure specific individual and family responses to stress or threat. We also need to keep in mind the notion of generational adaptation – a way in which each new generation of ethnic minority children and young people use the experiences of parents/grand-parents to screen or filter their own particular contemporary challenges. The evidence suggests a spectrum of adaptation to the psychosocial experience of discrimination from denial through to outright hostility. These have been captured and typified as the adopted black child found bleaching itself in the bath through to militant black power organisations seeking to influence younger generations of black children.

So in order to think more comprehensively about meeting the needs of children and young people from ethnic minority communities we need to start with the developing influences and interrelationships within their family. And we must understand these as fluid, organic processes rather than as static or *unidimensional*. In other words, within each separate family there will have been several periods of experiences and events that have shaped opinion and beliefs about themselves as a family and as a black family. For example, a prevailing belief about white people may have been challenged or even overturned in the light of a new experience – negative or positive. Equally, an assumption about the status of black people in society could have been reinforced and hardened over time.

This is where a mixture of systemic and psychodynamic concepts and practices can be most helpful in understanding the way individuals evolve and grow within a family environment. These are in turn influenced by the experience of being part of a community. In inner-city areas where there is a richer cultural and ethnic mix of peoples there is a context for black families to test out their beliefs and assumptions with those who have a shared understanding. Neighbourhood interactions, informal or formal support systems and sources of information help families measure their individual experiences. As part of our work, we need to be able to elicit these multiple levels of understanding in order to better assess the most effective culturally competent way to help.

Generational influences

Childhood and adolescence are today incomparable with previous generations' experience of these developmental periods in a person's life. Within cultures, the experiences are perhaps more acute because of the additional stressors and the context of children from different cultural backgrounds attempting to mediate between living relatives and their customs and expectations, and the external reality of urban street life characterised by an individualistic, materialistic child and youth culture. For the adolescent, the transition from childhood to adulthood is at its simplest a time of change, perhaps more intense than other bio-psychological stages, but a time of change nevertheless.

The link between the biological/physical and the psychological changes are manifested more acutely in terms of sexuality and the development of a sexual identity. Here, we have the ingredients for potential earlier traumas or interrupted infant development to resurface with a vengeance. The extensive literature offers the benefit of studies, research and case-history analysis to help inform our understanding of the deep-rooted processes at work that can produce psychological problems for young people. These are, in the main, based on classic texts that have served as a foundation upon which to build hypotheses, assessments and helping strategies aimed at alleviating the distressing symptoms through individual insight/awareness, behavioural changes or systemic interventions to mobilise family support.

As we have seen, developmental theories have applied a universal set of descriptions of the characteristics of these changes, each with their own focus (Freud 1905, Piaget 1953, Erikson 1965). These were of course based on observations and analysis of mainly white European infants and children at a time when mass immigration and migration were unknown. Critics refer disparagingly to dead white men's theories and their irrelevance to modern multicultural societies (Beckett 2002). However, they serve as a useful foundation on which to build a more refined and realistic set of tools to help us understand the lived experience of children and young people from a diverse set of backgrounds. They are after all part of the culture of scientific inquiry that as with all theories was relevant in its day but requires amendment and improvement to stay useful in modern contexts.

There is a useful literature on how children develop their own racial or ethnic identity as well as the origin of their racial attitudes towards others (Milner 1983, Robinson 1995, Madge 2001). Evidence suggests that children become aware of ethnic differences at an early age. Studies have claimed, however, that black and white children expressed white-skin preferences. Others suggest that the interpretation of these studies does not take sufficient account of the influence of adult attitudes or of the level of awareness of racial discrimination and prejudice. These questions are important for us seeking to work more effectively with all children and young people because of the impact these preferences have on self-esteem and ethnic identity.

Rodriguez et al. (2002) have constructed a useful schema for charting the stages through which ethnic minority children may develop as they progress towards forming a coherent ethnic identity. Mapping this against conventional developmental stages, we can note that in the early pre-school years the child begins to develop some sense of ethnic awareness but that it has little social significance. As the child moves through latency, she/he identifies with a specific ethnicity and understands the social significance. After latency the child comes to understand the social significance of ethnicity and realises that it is immutable and will not change. In late adolescence the maturing child is able to begin to build a strong sense of identity and can feel a commitment to a particular ethnic group.

The culture of self-esteem

According to some authors it is important to consider the specific meanings of subjectivation that emerge for adolescents in cross-cultural, multicultural and cultural contexts, who may be struggling to develop a cohesive sense of self (Cahn 1998, Bains 2001, Briggs 2002). If we accept that identity is based on issues of sameness and difference and consider the broad sense of culture meaning to fit in and be the same as other peers, then we begin to gain a sense of the *power* of being part of the majority and the fear engendered by being in the minority. For all adolescents the issue of fitting in – being the same and not standing out – is crucial, perhaps more so for females who require an element of gender solidarity to help manage the sexualised undercurrents of much school-based interaction.

We also need to distinguish between those black and other ethnic minority adolescents who live in multi-ethnic and culturally diverse communities and those who live outside major towns and cities or in rural areas where their difference is much more visible. Another variable is the length of time spent within a certain area or resident in the country. If a young person is still trying to orientate to the separation and disjunction caused by sudden relocation, perhaps under stressful or dangerous circumstances, then their experience will be qualitatively different to an adolescent born in the country into a settled ethnic community. The key is to avoid generalisations and assumptions about the way a particular adolescent is developing their own sense of self and unearthing some of the culture of self-esteem.

The brutal context of racism – both personal and institutional – has been conceptualised as a denial of the individual and a projection by those experiencing primitive and powerful feelings of unbearable aspects of themselves. Racist bullying has been quantified and identified as a risk factor in the development of self-esteem and in mental health problems in young black children (Aggleton et al. 2000). On its own it may not trigger depressive/anxious problems or conduct disorder, but combined with other risk factors such as poverty, bad housing and unemployment it could provoke the start of eventual serious mental health difficulties. As a reaction to this painful discrimination, the black adolescent may withdraw from contact with white peers and retreat to her/his cultural group. This can then lead to superficial assumptions by practitioners about different ethnic communities being 'inward-looking' and unwilling to interact with the majority culture. Thus a circular process begins whereby self-fulfilling beliefs are used as evidence of the failure of multiculturalism and as reinforcing notions of ethnic minority groups as separate.

At the individual level this personal and institutional discrimination will feel like persecution and resonate with a sense of badness within (Perret-Catipovic and Ladame 1998). At the developmental stage of forming an identity and beginning the process of separation from parental influence, the black adolescent is struggling to be understood within the family arena while absorbing an internal model of self-esteem of not being tolerated for being different. Thus the negative experience in this domain is anticipated, making it all the more important for us to assess in our therapeutic work whether, for example, a defence is dysfunctional or functional (Bains 2001). Indeed there may be more potential for psychopathology in certain individuals who resort to maladaptive methods of managing this contradiction. Evidence from North American systemic studies of ethnic minority children suggest that the Asian American adolescent fears rejection and being cast out by the family as a sanction against rebelling. This compares with the white American who fears being grounded or held within the family as a result of misdemeanours. Thus it is posited that the Asian young person has to struggle to stay within the family whereas the white young person has to struggle to get out (Berg and Jaya 1993).

Preventive practice

It is important not to be overly influenced by the negative connotations of causes, definitions and consequences. Too much emphasis on spotting emerging or established mental health problems in ethnic minority children and young people could unwittingly increase persecutory feelings and paranoia, thus provoking negative interactions that could lead to psychological disturbance. Focusing on pathology can distract from the critically important role of prevention. An ecological paradigm that understands the individual young person in an interactive relationship with their particular environment is a helpful point of departure in seeking to explain the internal and external stresses producing mental health problems. A health education framework that tackles the consequences of drug and alcohol misuse, combined with targeted early intervention and provision of accessible services in high-risk groups, is another important factor. Finally, given the significance in interpersonal problems as precipitating factors in the triggering of mental health difficulties, life skills education and training should be emphasised at known developmental crisis points such as pre-adolescence (Hawton et al. 1998). Psychodynamic and systemic practice can be harnessed in such preventive roles.

Prevention is better than cure. One of the difficulties in engaging children and young people as well as others in preventive practice is the stigma and prejudice attached to mental health problems. The statistics show how relatively common these problems are, and how very common for the less severe conditions or mild forms (ONS 2001). Yet the phenomenon is either cloaked in secrecy with people ashamed to admit to suffering in this way or it is portrayed in dramatic, dangerous and disturbing imagery. In the context of children and young people, it gets mixed together with other notions reflecting the demonisation and denigration of young people. With black children there is an additional factor that sees their behaviour in terms of outside normality, primitive and beyond control.

This is a powerful cocktail of ideas, and in the hands of a generally irresponsible media, it can feed the general public with distorted or unrealistic perceptions of child mental health problems. Further stigmatisation can occur when mental health problems are linked with aggression, criminality and unpredictability. This can exaggerate public fears about young black people with mental health problems. Also people find it easier to see mental health problems belonging to others rather than themselves or their children. This protects against powerful feelings of vulnerability and that most threatening of ideas – that everyone is capable of becoming mentally unwell. We need to achieve a high level of personal insight as therapists if we are seeking to enter the troubled lives of clients and not be deflected or distracted by our own internal vulnerabilities.

Culturally competent practice is about understanding apparent psychological difficulties in a broader context than narrow diagnostic criteria or the absence/delay of developmental stages. It means working more in partnership with the child, young person and their family to understand their perspectives, in their language and in their belief systems. It is also helpful to consider why similar children and young people in similar circumstances have not succumbed to emotional or behavioural problems. What stopped them from having the same experience, what protective factors within the culture worked for them and might be replicated? Discovering this kind of evidence can enable you to formulate preventive strategies and reduce the risk/vulnerability factors for others in the community.

Systemic and psychodynamic theories

Modern family therapy and systemic ideas that have developed from it are generally credited with emerging, in the 1950s, as a result of a number of developments in the fields of psychology, communication theory and psychiatry. At a broader level it is also important to acknowledge the socio-economic context of post-Second World War economic expansion, population growth and the significance of cultural changes affecting people's attitudes to sex, marriage, leisure and intimate relationships. The 1950s in the developed industrialised countries were therefore a time of rapid sociological change and economic growth, when new ideas were more easily articulated and received. Thus there was a broad cultural change and scientific ideas that sought improvements in the way psychological problems were addressed.

One of the important factors that stimulated the embryonic ideas that were to grow into a new form of psychotherapy was the need to build upon the traditional psychoanalytic model of individual therapy. This individual psychodynamic model was constructed on the basis of theories of the unconscious, psychosexual development and defence mechanisms that offered elegant explanations for internal conflicts leading to anxiety, depression and more serious problems resulting in interpersonal difficulties. New research that demonstrated effectiveness when groups of people were brought together to talk about their problems began to influence practice. Two key figures stand out as influential at this time in moving forward the ideas that were to crystallise in the practice of systemic practice. Ludwig von Bertalanffy (1968) was a German biologist who devised a general systemic theory that could be used to explain how an organism worked, by studying the transactional processes happening between different parts. He understood that the whole was greater than the sum of its parts and that we could observe patterns and the way relationships were organised in any living system.

Gregory Bateson (1973) and others in the USA took this concept of a general systemic theory and combined it with the new science of cybernetics and applied it to social systems such as the family. Cybernetics had introduced the idea of information processing and the role of feedback mechanisms in regulating mechanical systems. Bateson used this notion to argue that families were systems involving rules of communication and the regulatory function of feedback that influenced patterns of behaviour within them. In the UK, Ronald Laing (1969) challenged the orthodoxy in psychiatric practice by arguing that schizophrenia was a product of family dysfunction, while John Bowlby (1969) moved from treating individuals to treating families where an individual was displaying mental health problems.

The idea began to take root therefore that individual experiences within families were continually being shaped and influenced by the evolving interaction patterns of communication. Individuals were not therefore determined by early traumatic experiences or distorted developmental transitions, as the prevailing therapeutic orthodoxy argued (Freud 1973, Segal 1975, Yelloly 1980). Systemic thinking conceptualised that individual personality and identity could change along with changes in family dynamics. From this common root theory – systemic theory – a number of models and methods of family therapy practice evolved through to the present day (Walker and Akister 2004).

Family therapy practices

The characteristics of structural family therapy stem from the technique of observing the interactive patterns in a family. Once this baseline of behaviour can be understood as contributing to the problem, a structural approach would seek to highlight these, interrupt them when they are happening and then get the family to re-enact them in different ways that lead to different outcomes. The attraction to practitioners in this way of using family therapy techniques is that it aspires to provide families with problem-solving practical solutions while maintaining a strict normative structural hierarchy. In a family session therefore the task is to enable the family to try out different ways of doing things – for example by coaching a parent on how to maintain a boundary or limit the behaviour of their child.

The strategic family therapy approach, in contrast to the structural approach, does not have a normative concept of the family that should exist according to set hierarchies and sub-systems of parents/ children, etc. Rather, the focus with strategic family therapists is on the day-to-day interactions which have resulted in problems and the cognitive thinking being applied to solve them. The perceptions people have about these problems invariably influence how they try to tackle them. In this way a culturally competent therapist will focus on the perceptions within the family system rather than seek to impose one. Attempted solutions and behavioural responses that actually maintain the problem require challenging and shifting to alternatives promoted by the therapist.

The development of the Milan systemic model began in Italy, in the 1970s, where a group of psychiatrists were experimenting with treating individuals diagnosed as schizophrenic in a radically different way to the orthodox methods then employed. This is an example of a challenge to the prevailing culture within Anglo-American practices from a team influenced in their thinking by their particular cultural context. They reported better outcomes when they worked with the whole family rather than the individual patient. The central theoretical idea informing this approach is that the symptomatic behaviour of a family individual is part of the transactional pattern peculiar to the family system in which it occurs. Therefore the way to change the symptom is to change the rules of the family.

The goal of this therapy is to discover the current systemic rules and cultural myths which sustain the present dysfunctional patterns of relating, and to use the assumed resistance of the family towards outside help as a provocation to change. Change is achieved by clarifying the ambiguity in relationships that occur at a nodal point in the family's evolution. Milan systemic therapists do not work to a normative blueprint of how an ideal family should function (Burnham 1986). This approach furthermore emphasises the importance of the underlying cultural beliefs held by family members about the problem which affected behaviour. It avoids being perceived as blaming the non-symptomatic members of the family by working on the basis that the actions of various family members are the best they can do (Dallos and Draper 2000).

Systemic and psychodynamic work

Supervision – Family therapy has had a rare openness in relation to exposing practice to wider scrutiny. Apart from the use of video recordings as a way of analysing the complex family patterns of interaction that are impossible to track during an interview, they can also be used as a training tool. Family therapy sessions are usually supervised live, involving at least another person observing the session and offering feedback and suggestions during the work or at a planned mid-point break. The person/s observing are able to gain a different perspective to the worker involved with the family and spot important aspects that may benefit from a supportive suggestion. This notion has been developed to include the use of reflecting teams whereby the people behind the screen/mirror join the family and the worker in front to openly discuss their perceptions. Individual-oriented psychodynamic therapists or counsellors who have usually undergone intense personal analysis are also expected to open their practice to scrutiny and supervision whether in public or private practice. Convergence is occurring nowadays whereby family therapists are coming under pressure to demonstrate a degree of personal therapeutic experience before qualifying as registered therapists.

Context of problems – is more than anything perhaps the most defining characteristic of family therapy practice. It means that whatever the problem being presented to you as a practitioner using systemic or psychodynamic theory you will automatically begin to ask a series of questions that are linked to the context of the presenting problem. This relates to not just the family context but the wider professional, public, socio-economic and cultural context of the problem. In other words it is an ecological approach in that it posits not just individuals as inter-linked within families but families as inter-linked in communities that are in turn inter-linked to class, ethnic groups and cultures. It is a way of beginning the reframing process and looking at the problem from a different angle so that the concept of blame begins to be eroded and replaced with the concept of understanding the patterns that create and maintain the current problem. For example, one favourite question asked by many family therapists at some point to each member of a family is 'If this problem were to disappear what problem would be left to concern you?' This illustrates the different way of working compared to approaches that can unwittingly reinforce the family's dependence on a particular problem. Understanding the overall context of the problem offers another way of tackling it rather than seeking to change an individual or indeed trying to change a family.

Circularity/patterns – is a characteristic of psychodynamic or systemic styles of work. It is a foundational assumption of all therapists that problematic behaviour is conceived as forming part of a reflexive, circular motion of events and behaviours without a beginning or end. Being able to spot the circular process and articulate it in a meaningful way with the individual or family offers a positive way forward. This releases the therapist and the family to think beyond linear causality and blaming or scapegoating behaviour. The important distinction when using this conceptual framework is where abusive adults use grooming behaviour and their power to abuse children and young people. In these child protection cases and in domestic violence situations the motivation and responsibility need to be firmly located with the perpetrator. The circular understanding of problems offers an elegant explanatory tool for the reasons for the symptoms and other dysfunctional behaviour. Within a family, any action by one member affects all other members and the family as a whole. Each member's response in turn prompts other responses that affect all other members, whose further reactions provoke still further responses. Such a reverberating effect in turn affects the first person, in a continuous series of chains of influence (Goldenberg and Goldenberg 2004).

It is important not to take theoretical concepts to a level of abstraction where they cease to be useful. It is easy to be seduced into the technocratic skills and mechanisms of therapeutic working at the expense of missing individual human responses in families or individuals members and yourself to what emerges during a therapeutic session. You may become an efficient therapist in terms of technical ability, but will be experienced as cold, distanced and emotionally unavailable.

One way of guarding against this is to do some preparation before embarking on the work by reflecting on your own individual experiences within your family system. This includes early childhood memories which you may want to prompt with the use of photographs or familiar objects and places. Try constructing your own family genogram using the symbols and example in Figure 2.1. Draw connections between other family members you feel close to or distanced from. Think about the family history and culture going back several generations by drawing writing pen pictures of grandparent relationships and characteristics/behaviours/mannerisms. By recalling those poignant stories or significant events that affected you and your family, you can begin to appreciate the impact of your own interventions with families and individuals.

This exercise should help you maintain contact with the real feelings and experiences generated when working at a therapeutic level with client families or individuals. Some of you will find this exercise too distressing or uncomfortable while others will find it enlightening and empowering. You may find it helpful to conduct the exercise jointly with a trusted colleague or friend, or even a family member. Be prepared for a powerful experience and anticipate the need to talk it through with someone afterwards – this might be a team leader or counsellor or a friend who is good at listening in a non-judgemental way. Knowing yourself is a prerequisite for modern therapeutic practice, and is very much the case for working

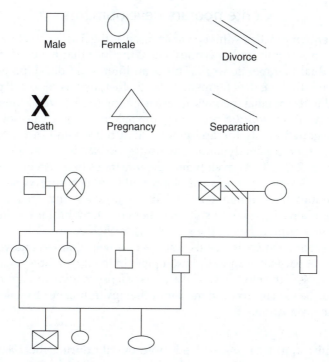

Figure 2.1   Genogram symbols and illustration of a three-generational family.

with families where you are engaging them at a deeper level. Understanding your own family culture and heritage and the events and issues that have shaped all the individuals within it offers you some personal insight into the meaning of culture and the deep feelings of identity it evokes.

Thinking about your own community and where you come from as well as the idea of what it feels like to expose the past and explore its impact on the present is a powerful experience. A thorough knowledge of your family process can help you avoid over-identifying with a similar family or help avoid persecuting a different family. Awareness of your own feelings of vulnerability and sensitive family issues can prepare you for negotiating these in a more sympathetic and thoughtful way with families and individuals you work with. A sophisticated understanding of culture will enable you to consider the multifarious nature of the term 'culture' and how it can protect you against assuming knowledge and understanding of similar people when in fact you are very different.

Contemporary developments

Convergent practice – this is characterised as the narrowing of the gap between systemic and psychodynamic theories that have informed individual therapeutic work. This is an interesting development in the sense that the development of family therapy has come full circle round to the original theoretical base it sprang from. Several contributors have discussed the previously unspoken notion of a combined or integrated family therapy practice that reflects and incorporates elements of psychodynamic therapy (Pocock 1997, Larner 2000, Donovan 2003). This development demonstrates that systemic theory is still a flexible, evolving paradigm within which approaches and techniques have remained fixed in some ways and changed in many others. This should suit practitioners who whilst interested in particular approaches to their work, nevertheless, are agile enough to incorporate ideas and skills that can best help children and young people at particular times. An example is in the use of interpretation. This is one of the most powerful aspects of a psychodynamic approach that can be seen mirrored in the family therapy technique of a reflecting team conversation.

Feminist approaches – evolved more overtly during the 1980s, as female family therapists began to discuss and write about power and gender relations within families (Perelberg and Miller 1990, Goldner 1991, Hare-Mustin 1991). Their feminist analysis of therapeutic work revealed that couples were strongly influenced by assumptions about gender roles and expectations within relationships and families. Despite 30 years of feminist theory and practice in other contexts, these writers and many female family therapists began to articulate a challenge to the gender-neutral concepts in orthodox family therapy theory and practice. Instead of assuming a parity between partners or married couples they incorporated an understanding of the inequality conditioned and socialised into heterosexual relationships that explained domestic violence at one extreme, or at the other a stereotype of passive/nurturing female and assertive/emotionally distant male.

Where problems occur in relationships, they can often be better evaluated through a gendered lens that highlights the contradictions and dilemmas between people who are constrained by powerful concepts of maleness and femaleness. When people fail to conform to the societal norm of working man and child-caring female it is usually expressed as the female failing. Orthodox family therapists however well-intentioned would try to reverse the stereo-type by seeking to engage the male partner in more child-care duties, but this in many cases simply reinforced the female's sense of failure. This attempted intervention neglected to understand that for many women success in childcare was an important defining characteristic of their femininity from which they gained enormous self-esteem and role satisfaction. The intervention also unwittingly reinforced the male as the problem-solver and the more successful partner.

Practitioners using an empowering anti-oppressive framework to their practice will find these concepts resonating with your way of working with women who are abused by violent partners and left to cope with children on their own. Feminist counsellors and psy-chotherapists have equally contributed a gendered perspective to the development of practice in psychodynamic work (Bollas 1987, Welldon 1988, Holland 1990). Helping children and young people recover from such traumas and build self-confidence requires patience as well as the ability to reframe them away from notions of individual fault/blame/failure towards an understanding of the social constraints affecting parental relationship patterns. These cultural issues can be acknowledged and reflected upon in positive and thoughtful ways without them inhibiting practitioners. If they are accessible to the consciousness of therapists then it must follow that these hidden cultures will become more available to clients to address.

Constructivism and Social Constructionism – these two related but different concepts are linked to postmodern theories that have recently begun to challenge some of the orthodox thinking and tech-niques of systemic and psychodynamic practice. The postmodern thesis rejects the notion that there is a fixed truth or single reality about individual or family process. The postmodern view suggests that each individual constructs his or her personalised views and interpretations of what the family might be experiencing together. Counsellors and therapists with a constructivist or social construc-tionist perspective emphasise the importance of cultural diversity, multiple realities and the acceptance of a wide range of belief systems (Goldenberg and Goldenberg 2004). Constructivism stems from the study of the biology of cognition which argues that individuals have unique nervous systems that permit different assumptions being made about the same situation.

Social constructionism is similar in that it argues that there is no such thing as objective reality, but that what we do construct from what we observe arises from the language system, relationships and culture we share with others. In practice, the constructivist and social constructionist practitioner therefore would be recognised by their more collaborative style of working. The focus is on helping the child or young person examine and reassess the assumptions individuals make about their lives rather than focusing on family patterns of communication. Using these approaches involves taking a position of safe uncertainty and not knowing, with the therapist joining in the search for workable solutions on an equal basis with the individual or family.

Narrative therapy – this recognises the natural ability children and young people have to possess, to generate and to evolve new narratives and stories to make sense of their experiences (Freeman et al. 1997). The focus of interest is the meanings that individuals and families generate to explain and shape possible courses of actions. Traditions within families and cultures are used to guide interpretations of events. Making these more explicit in a more conversational style of therapeutic process helps to validate the family experience rather than seeking to impose a solution or follow a therapist-determined path. The nature of the conversation is the key to this approach. The approach challenges the way children and young people are labelled because they are usually superficial, negative and one-dimensional descriptions. The child can begin to accept these limiting descriptions, and believing they are 'true' start to behave in ways that confirm the label. Narrative therapy aims to help children and young people by collaborating in developing alternative stories about their lives and replacing a single, problem-saturated belief with a number of different, complex beliefs that open up possibilities.

Systemic and psychodynamic theories and practice have developed over time to a confident, mature position where practitioners are beginning to relax and feel able to acknowledge more similarities and differences – especially by counsellors and psychotherapists. The evidence does suggest that it is possible to construct and continue to develop a synchronised therapeutic approach which offers a great deal to the practitioner seeking to work in more culturally competent ways. It may be that by opening our minds to different ways of working we can simultaneously open our minds to the cultural *multiverse* that exists in the increasingly ethnically diverse society we all inhabit. In this way our practice can become more flexible, creative, agile and accessible making it more likely that we can be perceived as useful and resourceful to every child and young person requiring help.

Summary

Counsellors and therapists need to find knowledge and learning resources that address in a comprehensive way the concept of culturally competent practice. In attempting to construct practices that can be applied universally, therapeutic approaches have tended to avoid the complexity and uncertainty of ensuring that the approaches can and should be accessible to every child or adolescent.

Children and young people vulnerable and at risk of psychological problems can be helped by unique or culturally generalised resilience or protective factors. Counsellors and psychotherapists seeking to intervene effectively should carefully consider the various ways potential mental health problems are thought about, understood and communicated in every family, in every culture.

For some refugee and asylum-seeking young people it could be a relief to have a psychological explanation for feelings and behaviour that they find hard to make sense of, whereas for others it could exacerbate feelings of blame, guilt and self-loathing. The enduring social stigma of mental health problems, combined with institutionally racist practices, provides an overall context for these feelings to be repressed, displaced or acted out.

Conventional developmental norms show how adults construct childhood, how to measure children's progress and detect mental health problems. They are, however, set down as solid absolutes. These theories have had positive effects but they have also restricted the field of vision required to fully engage with and understand children and adolescents from the diversity of cultures in a multi-ethnic society.

It is important to consider the specific meanings of subjectivation that emerge for adolescents in cross-cultural, multicultural and cultural contexts who may be struggling to develop a cohesive sense of self. If identity is based on issues of sameness and difference and the broad sense of culture meaning to fit in and be the same as other peers, then adolescents gain a sense of the *power* of being part of the majority and the fear engendered by being in the minority.

At the individual level, personal and institutional discrimination will feel like persecution and resonate with a sense of badness within. At the developmental stage of forming an identity and beginning the process of separation from parental influence, the black adolescent is struggling to be understood within the family arena while absorbing an internal model of self-esteem of not being tolerated for being different. Thus making it all the more important for us to assess in our therapeutic work whether, for example, a defence is dysfunctional or functional.

Feminist counsellors and psychotherapists have contributed a gendered perspective to the development of practice in systemic and psychodynamic work in domestic violence. Cultural issues of self-blame and patriarchal power can be acknowledged and reflected upon in positive and thoughtful ways without them inhibiting practitioners. If they are accessible to the consciousness of therapists then it follows that these hidden cultures will become more available to clients to address.

Systemic and psychodynamic practices have developed a confident maturity where therapists are beginning to relax and construct a synchronised approach seeking to work in more culturally competent ways. By opening our minds to different ways of working we can open our minds to the cultural *multiverse* that exists in our ethnically diverse society. Practice can thus become more flexible, creative, agile and accessible, making it more likely that we can be perceived as useful and resourceful to every child and young person requiring help.

3

INTEGRATING THEORY, SKILLS AND VALUES

Experience is not what happens to you. It is what you do with what happens to you.

– Aldous Huxley

Introduction

The increasing diversity of modern societies with multicultural characteristics has prompted both systemic and psychodynamic practitioners to reconsider their received ideas about individuals, families and family relationships. Both paradigms have evolved over time from their earliest theoretical and practical applications in response to influences and changes in the wider social economic and cultural environment. Psychodynamic ideas originated in the late 19th century period of scientific enquiry following the Enlightenment and answered the human predicament left wanting by religion. Systemic ideas arose in the late 20th century at a particular historical juncture within the growth of psychological efforts at healing troubled people, where the limits of individual-focused work were being acknowledged. Now at the beginning of the 21st century it should be possible to consider integrating theory skills and values from both sets of ideas as a means to developing culturally competent practice.

Feminist discourses for example that informed the critique of orthodox family therapy notions in the 1980s have themselves recently broadened in scope to incorporate critical reflection on the role of women in non-white non-Western households. The earlier discussion of family therapy criticised the approach as colluding with part of a Western cultured patriarchal society that sought to organise women into domestic roles. This has developed into a more complex understanding of women who can value and rejoice in the role of homemaker and child-carer without accepting a subservient role. The notion of a multiplicity of culturally specific feminisms rather than an overarching model explaining female oppression is now accepted (Dominelli 1997a). Counselling and psychotherapy in a similar way have evolved to embrace concepts derived from anthropology and sociology that focus on the significance of intimacies within larger kinship groups for secure family and gender identity (Gorell Barnes 1998). Both theoretical paradigms have recognised the need to move away from previous certainties about dysfunctional/functional families and individual pathology/normality.

In so doing they are seeking to enhance the fundamentals within their approaches with critical learning from modern human development and consider where a synthesised practice can meet certain needs of the clients. This means actively seeking out knowledge and information about the multitude of ways children and young people *experience* their family life and wider environment. It is both easy and dangerous to make crude assumptions about a person's culture based on their country of origin, gender, ethnicity or religion. Therapists using a systemic or psychodynamic approach need to experience families or individuals in the same room during therapy or counselling but they are also presented with an *idea* of the family or individual by the clients' narrative.

The version in their mind may not fit with that experienced by the practitioner because it is retrieved from an earlier *version* of themselves based on a unique history and culture-bound interpretation of feelings, behaviour and events (Elliot and Frosh 1995). For most children and young people their sense of self-legitimisation and identity is formed in the family crucible at an early stage in their development. Both systemic and psychodynamic perspectives offer a vehicle for exploring this terrain as it is shaped by the intra-familial constellation of relationships and external pressures and stresses of Western societies characterised by inter-ethnic tensions and oppression of minority cultures.

The family life cycle as a means to identifying particular developmental transitions in family functioning that are provoking an individual or interpersonal crisis in a child or young person is always constrained by cultural and social norms. What is and is not accepted and acceptable behaviour in a child's immediate family, the family's kinship structure and social network at any point in their lives, and the immediate social structure through which the life cycle of any child progresses are inevitably affected by differences in cultural expectations (Gorell Barnes 1998). There is thus a need for an integrated approach to articulate with these challenges in terms of knowledge skills and values.

These expectations are fluid and constantly changing as families previously rooted in old traditions underpinned by religious beliefs are constantly challenged by new social and economic circumstances, or affected by customs and practices in other countries. Newer family forms such as gay and lesbian parents are still developing a culture of traditions, beliefs and behaviours in the absence of any comparison while relying on their own upbringing in overtly heterosexual households. Lone parents, stepfamilies and divorced or separated parents may orient themselves towards former assumptions about family life and neglect the value of their own style or culture of doing things. Children and young people are constantly challenged to assess, adapt and incorporate new challenges and experiences in addition to the enormous developmental milestones they are negotiating. We also need to assess, evaluate and, where possible, integrate new concepts, knowledge and practices to maintain our therapeutic accessibility.

Integrating and complementing

Considering where and how to integrate changes in our methods and models of practice is challenging if we consider some of the obvious distinctions. A major defining difference between systemic and psychodynamic theories is the notion that problems can be as much about interpersonal matters as arising from within the individual. Especially for children and women in families, systemic theory was liberating because it offered a way out of the double abuse of being oppressed by the family dynamics and subsequently blamed for reacting to them. Systemic theory emphasises that individual experience and the development of identity are formed by relationships, communication and interaction. Personality and the self are not static in the systemic perspective – they are *malleable* and constantly subject to the changes in family process.

Practitioners can utilise the different theoretical perspectives offered by systemic and psychodynamic approaches by searching for those points of complementarity and harmony. For example, an assessment based upon psychodynamic knowledge may see a troubled youngster as suffering from poor early attachment with a depressed mother. This in turn leads to friction in the household between the parents, and between them and external education or youth justice agencies. An intervention using systemic theory to address the whole constellation of factors and people involved can link with the assessment and offer a non-stigmatising response that avoids scape-goating and pathologising the youngster.

Gorell Barnes (1998) suggests that the job of the family therapist is to understand the meaning-making particular to each family – the family culture of which the larger culture with its many layered meanings is a part. The therapist in these circumstances is required to maintain a clear head and avoid becoming confused, enmeshed or inappropriately confrontational when faced with beliefs that are at variance to her/his own culture. The temptation is to empathise with an oppressed woman, for example, and defend her against an abusive misogynist husband or partner during couple therapy. This will more likely result in the husband/partner not returning to therapy and endanger the woman to further abuse. However, combining this with a psychodynamic understanding enables a practitioner to address both adults' underlying conflicts and dilemmas and focus on the ambivalence within the woman in order to foster her own sense of self-preservation, ego strengths and decision-making skills.

This approach is exemplified in the work of Carl Rogers (1942), who offered a variant of a psychodynamic orientation focused on the client/therapist relationship in a way that reduces the notion of the expert role of the therapist. It fits with the aspiration of defining a more integrated practice drawing on the strengths of systemic and psychodynamic thinking. This person-centred therapy reflects an emphasis on the client's expertise instead of the problem, and highlights the spiritual or transcendental characteristic of the relationship. Rogers viewed differing cultural realities as a promising resource for humankind to learn from one another without fear. Postmodernists will recognise echoes of contemporary discourses in his much earlier writings.

The strength of the systemic perspective is its fundamental belief in the importance of context in seeking to understand personal difficulties. The strength of the psychodynamic perspective is its focus on the deepest fathoms of the psyche in order to enlighten an individual seeking help with psychological problems. Psychoanalysis seemed to make significant improvements in its theoretical structure during the period containing two world wars resulting in a generation of people marked by that destructive experience. Systemic understandings suggest that psychoanalysis therefore represents a set of explanatory metaphors into the psyche, developed from a historical context of human destructiveness (Woodcock 2001). Given the seemingly perpetual cycle of war, human conflict and the psychological consequences for families directly or indirectly, it is reasonable to think that for many children and young people these experiences are organising their unconscious world.

Whether actual or potential refugees and asylum seekers, the children of military personnel or civilians at risk of terrorist attack, modern young people perhaps as never before are touched by concepts involving loss, death and bereavement. Denial and displacement, anger, depression and anxiety within the rising numbers of mental health problems of children and young people perhaps testify to the impact of everyday discourse and media imagery that illustrate, in often graphic details, the depravity and horror of human conflict. This contemporary example of how the external context of war is shaping the developing internal psychic mechanisms of growth and survival requires consideration of a synthesis between systemic and psychodynamic practice offering a holistic response to troubled young people.

Culturally informed rituals and symbols have a power to import meaning into events such as ethnic conflict or invasion by hostile forces that would otherwise be invisible to therapeutic interaction. The spiritual and traditional are crucial elements that can be addressed with young people from other cultures and brought into the therapeutic encounter. They offer an accessible way for the therapist to make a connection between the external and the internal meaning for the individual (McGill 1992). By integrating psychodynamic and systemic perspectives the therapists are making themselves available to a rich source of material within the child or young person seeking an outlet. Thus the ability to heal such traumatic experiences lies not only in making the latent content of narratives explicit but also in doing it in a similar way as Bettelheim (1978) implies that complex fairy tales containing awful representations allow children to integrate what is less easily rendered into a more easily digestible narrative.

In terms of cultural competence the influence of the ethnographic traditions of anthropology and sociology exemplified in the works of Goffman (1969), Sontag (1979), Stewart and Roter (1989) and the concept of symbolic interactionism need to be understood (Jenkins 2002). Our study of and attempts to intervene in the human world are only best efforts, given the limits of knowledge and evidence that can be empirically verified. The advantage of an integrated approach to your practice is that by expanding your theoretical panorama you will feel more able to access intellectual and therapeutic resources to enhance your interventions. We can respond to the idea that individuals within these theories are essentially social beings emphasising the choices available in role playing and the importance of negotiation and interpretation of identity during the management of various social situations. Family life thus becomes best understood as a fluid process with roles not fixed by an implacable collective consensus, but as a reality constantly renewed and redefined by specific members of specific families (Bilton et al. 2002). Thus describing a group of people as living in a nuclear family says nothing about the cultural manifestations in which they specifically negotiate their relationships inasmuch as talking about an Asian family says nothing about their internal and familial norms of behaviour or beliefs.

The language of emotions and feelings pervades therapy whether with groups, families or individuals. It is the common vocabulary that contains dominant assumptions that help construct discussions and beliefs about emotions and mental health problems. However, social construction theory suggests that a range of culturally shared assumptions regarding emotions shape not only beliefs about emotions but serve to *construct* our experiences, including what are regarded as legitimate feelings and what courses of action are acceptable once particular feelings arise (Lutz 1990). We can begin to accept therefore that emotions are not just private, internal and psychologically driven according to psychodynamic thinking. Shared meanings in Western cultures perceive emotions as chaotic rather than ordered, irrational rather than rational, and uncontrollable rather than intellectual – hence the way some ethnic minority peoples who are less restrained with emotional expression are regarded as inferior, primitive and often dangerous.

Synthesising and blending

By combining the psychodynamic notions of feelings as arising from inner turmoil and conflict within the unconscious with the systemic concept of culturally determined and complex process of attributions made about the internal state of children and young people, we can begin to better understand their experience. When therapists ask a young person how they are feeling they are also perpetuating assumptions that the answer somehow only reflects some aspects of their real inner state; the question also reflects their relationship with their wider culture. With young people suffering severe mental health problems such as a first episode psychosis, the prevailing instruments for diagnosis and assessment include the concept of 'lack of insight'. However, several authors are critical of the concept of insight and subsequent diagnosis of psychosis, suggesting it is relative and open to comparative judgement based on Western, Eurocentric constructs (Beck-Sander 1998, David 1998, Saravanan et al. 2004). The imposition of such a stigmatising diagnosis has profound implications for the young person's self-esteem, future development, sense of loss and capacity for using therapeutic interventions.

An alternative construction of lack of insight suggests that the young person can make sense of themselves within their own terms, which can be interpreted as a divergent perspective rather than an 'incorrect' one. The notion of lack of insight as a defence mechanism protecting against the pain and confusion of a mental health problem is also challenged. Rather than a type of self-deception denying the threat to the self, it can be argued that the mechanisms underlying the concept of lack of insight as a defence lie not on an absolute but on part of a continuum encompassing all experiences whether 'normal' or 'pathological'. Young people may very well hold multiple beliefs about their problem, which are diverse and contradictory. They may both seek help from conventional therapeutic resources which can demonstrate insight and also access treatments from different sources that contradict each other.

Western explanations for psychological difficulties rely on a medical model that uses internal concepts such as illness, abnormality and pathology – whereas Eastern explanations include external concepts such as supernatural, causation, sin and punishment, and karma. Cultural concepts of a mental disorder such as psychosis are closely related to insight. If the individual self is a culturally mediated interpretation, then we might expect that cultures act through self-awareness to shape the natural course of schizophrenia (Saravanan et al. 2004). It is important to locate your use of these theoretical resources in anti-discriminatory and anti-oppressive ways to promote culturally competent practice.

It has been argued historically that therapeutic models have rarely sat easily with the concepts of empowerment and anti-oppressive practice – because they essentially reflect the existing power relationships dominated by white, middle-class, heterosexual, male, healthy, employed Westerners. The fundamental problem for workers attempting to practise in anti-oppressive ways arises because they are perceived as part of the superstructure of social control and state-sanctioned oppression. However, by integrating therapeutic approaches and paying explicit attention to the social circumstances of children and young people you can foster a more authentic and accessible relationship with them. Equally, it is argued that while government policies emasculate citizens and the economic system is inherently contradictory, there are many opportunities to satisfy your aim of practising in more empowering ways. Some of the features of anti-discriminatory or anti-oppressive practice are as follows:

- Work collaboratively with your client, parents, the family and other agency staff.
- View users as competent; resist a pathological label and enable the child or young person to communicate their needs.
- Help children and young people to see themselves as having some strengths.
- Develop their confidence by affirming their experiences rather than mystifying them.
- Help children and young people to seek diverse solutions including but not exclusively relying on insight development.
- Help them build and use informal networks among relatives, school friends, youth groups, friends and neighbours to increase access to resources.

The use and abuse of power is at the centre of culturally competent practice. It is a significant element in every relationship but is not necessarily negative. Rather than becoming monitors of sexism, racism, disablism or homophobia, you might find it more useful to think in terms of ensuring you and your clients have access to equal opportunities in your environment and in the assessment and intervention plan you formulate. Effective culturally competent practice requires a clear theoretical perspective to inform the value base that permits anti-oppressive work (Payne 1997). To practise in an anti-oppressive way means seeking to bridge the gap between you and the child or young person in order to facilitate a negotiation of perceptions. This can be a liberating experience for you and them. You are relieved of the burden of the knowing expert with the pressure to formulate interpretations designed to stimulate the client to engage with you. Equally, the client is liberated from the position of subservient patient dependent on another's expertise to reveal to them the 'truth' of their situation.

Developments in systemic theory and psychodynamic practice are showing signs of moving towards an integrated or synchronised position in this respect. Systemic practitioners have evolved from the rather narrow family therapy interventionists, with the need to exercise control and try to influence family behaviour in prescribed ways. They are increasingly able to evolve towards more dynamic, reflective and narrative co-constructionist methods. Equally, some former purist, analytically trained psychodynamic therapists and counsellors have been able to release themselves from rigid method-ologies and embrace contextual systemic issues with whole families (Pocock 1997, Gorell Barnes 1998). The combination might not sit easily with some who rely on tried and tested formulas, but for those intellectually agile enough, seeking alternatives and willing to incorporate new ideas into their practice, the prospect can be enlightening.

At the heart of a more enlightened practice is a consideration of the concept of power. An important element in the process of evaluating and reflecting on your practice is understanding that as practitioners or clients, men need to be made aware in every situation of their potential to oppress and how maleness, for example, affects their perception of problems and to be oppressed because of assumptions about masculinity. Feminist practice engages both the personal and the social by focusing on the whole person and examining the inter-connectedness between people and the structures they live within. It provides a powerful explanatory tool to use in assessing situations involving child abuse and domestic violence – for example, where practitioners inadvertently end up blaming mothers for failing to protect children, instead of understanding the cultural dilemmas and impossible predicament faced by women.

Gender permeates aspects of social, cultural, political and economic life and the organisations that maintain society. Culturally competent practice requires the active challenging of dominant masculine discriminatory attitudes, beliefs and practices. In practice, this means raising issues about which team member is the most appropriate to work with certain children or young people. It also means resisting the simple notion that a female worker should necessarily work with a female client. Cultural competence means challenging the assumption that a female client needs a female therapist to identify with or relate to openly. For some children or young women this might only be possible with a male counsellor or therapist. The important point is that the issue is acknowledged and discussed instead of being avoided. A wider theoretical perspective suggests that your practice should be informed by ideas about how people behave in relation to and therefore influence others and the effects of social factors such as stigma, stereotyping and ideology on behaviour in groups (Hogg and Abrams 1988). In this context, empowering prac-tice is both a goal and a process for achieving cultural competence.

Similarly, anti-racist practice requires an acknowledgement of the combination of institutional and personal racism that privileges white Western culture and norms of behaviour whilst denigrating and obscuring black culture. The effects of racism have been measured and quantified consistently over decades and as recently as the Macpherson inquiry into the murder of the black teenager Stephen Lawrence. Over the years, research detailing systematic discrimination against black people in terms of housing, employment and educational opportunities continues to reveal the reality behind rhetorical political slogans of governments of whatever persuasion (ONS 2002). In the youth justice system and the psychiatric system young black males are over-represented compared to other groups in Western societies, while in the public care system black children are likely to face multiple disadvantages – not least culturally insensitive practices. It is important to keep the issue constantly in mind so that in every proposed intervention you are actively considering how your practice can resist and challenge overt and covert racist assumptions and beliefs.

Establishing the therapeutic relationship

As counsellors or therapists working with children and young people, the issue of engaging and establishing the therapeutic relationship becomes challenging when trying to incorporate culturally competent notions. You may worry about whether you need to start from scratch and learn a host of new concepts, or you may feel that your existing methodologies and skills have stood the test of time and experience and require no change. As long as you accept that the issue is important enough to warrant examination of your existing practices, you have begun the process that will lead to a more culturally competent practice. The ability to engage with troubled children and adolescents is not easy at the best of times. At times of crisis or heightened anxiety from parents or other professionals it becomes particularly challenging. Paradoxically, by reflecting on cultural competence you may well find yourself managing these stressful events more easily. If we consider some of the potential barriers to engagement identified by, among others, Compton and Galaway (1999) we can begin to at least describe the elements likely to require particular attention:

Anticipating the other – this is connected to pre-judging the situation and happens when you fail to listen carefully because you believe you know beforehand what the other person is going to say. This might be because of information provided by another source or your own stereotyped imagery about the situation being presented. The message and subsequent communication is anticipated, and you drift into automatic language rather than reading between the lines of what the other person is saying.

Failure to make the purpose explicit – if you fail to make the purpose of contact explicit, then you and the client may have different, even contradictory, ideas of what the purpose is and will interpret each other's communication in the light of different ideas. This may occur because of your anxiety about the likely reactions from the child or young person. As the subtle distortions continue, both will be heading in entirely different directions.

Premature change activities – efforts to effect change will fail where you attempt change efforts without clearly understanding what the client wants and whether that change is feasible. Cultural competence requires that you make every effort to understand their point of view. To urge change prematurely may create a barrier to communication and can lead to directive approaches that are often ineffective in the absence of trust.

Inattentiveness – if your mind wanders during the contact, then the communication process is compromised. This happens when you are tired thinking about the last or next client, bored or even frightened and upset. The situation you are confronted with might remind you about your own family or a deeply personal experience that has suddenly come into your mind and is distressing or distracting.

Client resistance – the barriers that some clients create can be thought of as forms of resistance against entering into a problem-solving process. They can stem from discomfort and anxiety involved in dealing with a strange person and a new situation, or from cultural or sub-cultural norms regarding involvement with service agencies and asking for help; some clients may also be securing a degree of satisfaction from their problems.

In order to overcome these barriers to culturally competent engagement you need to prepare fully and follow some relatively simple guidelines during the initial contact. These first steps to effective intervention can lay the future direction and pattern for the child or young person's contact with your agency and other helping relationships. Do not underestimate the importance of this. You need to examine your own inner prejudices and assumptions about the clients' situation and try to suspend these to prevent them compromising good practice. Encountering early hostility, silence or non-compliance should be expected from reluctant or involuntary child and adolescent clients and should not be seen as reflecting your lack of skills.

An example of an integrated approach is offered if we consider the recent increase in drug and alcohol misuse by young people that is causing parents and government agencies a great deal of concern. Genetic, environmental and personality factors have all been identified as causal factors in determining the prevalence rates of alcohol abuse. Cross-cultural alcoholism prevalence rates show that the rates ranged from a high of 23 per cent for Native Americans to a low of 0.45 per cent in Shanghai, China. The high rate among Native Americans has been attributed to high unemployment, racism, poverty, depression and social alienation (MacNeil et al. 2000). Similarly, a meaningful understanding of adolescent substance misuse without consideration of cultural factors is impossible, since each culture has its own values, beliefs, customs and schema regarding the use of substances, which provide a context in which to evaluate such behaviour (Westermeyer 1995).

Castillo (1995) suggests that important cultural factors include the psychocultural characteristics of the individual, including the individual's personality traits, cultural beliefs about the behavioural effects of the agent and the cultural meaning attached to taking the drug. Also important is the socio-cultural setting in which the drug is taken, including the people present, their beliefs, moods and behaviours. The ingestion of *peyote* is a case in point. The effect of ingestion is intoxication when the drug is taken recreationally by Anglo-Americans, but similar effects have different meanings for Mesoamerican Indians taking *peyote* as a sacrament in their tribal religion.

Empowering by relinquishing

Previous negative experiences or the dynamics of the practice situation may not permit the child or young person to perceive you as an individual person, but rather as a representative of a potentially disempowering agency service. Remember, client behaviour in the early stages of an encounter is unlikely to have much to do with your specific actions. The best strategy is to be clear, honest and direct but in a non-defensive way – clarifying your role and the agency mandate and working hard to project a calm, patient, uncritical image will help in the long run. Avoid contradicting the child or young person even on matters of fact; it is much better to listen respectfully and acknowledge their right to express different values and preferences. The following characteristics reflect a synthesis of systemic and psychodynamic skills that are reliably identified as better at producing effective intervention outcomes are when counsellors and psychotherapists are (Smale et al. 2000):

Empathic – placing yourself in another person's shoes and convincing yourself that you understand the client's predicament is a start. Empathy is also about experiencing another person to the extent that they feel you understand the core issues of relevance to them. It is more than sympathising with their situation as well, it means having the capacity and courage to challenge a person's assumptions and perceptions.

Respectful – this is more than a token acknowledgement of difference or superficial knowledge of ethnic or cultural customs and practices. Respect is a fundamental psychotherapeutic value that comes through your humanitarian principles of concern for other human beings conveyed from your inner self.

Warm and friendly – children know when you are pretending to like them and they can spot false warmth a mile off. You need to harness your inner feelings of compassion combined with a desire to improve matters to enable the warmth and friendliness of a genuine equality of brotherhood or sisterhood to touch every gesture and tone of voice in your communication.

Authentic – behaving consistently as a rounded human being rather than adopting a stilted professional role or hiding behind an obscure therapeutic strategy. Demonstrating proper professional standards based on reliability, clarity and limitations need not be done in a cold matter-of-fact way. Bringing something of your own unique personality into the work reveals your humanity and can help a suspicious child or adolescent to re-examine their own assumptions about what to expect.

Rewarding and encouraging – do not be afraid to praise success where it occurs or even the effort if a task is not achieved. Children and young people especially thrive on encouragement, so make much of small successes and suggest that more is possible.

Confident – be sure of your ground and always strive to convey a sense of authority. You can be authoritative about *not knowing* something, provided you admit to this and can assure the client of your capacity to obtain accurate information. Knowing your own professional and legal boundaries will help establish the limits to your remit and enable you to be confident in what you are doing.

Interested – try to find something special or unique about the child or young person you are trying to help and show interest in this. Focusing away from the problem for a while might relieve a stressful situation and introduce information which helps them see themselves or the situation differently. You can concentrate on the problem of course, but if this is done in a routine or even indifferent way you may be creating unhelpful barriers to the process of change.

Challenge in a non-confrontational way – easier said than done especially in heated situations where the potential for harm or abuse exists in the child's home. Keeping a calm tone, maintaining appropriate eye contact and remembering to use positive language will help children and young people hear your perceptions of the situation. It is important to keep the flow of the conversation going and providing every available opportunity for the client to express themselves.

By relinquishing or temporarily suspending your statutory role during therapeutic work, the child or young person will be enabled to perceive the helping nature of the relationship. For counsellors and psychotherapists already in clinical and non-statutory work, clarity about the nature of the confidential therapeutic relationship needs to be explained thoughtfully. Appearing too bureaucratic and rule-bound could put them off opening up. On the other hand, presenting yourself as *laissez faire* in your attitude to agency regulations and administration might equally scare a youngster who requires a solid containing environment. As ever, the right balance is hard to strike but the use of your own feelings and the transference relationship during early meetings will guide you.

Attachment and loss

Cross-cultural attachment theories have employed an approach where Bowlby's conceptualisation of attachment and Ainsworth's operationalisation of attachment have been applied to various non-Western cultures (Van Ijzendoorn and Sagi 1997). Research shows that there are a number of differences that warrant consideration in seeking to understand a broader range of attachment styles and their relevance to the diversity of children and adolescents. Culturally competent practice requires constant re-evaluation of these fundamental paradigms in order to adapt them to specific children and young people's experiences. It is suggested, for example, that avoidant classifications are more prevalent in Western European countries and resistant classifications are relatively more frequent in Israel and Japan (Nakagawa et al. 1992).

The relevance of Western notions of predicting which children and young people are likely to benefit from therapeutic work is challenged by research that demonstrates flaws in the interpretation of children's capacity for emotional expression. Ferrara suggests that the stereotype of the Cree Indians of North West Canada as 'stone faced', reticent and therefore emotionally expressionless in their facial presentation which suffers from false cultural constructs. In Cree culture, children are socialised to be reticent and not verbally expressive of their feelings. They are instead encouraged to draw upon ancient ways of living and surviving, and channel feelings into hunting activity, art, craft and dreams. Thus a culturally competent practitioner would harness this cultural aptitude and use it to enable a troubled young person to access and express their emotional state through these media.

Concepts of ethnic identity development can be compared with ego identity formation in that it involves exploration and commitment to a defined identity (Marcia 1980). The child or young person's attachment to an ethnic identity will be mediated by internal processes, familial experiences and societal attitudes. The child between the ages of 2 and 5 becomes aware that there are different ethnicities. Between the ages of 3 and 6 the child is able to identify as a member of a specific ethnic group. When the child reaches age 9 it has usually realised that ethnicity is immutable and will not change with time. At about the same time and especially during adolescence the young person begins to develop an understanding and appreciation of the personal significance of ethnicity in her/his life (Dwivedi 2002). This could be a troubling time because in addition to a re-negotiation of significant attachment relationships a black adolescent may be feeling confused, awkward and guilty about feeling less attached to a culture than their parents or grandparents.

Increasing numbers of people fleeing from persecution and discrimination around the world are creating unique demands upon counselling and therapeutic agencies to respond with help that is appropriate and effective in situations of loss. The therapeutic context is necessarily *transcultural* in the host country and replete with loss and bereavement issues. Families have often been exposed to gross human rights violations and their exile status magnifies levels of stress. Referrals to helping agencies may imply or directly request therapeutic support but psychological treatment is not always what refugees expect or want. This response can be seen as a defence against the overwhelming feelings of loss and disorientation that can be met with a focus on practical and concrete matters such as housing and welfare rights information. However, the need for some engagement with counselling and therapy will in many cases be indicated. Sveaass and Reichelt (2001) devised a means of negotiating with refugees in these circumstances where there was a difference between the referrer and family with regard to the possible benefit of therapy.

Using a systemic model based on the work of Anderson and Goolishan (1992) the therapists in this example used a non-expert position to facilitate problem-solving and solution-focused conversations within the families. These were intended to trigger the families to use their past experiences of dealing with losses, traumas or difficult challenges and apply them to their current circumstances. It was acknowledged that with families who were generally feeling powerless and overwhelmed by their strange surroundings they needed to start to feel more in control of their lives. Declining therapy and preferring to deal with practical matters could have been immensely therapeutic. On the other hand, Sveaass and Reichelt noted that some families had an intrinsic affinity for therapeutic ideas and were relatively easy to engage in work. The key in this work seemed to have been to adopt the non-expert approach with an underlying understanding of assessing motivation for therapeutic engagement. This illustrates the potential of an integrated systemic and psychodynamic practice.

Systemic theorists have emphasised the importance of both individuality and connectedness in the development of the sense of identity or separate self. The model of individuation suggests that adolescents usually have an individuated relationship which displays a balance between individuality and connectedness. This is in contrast to the notion of adolescence as necessarily a period of storm and stress – particularly for the mother–daughter dyad because of the prolonged unresolved Electra complex. However, both concepts rely on Western constructs and need to be considered in the light of culturally competent practice. Recent research suggests that Pakistani mothers and daughters expressed more intimacy, relational harmony, connectedness and mutuality and lesser individuality than British mothers and daughters (Gilani 1999). Thinking about attachment and loss in these contexts in a culturally competent way means we need to appreciate the differences and distinctions between diverse family structures in this crucial dyadic relationship.

The symbolism of eating disorders

The example of eating disorders offers another means for considering how an integrated practice can be developed in response to a problem that appears to be increasing across class, cultural, ethnic and gender paradigms. It is challenging practitioners to reflect on the efficacy and usefulness of orthodox ways of conceptualising and intervening in the problem. The symbolism of food as a physical entity containing goodness, fuel, and the ability to prolong and maintain health is powerful. Thinking about it as representative of the internal state of a young person's psyche and their relationship with those parts of themselves that can offer enrichment or destruction can help us understand why it has become a major psychological problem (Lawrence 2001). It also offers a troubled youngster a means to exercise control over their life (and ultimately death), delay adulthood and a chance to regress to a baby state and be (force) fed if they reach a life-threatening physical state.

Eating disorders used to be thought of as a purely Western phenomenon and culture-bound to advanced industrialised societies with affluent lifestyles, a consumerist ideology and the influence of catwalk models emphasising thinness combined with sexuality. New evidence, however, is challenging this simple explanation as prevalence rates of anorexia nervosa and obesity are rising in boys and young men and in non-Western societies. A recent study of Hong Kong Chinese women and girls, for example, is providing a valuable insight into how culture affects the aetiology and treatment of this psychological problem (Ma et al. 2002). Systemic theory permitted a contextual understanding of the main symptom of self-starvation which offered some insight into the struggle of women in a modern society in transition characterised by tension between traditional Chinese values and Western values.

Practitioners in the West have many years' experience of intervening successfully in cases of anorexia nervosa (Dare et al. 1990, Fonagy and Roth 1997). The characteristics identified as causal factors include sexual abuse, enmeshment, overprotection, conflict avoidance, rigidity and family loyalty. However, this can in some instances result in families feeling blamed, guilty and subsequently demotivated and disempowered in therapeutic treatment. The family meaning of self-starvation in Chinese societies has rarely been examined. Thus by comparing Western and Chinese cultural assumptions and beliefs around anorexia nervosa, therapists have the opportunity of adapting their methodology to the client family as well as blending the two cultural concepts to increase motivation and optimise success.

In the Chinese tradition, women's roles and functions are culturally prescribed as submissive, subordinate and subjugated to the will of the father, husband and son respectively in three different life stages: as an unmarried daughter, as a wife and as a widowed mother (Pearson and Leung 1995). In work with anorexic families there are themes consistent with Western and Chinese clients except for the unique role of mothers in Chinese families. Here, there is a marked powerlessness and helplessness compared to mothers in Western families. This is reinforced by the traditional Chinese attitude to divorce, which means that it is extremely rare for a woman to initiate divorce. This would be viewed as shameful and lead to a loss of family face (*mian zi*) and mockery.

Young women suffering from anorexia nervosa – who tend to be better educated and more influenced by Western values – can find themselves in the role of supporting their oppressed mothers as part of Confucian filial expectations. This places added stress on the young woman struggling with serious mental health issues. A culturally competent model of working with such young women incorporates the reliable methodology associated with centres of excellence in the West combined with Chinese concepts that (Le Grange 1999, Ma et al. 2002)

- address the meaning of self-starvation at individual and family levels;
- empower the depressed mothers to address their own specific issues;
- harness the potential of the father to help change the parental matrix from reinforcing the mother–daughter dyad; and
- help the young women to redefine the Confucian filial ethic in the light of their own developmental needs.

An example of a culturally competent therapeutic approach illustrates the success that can be achieved when therapists and counsellors begin with the assumption that a combination of community organisation and social ideology can contribute to the genesis and maintenance of mental health problems, and also to their resolution.

A systemic team working on a kibbutz applied an integrated approach focusing on the family and community in a case of anorexia. The family and community's pathology narrative was addressed by expanding the field of support in a collaborative way, using members of the community and the family to offer long-term support.

Social and cultural understandings of eating disorders used to emphasise the gender-specific nature of these problems. Previous literature would focus on the images fed to young females emphasising the desirability of thinness as well as the sexuality implied in attracting attention from males. Females are thus acculturated to perceive of their bodies as representative of themselves in a psychological sense while wrestling at the same time with ambivalent feelings about identifying with their mothers. Young males, on the other hand, in the modern cultural context of changing masculine identity may find that there is a prerequisite that they are torn internally with ambivalence in social relationships and a fear of loss of control, rather than being split off emotionally (Briggs 2002).

Anorexia has been considered as a defence against emerging adulthood, with the maintenance of a child-like body and delayed menstruation as a symbolic rejection of the bodily world of adults. Eating disorders, in general, in adolescence are also regarded as cultural metaphors in contemporary developing societies. Bulimia and obesity are also ways for the young person to exert control of their bodies, which are readily amenable to physical control in a social environment. Thus they are able to contain their fears and anxieties about a plural, ambiguous and potentially risky world within their bodies (Williams and Bendelow 1998). While bulimia represents the unstable double bind of consumer capitalism, anorexia (i.e. the work ethic in absolute control) and obesity (consumerism in control) embody an attempted resolution of cultural contradictions. By integrating the powerful resources within psychodynamic and systemic theories, you will be able to comprehensively address the needs of a new generation of troubled children and young people presenting symptoms such as eating disorders, which seem to symbolise the *indigestible* psychic and social material they are struggling to comprehend in their contemporary culture.

Summary

Counselling and psychotherapy have evolved to embrace concepts derived from anthropology and sociology that focus on the significance of intimacies within larger kinship groups for secure family and gender identity. Systemic and psychodynamic paradigms have moved away from previous certainties about dysfunctional/functional families and individual pathology/normality. In so doing they are seeking to incorporate critical learning from modern cultural development and consider where a synthesised practice can meet certain needs of the client.

For most children and young people their sense of self-legitimisation and identity is formed in the family crucible at an early stage in their development. Both systemic and psychodynamic perspectives offer a vehicle for exploring this terrain as it is shaped by the intra-familial constellation of relationships and external pressures and stresses of Western societies characterised by inter-ethnic tensions and oppression of minority cultures.

Culturally informed rituals and symbols have a power to import meaning into events such as ethnic conflict or invasion by hostile forces that would otherwise be invisible to therapeutic interaction. The spiritual and traditional offer an accessible way for you to make a connection between the external and the internal meaning for the child. By integrating psychodynamic and systemic perspectives you can make yourself available to a rich source of material within the child or young person seeking an outlet.

Gender permeates aspects of social, cultural, political and economic life and the organisations that maintain society. Culturally competent practice requires the active challenging of dominant masculine discriminatory attitudes, beliefs and practices. This means thinking about which team member is the most appropriate to work with certain children or young people and resisting the simple notion that same-gender matching is required for effective therapeutic work to proceed.

A meaningful understanding of adolescent substance misuse without consideration of cultural factors is impossible, since each culture has its own values, beliefs, customs and schema regarding the use of substances which provide a context in which to evaluate such behaviour. Important cultural factors include the psychocultural characteristics of the individual, including the individual's personality traits, cultural beliefs about the behavioural effects of the agent and the cultural meaning attached to taking the drug. Also important is the socio-cultural setting in which the drug is taken, including the people present, their beliefs, moods and behaviours.

Eating disorders used to be thought of as a purely Western, female phenomenon and culture-bound to advanced industrialised societies with affluent lifestyles, a consumerist ideology and the influence of catwalk models emphasising thinness combined with sexuality. New evidence, however, is challenging this simple explanation as prevalence rates of anorexia nervosa and obesity are rising in boys and young men and in non-Western societies.

4

SOCIALLY INCLUSIVE PRACTICE

There are but two families in the world as my grandmother used to say, The Haves and The Have-Nots.

– Cervantes

Introduction

One of the persistent critiques of therapeutic practice is that it fails to address the broader social, economic, structural and *meta-cultural* issues that affect the way people live and the problems experienced by children, young people and their families. The discussion in some journals and books becomes limited to simplistic characterisations of therapeutic approaches as out of touch, or the converse argument that radical practice seeking to deal with the structural causes of psychological disturbance is naive. This is not helpful if you recognise that each approach has some merit and you have the intellectual flexibility to use approaches that fit with the circumstances presented. The task for the culturally competent practitioner is to find the right combination of methods and models of work that can make a difference to a particular young person with a particular problem, at a particular time. The systemic theorists call this 'both/and', in other words not ruling anything out that could conceivably be helpful and not privileging any one explanatory paradigm over another. This is preferable to wasting effort in justifying a universal approach or trying to suggest that all problems are due to social inequalities.

Another objection to using a psychotherapeutic orientation in public health and social care is that it is unrealistic or even dangerous to attempt such approaches. This is because either they (a) are not within the remit of the service specification of the agency or (b) that practitioners should not dabble in areas that require advanced training to be employed competently. As far as the first point is concerned there is ample evidence that modern practice in all its agency manifestations is expected to go beyond narrow resource-driven service. Practitioners understand the need to bring to bear a range of knowledge, skills and values to the problems faced by children and young people who, through no fault of their own, find themselves in need of help and support. Whether it is government guidance, legislation or professional ethical codes of practice, there are plenty of examples exhorting professional staff to work and think therapeutically.

The second point is disingenuous because many people enter health and social care training with experience and skills that ideally suit a counselling or psychotherapeutic approach. And you do not have to have completed advanced clinical training to be able to use some relatively simple concepts and techniques in your work with children and families that can reflect systemic or psychodynamic theory within the limits of safe, accountable practice. For example, access to a suitably qualified specialist for consultation or supervision ensures your work can be monitored and practice evaluated. It is possible to employ some of the key concepts and theoretical ideas in relatively straightforward pieces of work that can make a big difference. The key idea is that you are *thinking* systemically or psychodynamically and therefore using a reliable paradigm in which to practice – not that you are claiming expertise that you do not have or you are experimenting on powerless clients.

As we have already noted earlier in this book, the basic psychodynamic framework of practice is complementary to systemic theory and vice versa. No practitioner can be effective without combining the individual psychology of the child or adolescent with the social context of their problems to gain a holistic picture. Similarly, no therapist can properly work with a child and its family's internal problems in the absence of the wider context of their cultural experience. It is rather that you make an effort to find a means of engaging with clients at the level of their daily life. Grounding your work in the child's ordinariness can equally dismiss the criticisms of therapeutic approaches as being divorced from reality and grounded in abstract conceptual thinking. The skill is employing what can be perceived as obtuse ideas in a meaningful and relevant way. This is why it is crucial to consider socially inclusive and culturally competent ways of working with children and young people that invariably feel relevant to them.

In listening to the stories that children and young people tell us, we need to pay close attention to the way that aspects of the stories gain prominence in different contexts. Apart from their own internal hierarchies of discourse, children are influenced by their familial culture and the social *milieu*. Confusion may arise where within the family parents are treated with unquestioned respectfulness while outside children and young people witness others behaving quite differently. A child or young person's use of language and choice of subject matter is thus shaped by beliefs about what is legitimised in social exchanges between people of different generations, class and cultures (Gorell Barnes 1998). This contradiction can impact strongly on young people in families where values of parental respect are highly placed.

Social exclusion

The term 'social inclusion' gained rapid acceptance within the political lexicon at the beginning of the 21st century. It began to appear prominently in political discourse in the UK following the election of a Labour government in 1997 which regarded social exclusion as an impediment to its vision of a more open and equal society concerned with social justice and to economic progress (Walker 2003b). The concept of social exclusion has its origins in France in the 1970s where the idea of citizenship and social cohesion highlighted the plight of *les exclus*, who included immigrants from former French colonies in Africa and were relegated to the margins of society (Barry and Hallett 1998, Pierson 2002). Disaffection combined with poverty began to manifest in public protests – often violent. The social policy aim therefore is to advance a socially inclusive social and health care policy enabling every family to enjoy the opportunities offered by late capitalist Britain and the European Economic Community in an increasingly economically globalised world.

This fits with the aspiration to practise in culturally competent ways, whereby each family regardless of class, race, culture, age, religion, disability or gender should find the traditional barriers to their advancement being dismantled so that nobody is excluded from sharing in the wealth and resources being offered at a time of sustained economic expansion. These political aspirations fit with the value base of counsellors and psychotherapists who seek to embody anti-discriminatory practice, respect for persons, and equal opportunities for every citizen. Just as the earlier stages of capitalism resulted in new approaches to the social management of the disruption, impoverishment and alienation of the social casualties of economic progress, so too are the late stages of capitalism (Leonard 1997).

The evidence confirms that the gap between rich and poor is widening – there are more children living in poverty, the prison population is at its highest recorded level and disabled people are more likely to live in poverty or be unemployed than non-disabled people. Children from working-class families are less likely to receive a further or higher education and black families are more likely to live in poor housing. There are, however, differences within these broad examples of social exclusion that need to be taken into account when you are assessing strengths, resources and gaps in social networks where you are trying to help. For example, inner city deprivation, migration patterns and poorer health outcomes are factors also associated with class and are therefore likely to affect any family in disadvantaged social circumstances.

Those in the front-line services, faced with the consequences of the failure of this latest social policy aspiration and the raised expectations of families in need, are under considerable pressure. Evidence suggests that the process of exclusion continued in the 1970s as rising levels of poverty began to be quantified. In the process, a new role has evolved for statutory work, for example – not so much as a provider of services or even as a therapeutic intervention, but rather as a front-line service focused on the management of exclusion and rationing of scarce resources (Jones 1997). This has always been an uncomfortable position for social workers for example, who subscribe to an empowering model of practice that seeks to challenge social injustice such as racism while addressing the psychological impact. However, there are numerous positions in non-statutory, independent, voluntary or charitable organisations, where fewer constraints permit practice that is not defined in *reductionist* ways. And even within statutory contexts, there are more opportunities for using systemic and psychodynamic methods and models of practice than might at first appear to be the case.

There are few studies that have explored the role of discrimination with ethnocultural variables in order to ascertain less about why people are prejudiced, and more about how the experience of racism affects children and young people. A recent study sought to find out more about the psychological impact of discrimination on young people's ethnic identity and acculturation. A group of European American, African American, Mexican American and Vietnamese American adolescents were surveyed. Out of all these young people, the European Americans had less ethnic identity and more positive attitudes towards the other groups. In contrast, African American adolescents reported the highest levels of ethnic affirmation and perceived discrimination. However, contrary to popular belief, the survey found that high levels of ethnic identity and affirmation did not equate with high levels of negative attitude towards other groups (Romero and Roberts 1998). Thus social policy efforts at tackling race-hate crimes and institutional racism can be harnessed in work with young people feeling discriminated against and disadvantaged.

Social policy context

In a postcolonial world, the rights and expectations of indigenous people to reparation and how they are perceived are important issues in the context of achieving culturally competent practice. The disparities between developed and developing economies under the influence of globalisation are becoming more pronounced, incorporating new forms of cultural domination. The concept of cultural and social injustice can be illustrated thus (Powell 2001):

- *Cultural domination* – some people are excluded because they are subjected to ways of interpreting or communicating which originate from a culture which is not their own, and which may be alien or hostile to them.
- *Non-recognition* – some people are excluded because they are effectively rendered invisible by the dominant cultural practices.
- *Cultural disrespect* – some people are excluded because they are routinely devalued by the stereotyping of public representations or everyday interactions within the dominant cultural context.

The colonial legacy left by Western nations is part of the collective consciousness of the developing nations and the old post-capitalist imperial states. In Germany recently a proposal for a national guiding culture as the basis for immigrant integration is the political expression of a desire to construct a unitary homogeneous vision of German national culture that black and ethnic minority people should pledge allegiance to. This policy neatly obscures the fact that German history is replete with fundamental internal differences especially between Protestants and Catholics (Klusmeyer 2001). The colonial mentality left an indelible impression on generations of people who saw black people as potentially murderous, scheming, resentful and full of hate towards their white oppressors.

This can be read as a projection of those feelings white colonialists held towards the indigenous people, who in their benign passivity would have increased the paranoia of the colonialists fearing retribution for their oppressive behaviour. In some ways we can see the enactment of a paternal relationship with the child-like indigenous people, who require order and discipline to prevent a descent into chaos and mayhem. The example of a mixed-race child or young person of dual heritage offers a direct and indirect example of the ambivalence towards black people from former colonial countries that forms part of the covert relationship with *otherness*.

> Their mixed and split origin is what decides their fate. We may compare them with individuals of mixed race who taken all round resemble white men but who betray their coloured descent by some striking feature or other and on that account are excluded from society and enjoy none of the privileges. (Freud 1915)

The stereotypes that flow from this earlier colonial mentality even when challenged in modern historical texts or orthodox counselling and psychotherapy literature still pervade our consciousness. It is as if in trying to reject a crude, inappropriate and potentially damaging stereotype we are forced to consider it and be influenced to some extent by it. It is this force of ambivalence that gives the colonial stereotype its currency and (Bhabha 1994):

- ensures its repeatability in changing historical and discursive conjunctures;
- informs its strategies of individuation and marginalisation; and
- produces that effect of probabalistic truth and predictability for which, for the stereotype, must always be in excess of what can be empirically proved or logically construed.

Issues of citizenship and nationality, race and immigration provide the overarching context within legislation and public policy which sets the scene for racist and oppressive practice to go unchecked. In the United Kingdom the British Nationality Act provided legal rights to immigration, which have served as a focal point for a continuing racialised debate about the numbers of black immigrants and refugee/asylum seekers and the perceived social problems subsequently caused (Solomos 1989). The Race Relations (Amendment) Act (HMSO 2000) came into force in 2001, extending the scope of the Race Relations Act. The new Act strengthens the law in two ways that are significant to therapeutic practice. It extends protection against racial discrimination by public authorities and it places a new, enforceable positive duty on public authorities.

Like the Human Rights Act, the new Act defines a public authority very widely. Anyone whose work involves functions of a public nature must not discriminate on racial grounds while carrying out those functions. The most important aspect of the new Act in the long term will be the new positive duty on local authorities because it gives statutory force to the imperative of tackling institutional racism. The new general duty replaces section 71 of the Race Relations Act 1976 with a tougher requirement on public authorities to eliminate unlawful discrimination and promote equality of opportunity and good race relations in carrying out their functions.

At the 1991 census just over 3 million (5.5 per cent) of the 55 million people in Britain did not classify themselves as white. Half are South Asian (that is of Indian, Pakistani and Bangladeshi descent) and 30 per cent are black. There is rich diversity in Britain's minority populations, but importantly, nearly half of Britain's non-white population had been born in Britain, with three-quarters of these registered British citizens. Thus the overwhelming majority of non-white children under 16 were born in Britain. The latest 2001 census data reflect the continuing trend. In terms of addressing the wider context for working therapeutically with children and young people, this fact testifies to the stubborn and prevailing racist ideologies relying on provocative imagery of host countries being 'swamped' and overwhelmed by alien cultures.

The Nationality, Immigration and Asylum Bill (HMSO 2002) is the fourth piece of primary legislation attempting to reform the asylum system in the UK in 10 years. Previous measures related to dispersal and support measures and were widely regarded as harmful to children's psychological health because they resulted in sub-standard accommodation, isolation, discrimination and poverty (Dennis and Smith 2002, JCWI 2002). The new Law proposes the establishment of accommodation centres housing about 3000 people in rural areas. Protection of children in such places will be difficult due to the high turnover of residents, while these children will be emotionally disadvantaged by being impeded from opportunities to integrate and feel part of society. Counsellors and psychotherapists offering services to these communities need to consider this socially excluding context in their assessment and interventions.

In addition, the new Law proposes denying asylum-seeking children the right to be educated in mainstream local schools. Such segregation could contravene the Human Rights Act 1998 and the UN Convention on the Rights of the Child (UN 1989) because this is not in the best interests of the child and will very likely harm their development and mental health. Children who have suffered extreme trauma, anxiety and hardship need to feel safe, included and part of their community with their peers in order to begin to thrive and rebuild their fragile mental health. There are doubts that the quality of education offered in accommodation centres would properly meet even basic standards of pedagogic practice.

The proposals on marriage and family visits in the Law are another potential source of anxiety and psychological harm to children and young people. The subject of arranged marriage combines further attempts to restrict entry from abroad with a barely disguised racist attack on cultural practices in some black communities. A two-year probationary period for marriages is proposed in order to test the integrity of individuals who enter into marriages abroad with non-British citizens. The effect will be to increase the number of children confronting the prospect of separation from one parent because of doubts raised about whether their parents' marriage will subsist indefinitely. These discriminatory practices if allowed to be sustained without legal challenge are yet more evidence of the need for practitioners to advance a culturally competent practice that can resist the damaging consequences for children and young people's welfare.

Therapy and cultural development

The idea of therapeutic practice and cultural development is based on the premise that most people's problems are sorted out within and between their existing local network of friends, relatives and neighbours. Thus the link with systemic and psychodynamic theories can be drawn – the focus of attention is wider than the individual presenting difficulty or the intra-familial dynamics. Counsellors and psychotherapists have a role in seeking to reinforce and support those networks or helping to facilitate their growth where they have declined, as a protective and preventive strategy. Community practice informed by therapeutic concepts is therefore an excellent intervention strategy for promoting social inclusion and cultural understanding (Walker 2004). Thus, widening the focus means working with every possible part of the wider system that is part of the community experiencing social exclusion. It does not, as is sometimes assumed, exclude work with individuals. The spectrum of activity includes (Smale et al. 2000):

Direct intervention – work carried out with individuals, families and local networks to tackle problems that directly affect them.
Indirect intervention – work with community groups and other professionals and agencies to tackle problems affecting a range of people.
Change agent activity – this seeks to change ways that people relate to each other that are responsible for social problems whether

at individual, family or neighbourhood levels by reallocating resources.

Service delivery activity – providing services that help to maintain people in their own homes, to reduce risks to vulnerable people and provide relief to parent/carers.

Systemic theory that informs community practice is not just about transforming neighbourhoods whether in small or large scale but it can also enable personal change and growth in individuals through social action and the fostering of co-operative activity. The reverse of course is also true. Individual work using psychodynamic concepts that focus on the internal problems of children and adolescents can also contribute to wider cultural transformation in neighbourhoods. Once change occurs in separate families it can cascade throughout a street, tower block or estate. Defining community work in its widest sense and holding a multiple theoretical perspective includes anything from visiting lonely housebound people, setting up a food co-operative, individual or group therapy and establishing a collective resource such as a credit union. It could also involve helping to organise a protest march to the Town Hall to lobby for improvements in neighbourhood services and community safety (Adams et al. 2002, Thompson 2002).

With such broad definitional parameters it is not surprising to conclude that there is a shortage of evidence for effective therapeutic work or reliable empirical data about activity in this area of practice (Macdonald 1999). Without a common understanding of community practice it is hard to quantify and compare the outcomes for evaluative purposes. The available evidence does suggest, however, that it is community-oriented, proactive initiatives that are most valued by citizens and are doing most in helping to support families and individuals in need. Formal child and adolescent mental health services only deal with a small proportion of actual need in the community and still create large waiting lists for treatment (Walker 2003c). A modern, integrated therapeutic model offers the appropriate holistic perspective for us to engage with other professionals in the community, to work in partnership with families, and employ the personal relationship skills the majority of professional staff aspire to use. In this way practitioners will be reaching out to those children and families traditionally hard to engage and new families who are socially excluded.

A culturally competent practice can, for example, be helpful when addressing issues of loss and bereavement with ethnic minority families where earlier generations were split up during periods of economic growth. Caribbean women whose mothers left them with relatives as they took advantage of job opportunities overseas reveal tensions and complexities in their relationships as a result of being cared for first by adult relatives and then rejoining a mother from whom they were separated for years. The success or otherwise of this traditional provision of care was conditional on whether the child felt loved by them and how they understood their mother's leaving with increased well-being for the family. These experiences affect subsequent generational attachment relationships and need to be carefully and thoughtfully considered.

This illustrates how important it is that your practice should always take account of the impact the wider social policy context is having on you and the children and family you are attempting to help. As well as the internal dynamics of the individuals and their patterns of relationships, your assessment should include the effects of, for example, long-term unemployment or drug abuse, or poor housing conditions on the capacity to parent and family members to relate. Equally, it is helpful if you consider what impact various statutory regulations and procedural guidance are having on shaping your work and your beliefs about clients. This is not to add more confusion to possibly complex and difficult work, but to enable a more sensitive and tailor-made intervention to be designed so that it harmonises with the child's real day-to-day cultural experience. Clients will recognise this and feel properly listened to, valued, understood and be more ready to engage in therapeutic work than if you try to apply a rigid, inflexible model of practice.

Socially excluded groups

Inspection of services for black children and their families in Britain shows that despite years of rhetoric of anti-racist and anti-oppressive practice, and a plethora of guidance and training, assessments and care planning are still generally inadequate (SSI 2000). The guidance suggests

- ensuring that services and staffing are monitored by ethnicity to ensure they are provided appropriately and equally;
- involving ethnic minorities in planning and reviewing services;
- training in anti-racist and anti-discriminatory practice;

- Investigating and monitoring complaints of racial discrimination or harassment.

Explicit policies are in place for working with black families.

Skills in facilitating children and young people's empowerment are indicated in any vision of the future shape of service provision for troubled children and young people (Walker 2001c). A therapeutic practice framework employing systemic theory can enable black families and young people to support each other and raise collective awareness of shared issues. As noted earlier, by combining this perspective with a psychodynamic understanding of how we manage internal and external manifestations of the other, we can optimise the conditions for more culturally competent practice. Investigation of indigenous healing practices and beliefs will provide a rich source of information to utilise in the helping process. Advocacy skills in which young people are encouraged to be supported and represented by advocates of their choice with a children's rights perspective, would help contribute to influencing current service provision (Ramon 1999). Systemic theory and psychodynamic practice that links the internal and external world of the client, augmented with culturally competent skills, can thus better meet the needs of socially excluded children and young people.

In the context of the social policy aspiration of *multiculturalism*, young people from ethnic minority communities can be found straddling the traditional and modern division personified in the parent–child generation gap – for example, the Muslim teenager who wears the conventional dress of his school/college peers and regularly attends Friday prayers. In the East End of London these young people acquire the street talk and mannerisms of local working-class whites and are referred to as 'Bangladeshi cockneys'. Yet this attempt to construct a hybridised young person stereotype is as inaccurate as it is meaningless. Attempting to make sense of who these young people are requires us to enter a process filled with ambivalence and antagonism, because in so doing we reveal the inadequacy of our own systems of meaning and signification (Bhabha 1997).

As counsellors or psychotherapists, we therefore need to understand not just our own political or moral stance on racism and prejudice but at a deeper level our own tolerance of difference within ourselves. The capacity for tolerating difference arises from the early relationship between the infant and parents. According to Britton (1998, p. 42), 'If a link between the parents is perceived in love, and hate can be tolerated in the child's mind, it provides the child with a prototype for an object relationship of a third kind in which he or she is a witness not a participant.'

This concept has its links with the notion of the *meta-position*, discussed by family therapists when attempting to reach an observational position whilst in the process of therapy. Systemic theory posits that the worker can become inducted or absorbed into the family pathology and therefore rendered impotent. Achieving the meta-position permits the therapist being not only within the family process as an active participant but also able to step outside or to occupy the third place/relationship in the analytical sense. By demonstrating this ability to move between positions we can begin to model for young clients the capacity for tolerance and containment, and therefore be more likely to engage with them in revealing more of their own troubled and ambivalent feelings.

Continual reflection and evaluation of practice is required to maintain an anti-racist, socially inclusive practice. Recognising racial harassment as a child protection issue and as an indicator for subsequent potential mental health problems is evidence, for example, of how you can translate policy generalisation into specific practice change. Practitioners who make sure they take full account of a child's religion, racial, cultural and linguistic background in the decision-making process are demonstrating the link between social policy and socially inclusive practice. But taking full account must have explicit meaning rather than intentions that are well-meaning yet ineffective. Ensuring, for example, that black children in residential public care have access to advocates and positive role models can assist in challenging institutionally racist practice. Even the simple act of asking whether the young person would like such an advocate is transmitting a powerful message of cultural competence.

It is important in these contexts to be persistent because these young people will have learned compliance and the art of denying their own rights and how to avoid making a fuss. Skilled psychodynamic work and using transference feelings will guide you in how far to enable the child to seek fairer treatment and when to proceed without causing further embarrassment. Paying serious attention to anti-racist and anti-oppressive practice will help you and your colleagues develop strategies to overcome conscious and unconscious value judgements about the superiority of white British family culture and norms. Exploring the impact of white power and privileges in professional relationships with black people and drawing connections between racism and the social control elements of practice is another example. Rejecting stereotypes of black and ethnic minority family structures and relationships will enable you to assess the rich, cultural, linguistic and spiritual diversity of family life and permit the building of practice that is not based on a deficit model judged against an *Anglocentric* norm. Not only will your practice be enriched but also black families will more easily engage with your helping efforts.

Refugee and asylum-seeking children are among the most disadvantaged ethnic minority group for whom culturally competent practice is essential. Some are unaccompanied, and many affected by extreme circumstances might include those witnessing murder of parents or kin, dislocation from school and community and severing of important friendships. Lack of extended family support, loss of home and prolonged insecurity add to their sense of vulnerability. These experiences can trigger symptoms of post traumatic stress syndrome and a variety of mental health problems (Dwivedi 2002).

Parents-coping strategies and overall resilience can be diminished in these trying circumstances, disrupting the self-regulatory patterns of comfort and family support usually available at times of stress. Your involvement needs to take a broad holistic and integrated approach to intervention and not overlook the need for careful assessment of mental health problems developing in adults and children, whilst responding to practical demands. If these are not tackled promptly these children and adolescents may go on to develop serious and persistent difficulties which will be harder and more costly to resolve in the long term.

The scale of the level of need can be gauged by considering that the number of applications for asylum in the UK from unaccompanied under-18s almost trebled between 1997 and 2001 from 1105 to 3469. Department of Health (DOH) figures indicate that there were 6750 unaccompanied asylum-seeking children supported by local authorities in 2001. Further evidence shows that many of these young people were accommodated and receiving a worse service than other children in need (Audit Commission 2000). Very little research has been done to ascertain the psychological needs of this group of children. However there is some evidence of the symptoms of post-traumatic stress syndrome being present before they then experience the racist xenophobic abuse of individuals and institutions incapable of demonstrating humanitarian concern for their plight. This combination can shatter the most psychologically robust personality. It has been estimated that serious mental health disorders may be present in 40–50 per cent of young refugees (Hodes 1998).

Cultural dislocation

The sense of dislocation felt by individual children and young people and their families is illustrated by noting the experience of groups such as Roma, Gypsy and Travellers who may be included in recent groups of refugee and asylum-seeking families escaping ethnic 'cleansing' from the Balkan region of Central and Eastern Europe (Walker 2003a). These families have a long history of persecution and flight from discrimination. Roma, Gypsy and Traveller families who have for many years made their home in Britain are probably one of the most socially excluded groups of people living in Britain. Unemployment among Roma/Gypsies is in the region of 70 per cent, while increasing numbers of children are failing to complete even a basic education (Save the Children 2001). These factors – particularly the lack of proper education – are risk factors for the development of psychological problems in adults and children and young people. The overall context of social exclusion means an absence of contact with preventive services or the positive interaction with peers necessary for developmental attainment. Sensitive therapeutic work can help families begin the process of re-establishing patterns of behaviour that can sustain and nurture the personal growth of all concerned. Effort is required by counsellors and psychotherapists to enhance the engagement process with these families by

- gaining an understanding of the concept of culture;
- appreciating your own culture;
- a desire to facilitate effective communication;
- an appreciation of the varying perceptions of family process across cultures; and
- a desire to work with families considering their cultural values.

The experiences of children and young people uprooted by force or covert pressure can lead to a sense of loss which is magnified by a sense of not belonging. These twin feelings can result in a kind of cultural bereavement which can get mixed up with the adolescent developmental process that requires a sense of belonging (Eisenbruch 1990). Migration itself is a journey or transition and if the young person is simultaneously negotiating a crucial phase of transition from childhood to adulthood, problems may arise. It is argued that the yearning for belonging involves being able to risk relationship and loss, whereas it is probably more useful to be able to belong to multiple worlds rather than feel excluded from them (Noam 1999).

This sense of belonging is enhanced by the capacity for sharing language, customs and intersubjective experiences. A sense of sameness or identification begins to be developed in infancy when unacceptable emotions are taken in by another and the way they are returned. This secure base or containment is crucial in the child developing a tolerance of difference. The importance and subtleties of understanding the meaning of what is projected and what can be fed back mean that we have to work hard within the reflective therapeutic space when addressing issues of sameness and difference with children and adolescents (Briggs 2002).

Where adults may experience mental health problems, it is usually considered that the presence of a second parent in the home is a mitigating factor in moderating the impact on children and young people. However, this is based on Eurocentric studies that are not related to key relationships in different cultural family groupings. Research indicates that a grandparent relationship could be crucial or that access to a supportive adult outside the family home, contact with peers through school or sport and a reliable social life all help the child or young person cope (Gorell Barnes 1998).

An example of the importance of having a supportive adult is provided when we reflect on the way homosexuality is perceived by children and young people. This is an area about which little research has been undertaken, and is the subject of lively discussion and prescriptive policy from governments. In the context of rising levels of suicide among young males and the burgeoning literature on the widely reported crisis of identity among young men apparently usurped by years of feminist critiques of patriarchal society and gender abuse of power, we need to understand how children and young people construct and internalise concepts of gender (Laufer 1985). The invisibility of lesbian and gay role models or thoughtful discussion in social contexts conspire to construct a sense of danger and shame as adolescents experiment and explore different aspects of their sexuality.

An interesting research study recently explored the use of homophobic terms by boys and young men and the meanings invoked when they use them, in order to find evidence that might help explain masculinity and adult sexual identity formation in later years (Plummer 2001). The study found that homophobic terms come into currency in Primary School but usually with little connection with sexual connotations. Interestingly, this early use of homophobic terms such as 'poofter' and 'faggot' occurs prior to puberty, prior to adult sexual identity formation and prior to knowing much at all about homosexuality. The effect seems to be that early homophobic experiences provide an important reference point for boys and young men comprehending forthcoming sexual identity formation.

Elements of socially inclusive practice

Counsellors and psychotherapists have to assess needs, evaluate risks and allocate resources in a way that is equitable, as far as possible, for a wide range of service users in various situations (Walker 2003b). Challenging oppression in relation to key issues such as poverty and social marginalisation that underpin interactions in social welfare requires a holistic approach to change that tackles oppression at the personal, institutional and cultural levels (Dominelli 2002a). An empowering culturally competent practice can contribute to the defence of marginalised people using an overarching systemic and psychodynamic framework. A review of the elements that constitute a socially inclusive practice lists four core intervention skills necessary to build on an authentic and integrated practice that reflects your humanitarian values (Smale et al. 2000). These elements have much in common with counselling and therapeutic approaches.

Social entrepreneurship is the ability to initiate, lead and carry through problem-solving strategies in collaboration with other people in all kinds of social networks.

Reflection is the worker's ability to pattern or make sense of information, in whatever form, including the impact of her/his own behaviour and that of the organisation on others.

Challenging refers to your ability to confront people effectively with their responsibilities, their problem-perpetuating/creating behaviours and their conflicting interests.

Reframing is the ability to help redefine circumstances in ways which lead towards problem resolution.

These are all mirrored in the psychotherapeutic and systemic literature without perhaps the emphasis on social entrepreneurship. However, if we wish to promote the conditions for change within the person, we need to attend to the constraints *outside* the person. We must counteract oppression, mobilise users' rights and promote choice, yet have to act within organisational and legal structures which users experience as oppressive (Braye and Preston-Shoot 1995). Finding your way through this dilemma and reaching compromises, or discovering the potential for creative thinking and practice are the challenges and opportunities open to staff committed to a socially inclusive practice. This means treating people as wholes and as being in interaction with their environment, of respecting their understanding and interpretation of their experience, and seeing clients at the centre of what workers are doing (Payne 1997). The unique integration of systemic and psychodynamic perspectives offers a vast reservoir of knowledge and skills to bring to bear on the multiple problems of socially excluded children and adolescents. This ensures that the effort put in is more likely to address every possible cultural dimension and be more effective.

Anti-racist and anti-oppressive practice are repeatedly referred to in the literature and they have a long historical lineage as part of the social justice basis of modern health and social care practice. The concepts are backed up in counselling and psychotherapy codes of conduct, ethical guidance and occupational standards defined by central and local government requiring services to meet the needs of diverse cultures and combat discrimination. They are part and parcel of what attracts many of us into helping work in the first place. Translating good intentions into daily practice is, however, harder than it might at first appear.

For example, in the case of childcare practice there is still a tendency for social workers to proceed with assessment on the basis that the mother is the main responsible carer with the father taking a minor role. Women are perceived therefore as responsible for any problems with their children and for their protection. You may feel that this reflects the reality especially in cases of single parenthood, or domestic violence where fathers are absent or a threat. Anti-oppressive practice requires in these situations acknowledgement of the mother's predicament and multiple dilemmas. It requires an informed, culturally competent practice using feminist and psychodynamic theory to evaluate the situation and seek every small opportunity to support the mother and engage the father. The combination of personal guilt felt by women in these circumstances with a mother-blaming tendency in society can erode their precarious coping skills and paradoxically, increase child protection risk factors.

In this context it is important to consider the specific challenges faced by South Asian adolescent girls as members of immigrant families. A study of Indian, Pakistani and Bangladeshi families in Montreal, Canada, found that gender roles prevalent within each culture were maintained through segregation, control over social activities and arranged marriage. The adolescents felt that their parents and communities have more stringent rules for female socialisation than any other community. Because of the high levels of connectedness in the nature of family relationships, these adolescent girls perceived a high social cost attached to protest or dissent in relation to the cultural rules, resulting in elevated levels of stress (Talbani and Hasanali 2000).

A history of childhood mental health problems is strongly indicated in the risk factors for developing adult mental health problems. It is imperative therefore that the needs of all black and ethnic minority children vulnerable to mental health problems are addressed early and competently in order to prevent later problems. Your anti-racist work in multidisciplinary ways as part of inter-agency groups' co-ordinating efforts to support the child and family through temporary or moderate difficulties could be critical. As a worker using culturally competent skills, you can support other staff in statutory or voluntary resources by offering a more holistic evaluation and assessment of the family process adapted to take account of cultural diversity.

One way of demonstrating this is to exclude the risk of misinter-pretation or underplaying significant emotional and behavioural characteristics in black families. An understanding of the reluctance and resistance of black parents to consider a mental health explanation for their child's behaviour or emotional state is important when considering how to engage parents or carers from diverse cultural backgrounds in the process of support (Walker 2003c). It is equally important to make efforts to understand cultural explanations and belief systems around disturbed behaviour as part of risk assessment work. Respecting rather than challenging difference should be the starting point for finding ways of moving forward in partnership and co-operation. The dilemma in aspiring to practise in culturally competent ways is in balancing this respect with knowledge and evidence of the consequences of untreated emerging mental health problems.

The characteristics of non-Western societies such as collectivism, community and physical explanations for emotional problems are in contrast to Western concepts of individualism and psychological explanations (Bochner 1994). The Western model of mental illness ignores the religious or spiritual aspects of the culture in which it is based. However, Eastern, African and Native American cultures tend to integrate them (Fernando 2002). Spirituality and religion can be critical components of a family's well-being, offering a source of strength and hope in trying circumstances. You need to address this dimension as part of the constellation of factors affecting black children and adolescents, avoiding stereotyping, and bearing in mind the positive and sometimes negative impact spiritual or religious beliefs might have on their mental health.

Basing your practice on culturally competent principles is not a soft option, signing up to political correctness, or about being nice to black people. It is about how you define yourself as a worker and your relationship to service users. A recent powerful contribution to the literature on this issue makes the point that you cannot bolt-on a bit of anti-oppressive practice, it has to be part and parcel of all your everyday practice as a contribution to tackling poverty, social justice and the structural causes of inequality (Dominelli 2002b). This goes against theories of practice that advocate a maintenance or care management role for practitioners. Wherever you position yourself, you will probably find yourself occupying different roles at different times in your work, regardless of your explicit intentions. This is because if you are client-centred then you will engage with children and young people in partnership informed by psychodynamic and systemic theory to help meet their needs to maintain them in their current circumstances or support them in their struggle towards social inclusion.

Summary

The basic psychodynamic framework of practice is complementary to systemic theory and vice versa. No practitioner can be effective without combining the individual psychology of the child or adolescent with the social context of their problems to gain a holistic picture. Similarly, no therapist can properly work with a child and family's internal problems in the absence of the wider context of their cultural experience.

The evidence confirms that the gap between rich and poor is widening, there are more children living in poverty, the prison population is at its highest recorded level and disabled people are more likely to live in poverty or be unemployed than non-disabled people. Children from working-class families are less likely to receive a further or higher education and black families are more likely to live in poor housing.

In a postcolonial world, the rights and expectations of indigenous people to reparation and how they are perceived are important issues in the context of achieving culturally competent practice. The disparities between developed and developing economies under the influence of globalisation are becoming more pronounced, incorporating new forms of cultural domination.

Systemic theory that informs community practice is not just about transforming neighbourhoods whether in small or large scale, but it can also enable personal change and growth in individuals through social action and the fostering of co-operative activity. The reverse is also true. Individual work using psychodynamic concepts that focus on the internal problems of children and adolescents can also contribute to wider cultural transformation in neighbourhoods.

A culturally competent practice can be helpful when addressing issues of loss and bereavement with ethnic minority families where earlier generations were split up during periods of economic growth. Caribbean women whose mothers left them with relatives as they took advantage of job opportunities overseas reveal tensions and complexities in their relationships as a result of being cared for first by adult relatives and then rejoining a mother from whom they were separated for years. These experiences affect subsequent generational attachment, relationships and need to be thoughtfully considered.

Refugee and asylum-seeking children are among the most disadvantaged ethnic minority group for whom culturally competent practice is essential. Some are unaccompanied, and many affected by extreme circumstances might include those witnessing murder of parents or kin, dislocation from school and community and severing of important friendships. Lack of extended family support, loss of home and prolonged insecurity add to their sense of vulnerability. These experiences can trigger symptoms of post-traumatic stress syndrome and a variety of mental health problems.

The characteristics of non-Western societies such as collectivism, community and physical explanations for emotional problems are in contrast to Western concepts of individualism and psychological explanations. An understanding of the resistance of some parents to consider a mental health explanation for their child's behaviour or emotional state is important when balancing the knowledge and evidence of the consequences of untreated emerging mental health problems.

5

Assessment and Intervention

In all things success depends upon previous preparation, and without such preparation there is sure to be failure.
– Confucius

Introduction

Assessment is the starting point of engaging with children, young people and their carers – to begin a process of understanding what is causing them psychological difficulties or equally to help clarify why others are concerned about their mood or behaviour. *How* you assess in terms of culturally competent practice could make the difference between success and failure in the subsequent intervention. Assessment is not a science in that different helping professionals, parents and the child or young person themselves might offer a variety of explanations for a child or adolescent's emotional state and subsequent behaviour. A range of diagnostic or assessment tools exist to help us in the task of defining the problem/s and offering a treatment pathway including counselling and psychotherapeutic work (Milner and O'Byrne 1998). Assessment is often taken for granted, sometimes the subject of unwarranted attention, but *always* a potentially liberating and empowering experience for you and the child. However, you do need to incorporate cultural competence into your repertoire of assessment methodologies.

It is important that you understand how culturally competent assessment takes into account a child or young person's needs, rights, strengths, responsibilities and resources. You need to reflect on how your individual practice enables you to identify strengths rather than weaknesses, and work with children and young people's existing networks and communities. Organisational restrictions and resource constraints will militate against creative practice and probably seek to narrow your terms of reference but you need to overcome these. In much health and social care work, the process is to use assessment as a rationing device. Understanding how institutional and individual oppression and discrimination influence contemporary assessment practice and children's ability to function is an important task for your practice development. The psychological consequences of racism are acknowledged to be far-reaching, involving psychosocial processes which are diffuse, contextually bound and profoundly dislocating for victims.

The impact of institutional and personal racism is difficult to measure or assess accurately because of its cumulative nature; however, it can result in a decreased sense of optimism, displaced anger and a retreat into individualism for survival of the spirit. Constant victimisation and exploitation result in rage and conflicts between self-realisation and the restrictions imposed by membership of a minority group. The sense of limited control over external social realities and the subsequent feelings of helplessness and powerlessness lead to depression (Newnes et al. 1999). Black and other ethnic minority young women face a double disadvantage in a racist and patriarchal society where they attract the projected hate of those white women and black men who are subordinated to white men.

In the context of counselling and psychotherapeutic work, it is important to understand how public perceptions of mental health problems are organised in a multicultural society. Studies have reported that definitions of mental health problems are associated with extremely disturbed behaviour by individuals. A North American study found that public perceptions of schizophrenia were associated with emotional problems, depression and nervousness caused by stress and relationship difficulties. The public favoured psychosocial treatment such as psychotherapy and behaviour modification. This compared with mental health professionals who favoured explanations of symptoms of cognitive disorganisation caused by genetic and biochemical factors and drug treatment (Pote and Orrell 2002). In addition, it is argued that ethnicity and gender of the client and clinician are critical variables influencing diagnosis. High frequencies of psychosis and low frequencies of depression are diagnosed in black populations, combined with stereotyped perceptions that ethnic minority children and young people have less insight than their white counterparts (Lefley 1990, Johnson and Orrell 1996).

Assessment has been defined as a tool to aid in the planning of future work and the beginning of helping another person to identify areas for growth and change. Its purpose is the identification of needs – it is never an end in itself (Taylor and Devine 1993). Assessment is the foundation of the therapeutic process with clients. It can set the tone for further contact, it is your first opportunity to engage with new or existing clients, and it can be perceived by children and young people as a judgement on their character or behaviour. A good experience of assessment can make them feel positive about receiving help and their attitude to you and your agency. A bad experience of assessment can make matters worse, offend and make problems harder to resolve in the long term. You can regard it as little more than a paper-chasing exercise, involving form-filling and participating in a process that restricts eligibility; or you can see it as an opportunity to engage with children and adolescents in a problem-solving partnership where both of you can learn more about yourselves.

Effective assessment with black and ethnic minority communities is highlighted throughout the UK National Service Framework for Mental Health (DOH 1999c). Standard one notes that some black and minority ethnic communities have higher diagnosed rates of mental health problems than the general population and calls for specific programmes of service development for these communities. Standards two to six discuss the need for performance assessment to include the experience of service users and carers, including those from black and ethnic minority communities. These reflect the anxiety among politicians and professionals regarding the disproportionate numbers of black and ethnic minority people admitted compulsorily into psychiatric care. They suggest that in addition to the needs of black and ethnic minority children and young people being neglected, they also represent the institutionalisation of fear of the *other*.

In seeking to understand this you need to be able to review the social context of mental health, cultural variations in emotional expression, and the wider effects of racism in producing higher levels of stress and disadvantage among black and ethnic minority children and young people. This is then compounded by practices in psychiatric services that are perceived to be institutionally racist and insensitive to individual needs. The development of psychiatry and theories of human growth and development constructed in the 18th and 19th centuries were based on white ethnocentric beliefs and assumptions about normality. The Western model of illness regards the mind as distinct from the body and defines mental illness or mental health according to negative, deficit characteristics. In non-Western cultures such as Chinese, Indian and African, mental health is often perceived as a harmonious balance between a person's internal and external influences. Thus a person is intrinsically linked to their environment and vice versa.

The Western model of assessment of mental illness tends to ignore the religious or spiritual aspects of the culture in which it is based. However, Eastern, African and Native American cultures tend to integrate them (Fernando 2002). Spirituality and religion as topics in general do not feature often in the clinical literature, yet they can be critical components of a young person's well-being, offering a source of strength and hope in trying circumstances. Clients for whom family and faith backgrounds are inseparable may need encouragement to feel comfortable in multi-faith settings. Counsellors and psychotherapists need to address this dimension as part of the constellation of factors affecting black children and young people, bearing in mind the positive and sometimes negative impact spiritual or religious beliefs might have on their mental health.

Perceptions of child and adolescent problems

Practitioners seeking to assess and intervene effectively with children and adolescents from diverse cultures have to carefully consider the various ways potential mental health problems are thought about, understood and communicated in every family, in every culture. In particular, the following points should be kept in mind:

- Children do not have one essential identity, but switch identities in different situations and, subject to a diversity of cultural influences, can produce new identities.
- Practitioners employing anti-racist and anti-discriminatory principles may simplistically try to reinforce apparent cultural norms that are not applicable, or explain disturbed behaviour in terms of cultural features which are irrelevant.
- Understanding the culture within the culture – in other words, finding out what are the individual and family norms, preferences, styles, habits and patterns of relationships that make that family what it is in the particular context of psychological problems.

For example, there is an assumption that Asian families are close-knit with extended family relationships often living together in multi-generational households. This is a stereotype and may apply to a lot of Asian families but the danger is in applying the stereotype unthinkingly instead of using it to test a hypothesis about the particular family being helped. In many circumstances taking into account the concept of extended family relationships in close proximity can aid assessment of emerging mental health problems in an Asian child or young person. But assuming this is *always* a sign of family strength and harmonious supportive relationships is risking missing obscure, destructive dynamics that may be contributing to the child's mental health problems. These factors are beginning to emerge as some Asian youth struggle to balance loyalty to their history and culture with the different values and pressures in their environment (Fernando 2002).

A failure to recognise and acknowledge significant mental health problems could be just as damaging to the young person and others involved with them, as could seeking to explain their behaviour with a definitive psychiatric diagnosis. For some young people it could be a relief to have an explanation for feelings and behaviour that they find hard to make sense of, whereas for others it could exacerbate feelings of blame, guilt and self-loathing. The enduring social stigma of mental health problems in addition to racist experiences provides an overall context for these feelings to be repressed, displaced or acted out.

Very little of the research on the mental health consequences of black and other ethnic minority children witnessing domestic violence has examined the impact race and racism might have on these children. It has been suggested that the societal context of racism provides these children with a sense of refuge inside their own home. However, when violence occurs inside their home as well, this can have profound effects on the child's sense of security and vulnerability, triggering acute anxiety-related symptoms (Imam 1994). For these children there is no hiding place. Some of the negative impacts on black children are likely to be exacerbated by additional threats of abduction abroad, and/or by being asked inappropriately to act as interpreters or translators in situations where their protection is at stake.

A good grasp of the principles underpinning culturally competent assessment and intervention and an ability to translate these principles into practice is essential. Some guidance is offered in the context of safeguarding children and young people (Howarth 2002):

- Assessments should be child-centred and rooted in child development.
- Professionals should recognise and work with diversity.
- Assessment practice means working whenever possible, with children and families and building on the family strengths as well as identifying difficulties.
- The quality of the human environment is linked to the development of the child.

- A range of professionals are the assessors and providers of services to children in need, therefore assessments should be multidisciplinary.
- Assessment is a continuing process. Interventions and services should be provided alongside the assessment.
- Effective assessment practice is dependent on the combination of evidence-based practice grounded in knowledge with finely balanced professional judgement.

You will need to integrate multi-faceted knowledge of child development from knowledge and skills acquired from contemporary studies in human growth and development into your assessments to be able to confidently embark upon culturally competent practice (Beckett 2002). Psychodynamic theory and systemic theory are especially important tools to employ in this context. Two key concepts that are critical to the interrelationship between the inner and outer worlds reflected in these theoretical paradigms are attachment and self-esteem. Children who are securely attached to significant adults in early childhood have been shown to develop good peer relationships and cope well with problems. Therapeutic practice concerned with helping children who have lost attachment figures places great emphasis on providing these children with continuity of good alternative parenting experiences.

It is important to avoid being deterministic about some of these theoretical resources or to assume that adverse childhood experiences can cascade automatically through subsequent generations. Modern research has demonstrated the complexity and diversity of different children's responses to similar experiences. It is important to understand what may act as protective factors in children's lives which can mitigate the effects of negative experiences and promote resilience. And there are children who with ample social and family support have little capacity to cope with small amounts of stress. In other words, do not be tempted to ascribe a social causal relationship with the presenting difficulty just because your client is from an ethnic minority.

Children vary in their vulnerability to psychosocial stress and adversity as a result of both genetic and environmental influences. Family-wide experiences tend to impinge on individual children in quite different ways. The reduction of negative and increase of positive chain reactions influences the extent to which the effects of adversity persist over time. New experiences that open up opportunities can provide beneficial turning-point effects. Although positive experiences in themselves do not exert much of a protective effect, they can be helpful if they serve to neutralise some risk factors. And the cognitive and affective processing of experiences is likely to be a positive influence whether or not resilience develops (Rutter 1999a).

Evidence-based practice requires the gathering, testing, recording and weighing of evidence on which to base decisions and the careful use of knowledge gained during culturally competent assessment work with a child and family. This helps the task of determining what is most relevant in a family's situation, what is most significant for the child, the impact intervention is having and the judgement about when more or less action is required in the child's best interests. It is important to pay equal attention to all three domains and not be deflected by a child's emotional or behavioural symptoms to the extent that parental capacity and environmental factors are neglected.

Recent research demonstrates that assessments can become dominated by the agenda of social services departments when issues of protection or neglect are at stake thereby undermining the concept of inter-agency co-operation (Howarth 2002). Also, in the drive to complete recording forms within specified timescales, culturally competent practice is given a lack of attention, while the pace of the assessment is inconsistent with the capacity of the family to cope. Counsellors and psychotherapists have a crucial role to play in engaging with other agencies such as social services where anxieties can tumble out of control in the climate of stress, blame and persecution surrounding their practice. A therapeutic intervention in the context of case conferences or agency meetings combined with insights developed in culturally competent work can go a long way to mitigate or contain potentially destructive processes.

Assessment as process

A wide definition of assessment will ensure your practice is empowering and culturally competent. It is important to think of assessment as a process rather than a one-off event. There should be a seamless transition from assessment to intervention in a circular process that includes the crucial elements of planning and reviewing. Once completed, the circle begins again at the assessment stage of the process and so on. Think of it as a continuous, perpetual movement punctuated by a range of activities involving major or minor interventions in the lives of children and young people. Rather than adopting a *one-dimensional* view of assessment you could also perceive it as an intervention in itself – the very act of conducting an information-gathering interview could have a significant positive impact on a young person's well-being. The simple idea that someone cares and is prepared to listen to their story could be enormously comforting to a child or adolescent feeling lonely and isolated and with low self-esteem.

No discussion of assessment can be complete without addressing the concept of need, as it is a word that frequently appears in much legislation, practice guidance and service providers' documentation. There are universal needs expressed in global documents like the UN declaration on the rights of children, and there are special needs which although clearly discriminatory appear to be accepted as a useful signifier for certain groups in society. What this does is to permit rationing to occur under the guise of benign motives. If you consider the idea that every child or young person has special needs, in the sense of their individual uniqueness, and replace this with the notion of rights then the concept of special needs becomes redundant. In our therapeutic context the concept of need has a powerful impact on assessment practice. It has been categorised in the following way to help us distinguish the subtleties in meaning and the way need can be defined (Bradshaw 1972):

- *Normative need* – decided by professionals or administrators on behalf of the community. Standards are set to minimum levels of service with stigma attached.
- *Felt need* – limited by the individuals' expression of wants based on their perceptions, knowledge and experience.
- *Expressed need* – these are felt needs translated into service demand but restricted by what the client feels is likely to be offered.
- *Comparative need* – a comparison of need between two areas or client groups in order to reach standardised provision; results in levelling down rather than up.

It is useful to bear these definitions in mind during the process of your assessment practice. They can help guide you and enable you to position yourself as you move from the role of client advocate, articulating their needs, through the agency representative, who is expected to place a boundary or limit on resources, and finally to counsellor or psychotherapist, working systematically to service specifications.

Accepting that assessment is an imperfect science is a good starting point for creative culturally competent practice. Also understanding that it is a dynamic process requiring high quality communication skills is very important. Dynamic in the sense that it is not static – information can become out of date, a family's functioning can deteriorate quickly, while the very act of assessment can affect that which you are assessing. Assessment is therefore a purposeful activity. It is the art of managing competing demands and negotiating the best possible outcome. It means steering between the pressures of organisational demands, legislative injunction, limited resources and personal agendas. It includes having the personal integrity to hold to your core values and ethical base while being buffeted by strong feelings.

An assessment should be part of a perceptual/analytic process that involves selecting, categorising, organising and synthesising data. If it is conducted as an exploratory study avoiding labels, it can result in a careful deliberation of a young person's needs and not just fitting them into whatever provision exists. Remember that all assessments contain the potential for error or bias. These can be partly counteracted by following these guidelines:

- *Improving self-awareness* so as to monitor when you are trying to normalise, be over-optimistic or rationalise data.
- *Getting supervision,* which helps to release blocked feelings or confront denial of facts or coping with the occasional situation where you have been manipulated.
- *Being aware* of standing in awe of those who hold higher status or power and challenging their views when necessary.
- *Treating all assessments* as working hypotheses which ought to be substantiated with emerging knowledge, remembering that they are inherently speculations derived from material and subjective sources.

With government policy and organisational changes moving in the direction of more multidisciplinary teamworking it is imperative that therapeutic assessment skills in the context of practice with other professionals is both authoritative and creative. The values and knowledge base of different staff from other agencies will be reflected in the way they think about and undertake assessment. Your contribution is crucial and depends on having the capacity to work with other colleagues in partnership. Negotiation skills are paramount in order to enable you to challenge and confront when and where necessary to defend children and young people's therapeutic needs. Networking is considered a valuable attribute and you should be developing expertise in liaison, linking, communicating and convening meetings.

Multidisciplinary teams can become stressful places to work, particularly when the service is under pressure and energies are drained by resource shortages combined with high demand. It is easier to keep a low profile and grit your teeth in these circumstances rather than open up a painful or uncomfortable issue for discussion. However, you will gain respect by voicing concerns about the service or the clients and showing a willingness to tackle difficult issues. Being open, child-centred and demonstrating sensitivity to the team dynamics will be helpful to others who probably feel the same. Your broader understanding of children and young people in their cultural and socio-economic context together with your specific knowledge of psychotherapeutic processes will help clarify your distinctive and valued contribution.

Integrated intervention

An integrated culturally competent therapeutic model offers a concept of the mind, its mechanisms and a method of understanding why some children behave in seemingly repetitive, destructive ways. It offers the essential helping relationship involving advanced listening and communication skills with individuals or families. It provides a framework to address profound disturbances and inner conflicts within children and adolescents around issues of loss, attachment, anxiety and personal development in their authentic cultural context. Key ideas such as defence mechanisms, and the transference in the relationship between worker and client can be extremely helpful in reviewing the work being undertaken and in the process of supervision. The psychodynamic model, in particular, helps evaluate the strong feelings aroused in particular work situations where, for example, a young person transfers feelings and attitudes onto the worker that derive from an earlier significant relationship. Counter-transference occurs when you try to live up to that expectation and behave, for example, like the client's parent.

It is a useful way of attempting to understand seemingly irrational behaviour based on Eurocentric assumptions and beliefs. The notion of defence mechanisms is a particularly helpful way of assessing male adolescents, for example, who may have difficulty expressing their emotions. The integrated model acknowledges the influence of past events/attachments and can create a healthy suspicion about surface behaviour while addressing the complexities in family interactions. The development of insight can be a particularly empowering experience to enable ethnic minority children and young people to understand themselves and take more control over their own lives.

A recent study found that parenting styles have an influence on whether young teenagers, age 12–13, years engage in delinquent or anti-social activity (Smith et al. 2001). The study linked smoking and drinking to delinquency and identified a substantial use of drugs in the age group. It also suggested that young people who had been victims of bullying, robbery or assault were more likely to commit offences. Researchers measured three personality dimensions: impulsivity, alienation and self-esteem. Those who were victimised and those who offended tended to have lower self-esteem. The study concluded that young people who witness parenting as arbitrary and inconsistent have a higher incidence of delinquency. This compares with the fact that parents who supervise children closely, but are happy to negotiate some degree of autonomy are more likely to avoid teenage difficulties.

The popularity of parent education or training programmes seems to be a response to a demand for a variety of support, including information, child-development knowledge and skills development in managing children of all ages. It is a role undertaken in practice in the context of other work, most likely general family assessments or specific risk assessments where concerns have reached the threshold of statutory intervention. The gap between the demand and provision is currently met in the voluntary and private sectors, who are absorbing more and more complex work with fewer qualified staff. Yet counselling and psychotherapeutic skills deployed early enough are ideally suited to provide appropriate family support grounded in psychodynamic and systemic theory and based on best practice evidence.

Families for whom parent education is unlikely to be a sufficient response to child management difficulties are those which feature maternal depression, socio-economic disadvantage and the social isolation of the mother. Extra-familial conflict combined with relationship problems also contributes to the problem severity and chronicity and therefore affects the ability to introduce change. Parental misperception of the deviance of their children's behaviour is also a significant impediment to engaging in constructive family support (Macdonald and Roberts 1995). In other words, simply referring any parent/carer to a parent education resource or offering to convene a therapeutic group to parents/carers who cannot make use of the experience is offering false hope. It can emphasise feelings of hopelessness and failure, reinforce guilt and undermine the relationship between client and practitioner.

Early intervention

The evidence demonstrates conclusively that one of the biggest risk factors in developing adult mental health problems is a history of untreated or inadequately supported childhood mental health prob-lems (Department of Health 1998b, Howe 1999, Department of Health 2001b). Therefore it is imperative that counsellors and psychotherapists address this growing problem and offer their own distinctive contri-bution in the context of early intervention practice and various government health improvement programmes. Early intervention is often synonymous with preventive practice in child and adolescent mental health work (Walker 2001a).

The principle of preparing people for potential difficulties is useful and resonates with proactive initiatives in schools, youth clubs and resources, such as telephone helplines/Internet discussion groups and campaigns, to reach out to children and young people before they reach a crisis. Linking specific therapeutic interventions with agreed outcomes is problematic due to the network of variables potentially impacting on a child or young person's development. It is notori-ously hard to accurately predict the effect of specific interventions espe-cially when there is a lack of a research and evaluation culture in an agency. Equally, it is even harder to measure the impact of preventive or early intervention programmes because of the impossibility of proving that something did not happen.

Children and adolescents acquire different risk labels such as 'looked after', 'excluded' or 'young offender', affecting the variety of perceptions of their needs from the care system, education system or youth justice system. This can have a detrimental effect on efforts to build a coalition among different professional staff to intervene preventively. Each professional system has its own language and methodology with which to describe the same child, sometimes resulting in friction between agencies and misconceptions about how to work together and integrate interventions. Arguments over the *real* nature of a child's behaviour or the *correct* theoretical inter-pretation are a wasteful extravagance. In this climate the mental health needs of such children can be neglected and the opportunity for thoughtful, preventive work missed.

In addition to understanding why some children develop mental health problems, it is crucially important to learn more about those who in similar circumstances do not. Research is required to analyse the nature of these resilient children to under-stand whether coping strategies or skills can be transferred to other children. Positive factors such as reduced social isolation, good schooling and supportive adults outside the family appear to help. These are the very factors missing in socially excluded fam-ilies who generally live in deprived conditions and suffer more socio-economic disadvantages than other children. Yet many of these children will not develop mental health problems.

One of the most important preventive approaches is helping children and young people cope with the stresses they face in modern society. Every generation has to negotiate the manifestations of stress in their wider culture, therefore relying on ways used by former generations is not useful. This is challenging to practitioners who will naturally draw from their own experiences as an instinctive resource. However, the evidence suggests first in understanding the different *levels of stress* experienced by children and young people. Stress is a broad concept and includes a diverse range of experiences. The key is to ensure that the child themselves can categorise the level of stress according to their own cultural norms – for example, whether a bereavement is an acute or moderate stress, or whether parental separation/divorce is a severe and longer-lasting stress. What helps is enabling the child or adolescent to focus on what can be done to improve the situation rather than concentrating on negative feelings (Rutter 1995).

Postmodernism, culture and therapy

Postmodern ideas have been influencing practice in recent years as therapists seek ways of resolving the dilemmas inherent in modern practice that is constrained by managerialist values while demand for services increases. Postmodernism seeks to challenge received wisdom about what interventions are valid, based on apparent empirical certainty. Postmodern theorists have articulated a theory that requires us to continually question the prevailing cultural orthodoxy and to deconstruct theories and practices based on old certainties. For counsellors and psychotherapists aspiring to culturally competent practice, this is a valuable paradigm. Replacing conventional notions with a more flexible and less constrained perspective enables practice to embrace a plurality of intellectual resources from which to guide your work. The growth of the voluntary sector, devolved budgets, and decision-making, horizontal management structures and retraction of local authority social services departments are all stimulating the expansion of postmodernist thinking, as creative and innovative ways of delivering interventions are being engendered (Walker 2001b).

Postmodern theorists are also highlighting the significance of power relationships within practice and arguing for an analysis of how this impacts on intervention practice refracted through the prism of a commitment to social justice and human rights (Leonard 1997).

By attending more closely to the barriers constructed between yourself and clients you can begin to appreciate how professional language is a way of preventing cultural understanding rather than enabling useful communication. Narrative as a root metaphor can replace old modernist certainties derived from classic theoretical paradigms and medical models informing assessment and intervention practice. A more refined practice can become a dialogic–reflexive interaction between client and worker using language and the cultural construction of meaning to define the cultural parameters of the helping process.

If you are interested in a practice that seeks to challenge social inequalities and embrace radical ideas based on, for example, feminist or green politics, then you can begin with a structural analysis of power in society that produces exploitation of marginalised citizens. The postmodern paradigm advocates the importance of diversity, devolution, decentralisation and cultural interdependence. An integrated culturally competent model of practice drawing upon these notions searches for an understanding of the experience of the service user. Explanation or interpretation is still important but in the context of social understanding that is pluralistic, where a range of cultural explanations can co-exist and be part of a larger chain of enquiry that challenges discrimination in all its manifestations (McLennan 1996).

Therapeutic practices have become burdened by the managerial demands for efficiency, calculability, predictability and control. The relentless obsession with cost-effectiveness implies that only things that can be counted are important, and that the standardisation controlled by technology ensures predictability. The ensuing conformity and globalisation of practice has been highlighted by Dominelli (1996), who challenges the privatisation of welfare services, new organisational structures in helping agencies and a redefinition of the therapeutic task that leads to a deterioration in the relationship between worker and client. This conflict between the bureaucratic context of your practice and the values that attracted you into helping work in the first place lie at the heart of contemporary intervention practice. Postmodernist thinking offers a liberating perspective to help you locate your practice in the wider cultural context and within your personal value system.

Bonding and attachment

Bonding and attachment are probably among the most widely used concepts in assessment and intervention when considering issues such as whether a child remains with their carers, or to gauge the extent of fundamental problematic experiences in a child or young person presenting with difficulties. There is a paucity of information on culturally competent assessment of children and young people in relation to bonding and attachment. Previous research tends to focus on the evolutionary and biological predispositions underlying attachment while downplaying the culturally laden *meanings* that behaviour has for different societies. For example, new research illustrates that Aboriginal children are significantly overrepresented in the substitute care population in Australia by a factor of ten (Vicary and Andrews 2000, AIHW 2001).

It is argued that the long-term mental health consequences for an Aboriginal child to be brought up in a non-Aboriginal household far outweigh concerns about the immediate needs of disadvantaged children in the context of racism and culturally inappropriate assessment measures (Yeo 2003). The interplay between ideas from attachment theory, which is largely concerned with dyadic relationships, and systemic theory, which is more concerned with the whole family, can be explored in a more integrated manner to foster a richer assessment and intervention process.

Bowlby recognised that attachment relationships and family life were intertwined and that human beings of all ages are happiest and able to deploy their talents to their best advantage when they are confident that, standing behind them, there are one or more trusted persons who will come to their aid should difficulties arise. The person trusted, also known as an attachment figure, can be considered as providing his/her companion with a secure base from which to operate.

He argued that the main aim of family therapy is to enable all members to relate together in such a way that each member can find a secure base in his/her relationships within the family, as occurs in every healthily functioning family. To this end, attention is directed to understanding the ways in which family members may at times succeed in providing each other with a secure base but at other times fail to do so – by misconstruing each other's roles, by developing false expectations of each other or by redirecting forms of behaviour that should be appropriately directed towards one family member towards another (Bowlby 1979).

Since Bowlby described these concepts, there has been enormous effort to understand the different types of attachment relationships and their significance for the individual. More recently attention has turned to how these relationships are played out in the drama of family life. Attachment theory is included in government guidelines for assessing families (Bentovim and Bingley Miller 2002) and as a tool for understanding a child's developmental experiences. Systemic theory and attachment theory share common origins: both developed in opposition to the limitations of prevailing perspectives in the treatment of children or individuals, emphasised the importance of relationships and children's environments and both were influenced by general systemic thinking. Attachment theory offers unique data about the dyadic relationship (Walker and Akister 2004).

Being able to recognise the strategies children use within a dyadic relationship provides useful information about how the dyad has related in the past, and helps clinicians formulate questions, hypothesise and plan family interventions. Attachment patterns are observable. They do not require the infants or young children to articulate verbally their contribution to the relationship, but do require the child to relate to the parent as he/she always does, thus telling a story about the parent–child relationship. In other words, in attending to the attachment relationship, clinicians take into account the young child's non-verbal story of their experiences in the child-carer context (Kozlowska and Hanney 2002).

Integrating systemic and attachment theories

The question of how to develop these two theories, both of which are fundamentally focused on family relationships and their impact on children's development is taxing researchers. In terms of their relevance to practice, government and health and social care agencies are keen to standardise assessments of children and families. The theoretical underpinnings are critical here as standardising the collection of information is relatively simple but making sense of the data requires complex theoretical frameworks if cultural competence is to be achieved. Children have different attachments to each of their parents, so it is not possible to understand a family based on just one of these relationships. Similarly, adult attachment security relates to specific relationships and may alter or develop over time. Recent research increasingly indicates that both child and adult categorisations are subject to change rather than remaining fixed over time (Cook 2000, Feeney 2003). Ideas from both attachment and systemic theories are needed to aid practitioners in their assessment of a family.

There is considerable debate as to how these theoretical ideas might be combined or integrated. Three models are described below:

- *Dynamic Maturational Model* (DMM) which proposes expanding the attachment categories in a way which is helpful to therapeutic practice with families.
- *Network Model* which proposes keeping the ideas separate but valuing their differing contributions.
- *Family Attachment Measure* (FAM) which proposes an integration in order to assess family attachment.

All three models have useful contributions to further our culturally competent understanding of family processes and the importance of attachment relationships.

Crittenden (1999) suggests that from a clinical perspective the normative classifications are rarely found when working with disadvantaged, traumatised populations. Crittenden's expanded classifications are helpful, for practitioners working with families, in emphasising the adaptations which people make to deal as best they can with the difficult circumstances they find themselves in. The DMM emphasises the notions of adaptation, development and change. In contrast to other attachment models, which emphasise continuity of attachment classification, this model emphasises the dynamic interaction between maturation and experience.

In the DMM all attachment strategies are seen as adaptations to a particular relationship. In other words, children's behavioural and mental strategies are seen as organised and biologically determined, and function to increase the probability of safety and survival. The child's behaviour is understood as adaptive in the light of their relationships and other factors such as illness, loss or trauma. (This conceptual approach is similar to the family therapist technique of positive reframing.) In practice, this is important because the model focuses on the strengths and strategies that the child has developed rather than on weaknesses or deficits. It has an innate respect for black and ethnic minority children and adults who have had to contend with difficult circumstances. It also conceptualises attachment strategies or ways of relating to caregivers as becoming more complex over the lifespan.

Although treatment/intervention is often informed by attachment data it may occur at the individual, dyadic, marital or family system level. Using attachment-derived data does not necessarily result in an attachment intervention. Because of the connections between systems, interventions on family or marital levels can bring about change in the child's attachment relationships. This is compatible with the network model which takes information from different levels in the family system to inform interventions.

The network model (Capra 1997) refers to the application of general systemic theory to living systems. A key characteristic of living systems is the tendency to form multilevelled structures of systems within systems. Although each system remains distinct, it is simultaneously part of a more complex system that is distinct in its own right. This concept is synergistic with culturally competent practice. Inherent in the network model is the understanding that although the information from different levels of complexity is unique, it is neither more nor less fundamental than information from another level.

With this model, integration of family and attachment theories implies the ability to recognise each level of complexity as distinct yet interconnected. Using the network model, the integration of attachment and systemic theories does not mean either merging them or keeping them distinct. Rather, integration refers to the ability to recognise each level of complexity (e.g. dyad versus family) as distinct yet interconnected, and it enables our attention to move through different levels of complexity as required (Walker and Akister 2004). Figure 5.1 illustrates this complexity.

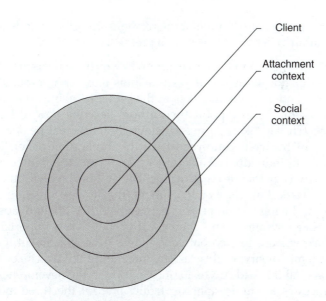

Figure 5.1   Integrated model of practice theories.

This model therefore means that the practitioner is able to consider the unique properties of a dyadic relationship together with the unique properties of the family system, as well as the relationship between them. This is essentially a simple model but vital in practice as it is easy for the complexities of family relationships to become impossible to disentangle, and this offers a way to separate key components. For example, it may be that one of the attachment relationships in a family is key to the problems being experienced by the whole family. In this situation the intervention will need to pay attention to the specific dyadic relationship as well as the family system.

In contrast to the network model the FAM is based on a proposed integration of attachment and systemic theories as a way of assessing family attachment. The approach argues that the key elements of attachment processes are affect regulation, interpersonal understanding, information processing and the provision of comfort within intimate relationships. They see these as equally applicable to family processes provided that

- attachment processes at the individual level are linked to family processes using the shared frames or representations of emotions, cognitions and behaviour;
- there is explicit consideration of the nature and quality of the dynamic between attachment and other processes in family life; and
- there is a conceptualisation of the relationship between individual and family processes. (Hill et al. in press)

The FAM is given to the family group in which members are asked to consider questions about relationships and a range of safety, discipline and attachment issues in the present. Taking attachment theory as the starting point the authors describe how although the research has taken an overwhelmingly individual perspective, attachment theory is concerned with the implication of relational processes for individuals (Hill et al. in press). The idea of integration of these two key theories is attractive. The authors highlight the fact that the classical measure of attachment (the Strange Situation Test) looking at the interaction process between mother–infant dyads has always been systemic. This theoretical proposition is important in again taking steps to incorporate the ideas from attachment theory into systemic theory, in this case by integrating the two theoretical positions. All this adds up to a critical period in the development of the processes for understanding family life. All the three models described contribute to our ways of assessing and interpreting the dyadic relationships which exist within the family and which have previously tended to be studied in separate domains (Walker and Akister 2004).

A culturally competent theoretical model

Using an integrated psychodynamic and systemic model means understanding that changes in any aspect of the family system affect other parts of the system. Attachment insecurity in one member is likely to have ripple effects through the whole system. These dynamics mean that changes which occur in one part of the system (e.g. parent–child relationship) can alter some aspect of the association between secure attachment and couple relationship quality.

A growing body of research finds concordance between mother's adult attachment and their attachment relationship with their child. It has been widely assumed that quality of the parent–child relationship is the linking mechanism – that adults who are securely attached themselves tend to provide a secure base for their children (Byng-Hall 1998). It is also suggested that the relationship between the parents plays a central role in the generational transmission of working models of attachment – that marital quality may play a causal role in affecting parenting style and children's adaptation. In other words, the family system plays a part as well as the dyadic parent–child relationship.

Extrapolating from recent research findings some authors conclude that the transmission of attachment relationships from grandparents to parents to children is not simply a matter of parenting. When a person learns early on that he/she is worthy of love, and that adults will be responsive and available in times of need, he/she is more likely to establish satisfying relationships with other partners, and to have the inclination and ability to work towards solving relationship problems and regulating emotions so that they do not escalate out of control (Mikulincer et al. 2002).

This leads to the place for cultural competence in working with children and adolescents on the difficulties not only for problems which are clearly involving the whole family but also where problems arise in dyadic relationships. For example, a young person may be in conflict with family cultural values – perhaps because of their developmental stage, and also in dispute with the same-gender parent. It also raises the question of how to help adults move on and restructure their adult attachment where this is part of the problem.

There have been enormous steps in the last 5 years in looking at the interactions between attachment and systemic theories. The contribution to understanding the dilemmas faced by individuals throughout the life cycle by the two theories is well established. That attachment style can develop and may change throughout a child or young person's life, in the context of their experiences in relationships, enhances the understanding of family systems and thereby offers a valuable tool to help construct a culturally competent practice.

Overall there is wide support, in the research findings, for practitioners working with either individuals or families to pay close attention to the attachment styles and relationships (dyadic) within the family as well as working with the whole family system. The duality of approach enables a more detailed understanding of the family dynamics. Utilising the concepts embodied in the network model also supports the practice of combining systemic and individual therapies as appropriate. While there is still a long way to go it is clear that thinking about the family system alone or about the attachment dyad alone is limiting and we should try to consider both paradigms (Walker and Akister 2004).

This is easy to say and hard to do. How to work with attachments is unclear. Systemic and psychodynamic therapies offer clear ways of working with a family or child and can include work focused on dyadic relationships which may alter attachments. The counsellor or psychotherapist needs to consider the place for individual, couple and whole family interventions and their potential impact on the attachment relationships in order to enhance cultural competence. Furthermore, there is increasing evidence that the specificity in the associations of psychopathology items and cultural factors indicates that the relationship between ethnicity and perception of mental health problems in children and adolescents is complex and cannot be understood in isolation from other factors or a more culturally competent understanding of conceptual models.

Thus cultural variations affect the prevalence rates, similarities and differences in children and young people's mental health. The use of ICD 10 and DSMIV medical classifications offers a limiting paradigm with which to understand many problems. Not all children with symptoms of mental health problems show marked impairment, while conversely some children experience significant psychosocial impairment without reaching the clinical threshold for diagnosis (Silberg 2001). The way forward is to continually question and critically examine the assumptions we make about assessment and intervention methodology to ensure we keep pace with the constantly changing cultural environment of children and young people.

Summary

Assessment is a tool to aid in the planning of future work and the beginning of helping another person to identify areas for growth and change. It is the foundation of the therapeutic process with clients. It can set the tone for further contact, it is your first opportunity to engage with new or existing clients, but it can be perceived by children and young people as a judgement on their character or behaviour. A good experience of assessment can make them feel positive about receiving help. A bad experience of assessment can make matters worse, offend and make problems harder to resolve in the long term.

The psychological consequences of racism involve psychosocial processes which are diffuse, contextually bound and profoundly dislocating for victims. The impact of institutional and personal racism can result in a decreased sense of optimism, displaced anger and a retreat into individualism for survival of the spirit. Constant victimisation and exploitation result in rage and conflicts between self-realisation and the restrictions imposed by membership of a minority group.

Practitioners employing anti-racist and anti-discriminatory principles may simplistically try to reinforce apparent cultural norms that are not applicable, or explain disturbed behaviour in terms of cultural features which are irrelevant. It is better to understand the culture *within* the culture by finding out the individual and family norms, preferences, styles, habits and patterns of relationships that make that family what it is in the particular context of psychological problems.

A structural analysis of power in our society where exploitation of marginalised citizens occurs is necessary. The postmodern paradigm advocates the importance of diversity, devolution, decentralisation and cultural interdependence. An integrated culturally competent model of practice drawing upon these notions can better understanding the experience of the client. Explanation or interpretation is still important but in the context of social understanding it is pluralistic, where a range of cultural explanations can co-exist.

The interplay between ideas from attachment theory, which is largely concerned with dyadic relationships, and systemic theory, which is more concerned with the whole family, can be explored in a more integrated manner to foster a richer assessment and intervention process. Although treatment/intervention is often informed by attachment data it may occur at the individual, dyadic, marital or family system level. Because of the connections between systems, interventions on family or marital levels can bring about change in the child's attachment relationships.

As well as understanding why some children develop mental health problems, it is crucially important to learn more about those who in similar circumstances do not. Research is required to analyse the nature of these resilient children to understand whether coping strategies or skills can be transferred to others. Positive factors such as reduced social isolation, good schooling and supportive adults outside the family appear to help.

Evidence-based practice requires the gathering, testing, recording and weighing of evidence on which to base decisions and the careful use of knowledge gained during culturally competent assessment and intervention with a child and family. This helps the task of determining what is most relevant in a family's situation, what is most significant for the child, the impact intervention is having and the judgement about when more or less action is required in the child's best interests. It is important to pay equal attention to all three domains – a child's personality, parental capacity and the environmental factors.

6

RELIGION AND SPIRITUALITY

In India two figures characterise religious attitudes. The way of the kitten – carried to safety by its mother clasping the scruff, and the way of the monkey – hanging on to its mothers' back.

– Campbell

Introduction

Religion and spirituality are dimensions of cultural diversity which must be actively considered in order to practise in a culturally competent way. The principles underpinning the counselling and psychotherapeutic helping relationship offer a complementary model to build on the capacity for healing that is associated with religious and spiritual experience. They also fit with the concept of personal growth and social justice enshrined in psychosocial practice. It is suggested that religion and spirituality can be equated together or seen as quite distinct concepts. Spirituality, it is argued, refers to one's basic nature and the process of finding meaning and purpose, whereas religion involves a set of organised, institutionalised beliefs and social functions as a means of spiritual expression and experience (Carroll 1998).

Religion and spirituality have traditionally been separated in their application to an understanding of the human condition employed by counsellors and psychotherapists. It is as if our desperate need for recognition and importance has to be privileged over all other influences – particularly those that impinge on the realm of the unconscious and psychological. Some go further and suggest that religions typically act to increase anxiety rather than reduce it, or they are an instrument of oppression and control over women and the poor (Sinha 1988, Guerin 2002). On the other hand the often criticised Islamic codes contained in the Qur'an on closer inspection reveal equal rights prescribed for Muslim women in terms of property, education, inheritance and employment far in advance of Western statutes. The complexities and subtleties of different cultural manifestations of relationship dynamics are lost on those relying on media stereotypes. The central features of spirituality have been described as follows (Martslof and Mickley 1998):

- *Meaning* – the significance of life and deriving purpose in existence.
- *Transcendence* – experience of a dimension beyond the self that opens the mind.
- *Value* – standards and beliefs such as value, truth, beauty and worth often discussed as ultimate values.
- *Connecting* – relationships with others, God or a higher power and the environment.
- *Becoming* – a life that requires reflection and experience, including a sense of who one is and how one knows it.

These spiritual needs can be explained in psychological terms as well. The conventional literature available to counsellors and psychotherapists can be used to explain these ideas in many ways using evidence from orthodox science and theories that have stood the test of time and served professionals well. Yet there is a lingering doubt perhaps that, on deeper reflection, the concepts of faith, purpose and the search for meaning are inadequately quantified in the language of scientific certainty that asserts they are just thought processes or embroidered survival needs. Even in this age of evidence-based practice we know that to ignore our intuitions and gut feelings risks denying us and the children and young people we aspire to help a most valuable tool.

It cannot be co-incidental that the further the human race moves towards scientific and rational certainty aided by the bewildering power of computers and technology, able to explore and manipulate the biological foundations of life using genetic research, the more people seem determined than ever to seek answers to fundamental questions about existence whether from organised religions or alternative forms of spirituality. Jung believed that therapists needed to recognise the relevance of spirituality and religious practice to the needs and workings of the human psyche. He suggested that a psychological problem was *in essence* the suffering of a soul which had not discovered its meaning – that the cause of such suffering was spiritual stagnation or psychic sterility.

Religions are psychotherapeutic systems in the truest sense of the word, and on the grandest scale. They express the whole range of the psychic problem in mighty images; they are the avowal and recognition of the soul, and at the same time the revelation of the soul's nature. (Jung 1978)

Jung's concept of archetypes suggests that unconscious components of the psyche are revealed through dreams and fantasies at critical points of internal conflict. This transcendent process mediates between oppositional archetypes in order to produce a reconciling symbol. This experience enables children and young people to achieve gradual individuation and the revelation of the self. Some of the central experiences of individuation such as the hero's journey, the metaphor of death and rebirth or the image of the divine child are paradigms of religious experience (Nash and Stewart 2002). They migrate into myths, fairy stories and legends, as we shall see in Chapter 7, and are therefore accessible for work with troubled children and adolescents.

A sense of religion or spirituality has the capacity to inhibit or enhance culturally competent therapeutic work with children or young people. You may feel that an over-reliance on beliefs of this nature are symptomatic of a denial defence and a fatalistic outlook in your clients. On the other hand you may believe that having faith in something outside of themselves permits a child or young person to experience a sense of purpose and greater good that can enhance a therapeutic intervention. As a counsellor or psychotherapist you may also have religious beliefs or a sense of spirituality that helps you in your therapeutic work. It might also hinder your work if you encounter an atheistic belief system in a young person or a religious affiliation that contradicts your own. The evidence, although yet to be fully developed, does suggest that spirituality has a protective function against developing psychological problems. Children and young people who possess such a sense of spirituality are considered more resilient in the face of traumas including sexual abuse and less prone to mental health and adjustment problems in adolescence (Resnik et al. 1993, Valentine and Feinauer 1993).

Religion and belief

The relevance to counselling and psychotherapy of religion and spirituality cannot be underestimated as they form a part of the covert or overt belief systems of children and young people that will to a larger or lesser extent impact on the work at hand. This is not to say that only those who have a religious faith or a belief in spirituality will have their therapy affected. The impact of *not believing* or of having firm ideas about the absence of spiritual feelings can be just as important. What is relevant is the existence of the ideas of religion, gods and spirituality in society and how individuals and families orientate to them – or not. Most cultures can trace back into deep history evidence of their ancestral heritage and the ways early civilisations sought to explain the world around them. These tend to involve the intervention of a supreme being or power with the capacity to control the natural elements vital for the survival of the species.

We can understand how, without the tools to predict the climate and manipulate food production methods, primitive people thousands of years ago felt vulnerable and frightened by natural phenomena. Seeking explanations for unpredictable events – good or bad – was perfectly natural. These ancient understandings echo throughout history. They form part of the fabric of world heritage. They have evolved, changed or in some cases stayed more or less the same. Settlers in developed countries embrace unorthodox and ancient customs while some native cultures in developing regions absorb modern theological concepts and spiritual practices. There are pockets of Christianity in strict Islamic states and places where minority religious beliefs are persecuted. Thus for many children and young people these frightening experiences will already have become part of their psychological lives.

The age of Enlightenment and the scientific paradigm provided an alternative set of explanations for why things happened as they did. Thus began a perennial tension between rationalism and religious divinity, symbolised in the creationist versus evolutionist debate about the origins of humanity. The polarisation of these two ideas should intrigue the inquisitive therapist – the need to find extreme opposites to charge an argument or debate might mask deeper ambivalence that is too uncomfortable to bear. In the same way that certain religions seek to claim a single truth or denounce others as *heretical* should serve as useful material for engaging with certain children and young people. What meaning does this have for the child's temperament of problem-solving skills? What are the advantages and disadvantages to hold such profound beliefs? The certainty of a person's belief could be measured by the depth of their mixed feelings and/or their absolute terror of the other point of view.

Here again we encounter the concept of the other – the opposite which is not part of us and must be avoided, rejected or overwhelmed. In earlier centuries, countries went to war and mass murders took place with official sanction on the strength of one's religious beliefs. The history of modern societies has been shaped as much by the religious struggles of previous stages of development as by the economic and political forces motivating people to embark upon social change or revolution. To try to better understand these processes systemic theorists would look for the interactive nature between religious development and political and economic movements – how one influences the other and vice versa. Psychodynamic theorists might formulate an explanation based on the primitive insecurities driving those individuals leading these mass movements and ideologies. Either way or a combination of the two offers us a therapeutic understanding of these powerfully important contexts within which individual children and young people evolve their own psychic road map.

Today, the world is said to be constructed into geo-political blocks based on economic power and geographical position. But there are the equivalent and much more complex *theo-political* blocks which have the capacity to invoke strong feelings and mass change in whole nations or significant sections of them. Table 6.1 illustrates the

Table 6.1 Religions and sects (ONS 2002)

Baha'I	African Orthodox	Calvinistic
Babism	Church	Methodists
Buddhism	Agapemone	Cameronians
Falun Gong	Albigenses	Camisards
Hinayana	American Baptist Church	Catholic Apostilic
Lamaism	American Orthodox Church	Church
Mahayana	Amish	Catholics
Nichiren	Amish Mennonites	Celtic Church
Rinzai Zen	Anabaptists	Chaldaen Christians
Soka Gakkai	Anglican communion	Cherubim &
Soto Zen	Anglo-Catholics	Seraphim
Tantrism	Apostolic Brethren	Churches
Theravada	Armenian Church	Christadelphians
Tibetan Buddhism	Assemblies of God	Christian Brethren
Zen	Assumptionists	Christian Science
	Assyrian Church	Church Army
Christianity	Baptists	Churches of Christ
Abode of love	Bogomils	Churches of God
Adventists	Bohemian Brethren	Church in Wales
African and	Brethren (Dunkers)	Church of Christ
Afro-Caribbean	Brethren in Christ	Scientist
Churches	Buchanites	Church of England

Table 6.1   (Continued)

Church of Ireland	Free Will Baptists	Rosicrucians
Church of Jesus Christ of Latter Day Saints	Gideons	Russian Orthodox Church
Church of North India	Greek Orthodox Church	Salvation Army
Church of Scotland	Huguenots	Seventh-Day Adventists
Church of South India	Hussites	Adventists
Church of the Nazarene	Hutterites	Shakers
Church of the New Jerusalem	Independent Methodists	Society of Friends
Congregationalists	Jehovah's Witnesses	Southern Baptist Church
Conservative Baptists	Jesus People	Swedenborgians
Coptic Orthodox Church	Jumpers	Syrian Orthodox Church
Countess of Huntingdon's Connexion	Lollards	Uniates
	Lutherans	Unitarians
	Malabar Christians	Unitarian Universalists
Covenanters	Maronites	Unitas Fratrum
Cumberland Presbyterian Church	Mennonites	United Free Church
	Methodists	United Reformed Church
Disciples of Christ	Millennial Church	Waldenses
Doppers	Moravian Church	Wesleyans
Doukhobors	Mugggletonians	
Dunkers	Nazarenes	**Confucianism**
Dutch Reformed Church	Nestorians	Neo-Confucianism
Eastern Orthodox Church	New Testament Assembly	**Hinduism**
	Old Believers	Brahmanism
Episcopal Church of Scotland	Old Catholics	Krishna Consciousness
Episcopal Church of USA	Oriental Orthodox Churches	Saivism
	Orthodox Church	Shaktism/Saktism
Ethiopian Orthodox Church	Particular Baptists	Shivaism/Sivaism
	Paulicians	Tantrism
Evangelical Churches	Pentecostal Churches	Vaishnavism
Family of Love	Plymouth Brethren	Vedantism
Fifth Monarchy Men	Presbyterians	Vishnuism
Free Church	Primitive Methodists	
Free Church of Scotland	Protestants	**Islam**
	Puritans	Druzes
Free Presbyterian Church of Scotland	Quakers	Ismailis
	Reformed Churches	Mahdism
	Religious Society of Friends	Senussi
	River Brethren	
	Roman Catholics	

Shia
Sufism
Sunni
Wahhabism

Jainism
Digambara
Svetambara

Judaism
Conservative Judaism
Essenes
Falashas
Hasidism
Kabbalah
Karaism
Messianic Judaism
Orthodox Judaism
Pharisaism
Rabbinism
Reconsructionism
Reform Judaism
Samaritanism
Zionism

Shinto

Taoism

Zoroastrianism
Mazdaism
Parseeism

Other
Ancestor worship
Animism
Candomble
Cargo cult
Druidism
Eleusinian mysteries
Ghost dance cult
Hau-hauism
Macumba
Mithraism
Myalism
Neopaganism
Orphism
Paganism
Pocomania
Rastafarianism
Ratana church
Sabaism
Scientology™
Shamanism
Shango

Spiritualism
Subud
Theosophy
Totenism
Umbanda
Unification Church
Voodoo
Wicca
Yezidism

---

contemporary range of known religions and sects. This offers evidence of the incredibly rich tapestry of religious material available to incorporate within our comprehension of the enormous culturally diverse world our clients inhabit. It also demonstrates the potential for inter-faith rivalries and offers a fertile seed bed for those charismatic figures seeking to influence young people towards a religious and spiritual certainty that claims priority over all others. As with any strong belief, when it turns into obsession it has the potential for great destructiveness.

Culture and spirituality

The decline of organised religious expression in the Western world has been documented in recent years and to some extent is blamed on the increasing prevalence of emotional and behavioural problems in children and young people who are a generation supposedly without moral guidance or social values, according to reactionary pundits. But what is less well documented is the evidence that experiences of the sacred or spiritual remain widespread especially among children (Cobb and Robshaw 1998). Evidence suggests a strong underlying belief system in young people in the concept of spirituality – even by those avowed atheists. Spirituality goes beyond the narrow definition of religion and offers a different and arguably *more difficult* paradigm within which to understand the troubles of children and young people. There are identifying characteristics that can help us in our therapeutic work but with such diverse meanings and interpretations that it becomes harder to be certain about what spirituality is, how it can be defined and whether there are universally accepted categories (Swinton 2003).

We are in effect entering an aspect of children's experience that transcends description and is difficult to adequately express in words. The very nature of the spiritual is inexpressible because it springs from the innermost depths of the human experience. If we are to engage with the religious and spiritual aspects of children and young people's culture then we need to find a way of accessing this rich reservoir of material within which important therapeutic work is ready to be done. The orthodox medical model, whether employed by clinicians or adhered to by parents/carers, may frame a child's psychological difficulties in a bio-psychosocial formulation that encapsulates all the intrinsic and extrinsic variables thought to explain the problem. But when working in a culturally competent manner we need to consider the various ways different cultures conceptualise psychological problems and if that means using a spiritual explanatory framework then so be it.

The recent ban on girls wearing the *hijab* at school in France has served to illustrate the potential destructiveness in the underlying tensions between the former colonial countries and their legacies of immigration and cultural diversity. The French state education system reflects the secular model of society created in the aftermath of the revolution. The strict separation of religion from the state has provided the context in which the wearing of the *hijab* is perceived as a religious symbol and therefore disallowed in school. Following the French example, some schools in the UK have also banned the wearing of the *hijab*. For some girls this may represent an attack upon their religion and result in considerable anxiety and depression. Evidence suggests that the wearing of the *hijab* in Western societies is a complex act involving a desire to remain within their tradition and to challenge it at the same time while also seeking to create a space for equality (Ghuman 2004).

If the child or young person, from whatever culture, has a belief system that accepts and takes account of a spiritual dimension then, rather than *pathologising* this, a counsellor or psychotherapist needs to reflect on how this meaning may be affecting the problem concerned. It could be part of the problem or it could be maintaining the problem or it could be stopping matters getting worse or it could offer a way out of the problem. Resisting the impulse to make untested and unfounded assumptions may be hard but bearing uncertainty and keeping open all possibilities will be more helpful in the long run. Spirituality therefore can be seen as an intra-, inter- and transpersonal experience that is shaped and directed by the experiences of individuals and of the communities within which they live out their lives (Swinton 2003).

An example to illustrate this is provided by the development of the Family Group Conference approach to child welfare in New Zealand, which is based on a cultural-religious indigenous concept among Maori people emphasising the relationship between Celestial and Terrestrial knowledge. The origin of the Family Group Conference was, according to Maori belief, a rebellious initiative by the children of Ranginui, the great Sky Father, and Papatuanuku, the matriarch Earth Mother. Protected in a darkened cocoon by their parents the children desired freedom to explore the outer limits of the universe. The family conference that was convened included close and distant relatives and grandparents who were all regarded as part of a single spiritual and economic unity (Fulcher 1999). Thus each Maori child's cultural identity is explicitly connected to their genealogy or *whakapapa*. The Family Group Conference is now being incorporated into mainstream child protection and adult mental health services in the United Kingdom, where extended family members are invited to participate in care planning.

Child development

Is there a point at which a child develops a sense of spirituality? Can we relate this to Western orthodox developmental instruments? One of the central tenets of religious belief is that of death and a belief in an afterlife. Jung considered that belief in an afterlife was important for mental health, whereas Freud suggests it was an unhealthy denial. In the context of the rise in self-harming behaviours and suicide rates among young men and the life-threatening risks in anorexia nervosa, it is clear that the subject of death and its connection with belief or lack of belief in an afterlife must be an important variable. The terms 'intrinsic' and 'extrinsic religiousness' have been coined in order to more closely define the complexities behind religious belief. Intrinsic religiousness is characterised by a young person extending their beliefs beyond acts of worship into every aspect and behaviour in their life. It is foundational to their concept of self. However, a young person with extrinsic religiousness is motivated by a self-serving instrumental approach to life that uses religion to provide status and social support. It has been compared to a neurosis in the sense that it is a defence against anxiety, whereas intrinsic religiousness makes for positive mental health (Paloutzian 1996).

Until about the age of ten, children are generally understood to be unable to grasp abstract concepts. If we accept the more abstract and non-literal aspects of religion then it follows that before that age religious education in schools is failing to connect with children. This has to some extent been acknowledged in studies examining difficulties in establishing in-school educational programmes aimed at tackling social exclusion and using religious studies as a means to enhance cultural respect (Larsen and Plesner 2002, Jackson 2004). Recent evidence suggests that religious education in schools that fosters knowledge about and respect for freedom of religion or belief as a human right is now a focus for policy makers seeking to increase understanding and respect between children of different religions or world views (Jackson 2003). It is argued that older-age school children can, in classroom discussion about different religions, by developing their ability to handle new and unfamiliar cultural material with skill and sensitivity demonstrate *meta-cultural* competence (Leganger-Krongstad 2000).

However, this relies on a narrow definition of religious development and cognitive capacity. Perhaps the concept of spiritual development enables us to begin to understand that such a process begins at a much earlier stage of development, when children are trying to make sense of the multiplicity of sensations and experiences bombarding them. The cognitive complexity in religious language is more a barrier to children's spiritual expression and in order for us to better understand it we need to learn how to listen to the language of children and young people within which is ample spiritual expression. Studies of children's spirituality using cross-cultural and multi-faith samples confirm the profound nature of spirituality and that spirituality is not only about what children talk about but also how they talk, act or feel about all sorts of things (Coles 1990, Hay 1990). It is important to bear the following points in mind when seeking to assess whether religion and spirituality are relevant to your work with a child or young person:

- Do not initiate discussion about religion – this will invariably elicit learned facts rather than the natural associated images and metaphors actually used by children.
- Accept that children may spontaneously introduce religious or spiritual concepts consistent with heightened states of awareness similar to meditational experiences.
- Create accepting conditions and an open environment to encourage the child to speak freely without censure or dismissal.
- It is important to respect and value the child's religious beliefs and statements in order to reinforce the validity of expressing a personal point of view.
- In some situations you can initiate discussion about spirituality as a way of demonstrating that the conventional secular taboo which suppresses these matters can be challenged.
- This may encourage the child to share their most private and confusing thoughts in other areas of life.

Research in the area of development and spirituality has been undertaken and a useful three-stage model of faith development has been described (Table 6.2) that can be matched against developmental stages to enable you to conceptually orientate your therapeutic process (Fowler et al. 1991).

Table 6.2 Fowler's Stages of Children's Faith Development (Fowler et al. 1991)

Stage	Age	Characteristics
One	3–7	Children live in worlds of fantasy, images, mood, story, action and examples. To move out of this, they need to develop rational thinking and a distinction between fantasy and reality
Two	7–11	Mythic-literal stage. Story is of central importance; fairness and justice are central concerns. Children may become convinced of their exceptional goodness/badness
Three	11–18	Synthetic-conventional faith. To reach this, children need good personal relationships and more awareness of the larger environment

Psychology, religion and spirituality

The Western model of psychological illness tends to ignore the religious or spiritual aspects of the culture in which it is based. However, Eastern, African and Native American cultures tend to integrate them (Fernando 2002). Spirituality and religion as topics in general do not feature often in the therapeutic literature, yet they can be critical components of a child and young person's psychological well-being offering a source of strength and hope in trying circumstances. Children for whom family and faith backgrounds are inseparable may need encouragement to feel comfortable in multi-faith settings. You need to address this dimension as part of the constellation of factors affecting children and adolescents, bearing in mind the positive and sometimes negative impact spiritual or religious beliefs might have on their mental health. It is well understood that children communicate about feelings and experiences more easily through responses to stories. Direct work that allows them to use their *imaginations* and access their own spirituality through stories can be liberating.

The therapeutic value of Western individualistic concepts is incomplete in attempting to alleviate suffering and alienation for collectivist and land-based cultural groups. Beatch and Stewart (2002) in their work with aboriginal communities in the Canadian Arctic show how significant problems related to depression, addiction and family violence are linked with cultural loss through colonisation, environmental destruction and assimilation by Western influences. Aboriginal healing includes strengthening cultural belonging, identity and community-based self-determination. Indigenous outlooks indicate a preference for ecological systems, holistic processes, belonging at the community level and reliance on traditional beliefs and values. A culturally competent approach embracing this context requires practitioners using counselling and psychotherapeutic skills to adapt and synthesise their work with prevailing indigenous ideas in order to maximise effectiveness.

Multiple caregiving to young children in Australian aboriginal culture has attracted concerns based on Western notions of attachment theory and the need for secure attachment relationships with primary carers. However, this concept is inappropriate when we consider that research has demonstrated that Aboriginal children can sustain and thrive with multiple attachment figures that are wholly consistent with societal norms (Yeo 2003). Indeed, there are sometimes lengthy absences from parents related to important sacred initiations or religious ceremonies necessary for the child or young person's spiritual development. These findings resonate with research in the UK and elsewhere studying the developmental progress of black children raised in single parent households with multiple attachment figures (Daycare Trust 2000).

In South American countries the influence of the Catholic Church and family planning combined with poverty, a history of military dictatorships and a culture of *machismo* has produced a culture of extreme social inequality where children can easily drift into prostitution, child labour or become homeless. In these conditions, authoritarian family structures create a climate where domestic violence thrives (Ravazzola 1997). Here liberation theology translates Christian concepts into activity that challenges the prevailing order offering hope of better circumstances and prospects through revolutionary struggle. Children and young people can thus link religion with empowerment and liberation from inequitable and socially unjust conditions.

Children and young people may well wonder about religion and spirituality either directly or indirectly. They may encounter friends, family members or others for whom such beliefs are an intrinsic part of their lives. In our work as counsellors or psychotherapists these people may well enter into the conversations and reflections ventilated by clients. This could trigger an interesting exploration by the child or adolescent about the meaning of life or a search for the answer to the question, what is religion? Your own perspective and theoretical orientation will guide you in considering how to respond. Do you take this literally or metaphorically? Do you enable the client to speculate, describe their hidden fears about such matters or suggest an interpretation that seeks to address underlying dilemmas or conflicts around the issue? The following list attempts to bring forward a definition or to describe the common characteristics of religions around the world:

- They look for the something else or somebody beyond the world of senses and scientific measurement. This something or somebody controls all.
- They have great figures, men of vision who seem to perceive the something else more than other people.
- They all express themselves in the written word trying to encapsulate what they believe in.
- Each religion gives to its own people advice on how to behave and what to do to draw close to the something else or somebody.

- Religions are often practised by people coming together in common worship at special places.
- Religions often bring people together at special times for particular celebrations.
- All religions hold special funeral ceremonies and grapple with the problem of whether there is life after death.

The inner world of the child

Research findings that explored the concept of spirituality with several groups of school-age children, some of whom held deep religious convictions and others who belonged to no formal religion, discovered that it is rare to come across a child who does not have at least an *implicit spirituality*. Even in the most resolutely secular boy evidences of spiritual sensitivity emerge, sometimes through self-contradiction, or allusive metaphor or through Freudian slips of the tongue. Our task is not to detect the presence of spirituality, but to understand how it becomes suppressed or repressed during the process of growing-up (Hay 1990).

Four core qualities of spiritual experience have been identified – awareness, mystery, value and meaningfulness/insight. They are often assumed to be consistent with positive life-affirming experiences. However, children who experience wonder, awe and mystery can quickly become distressed and fearful – even terrified if a secure and stable main carer is not available to contain those negative feelings. Many religions contain concepts of hell and punishment which could trigger profound feelings of despair that are experienced as completely overwhelming physically and psychologically.

Sin is defined variously in many religions and for a child or young person comes with the sense of failing to be satisfactory – for example, from early toileting experiences through to exam performance or adolescent sexuality. The sense of sin and failure is quickly transformed into guilt and shame resulting in feelings of depression, distress and despair unless there is some balancing influence. Children and young people without this balancing experience and with deficits in their environment and personal temperament are likely to develop mental health problems at the time or later on in life. It is easy for children to feel that they are failing or cannot fit easily into the world. This is the opposite of spiritual experiences of value, insight and relatedness. A persistent sense of sinfulness or failure prevents the development of healthy relationships (Crompton 1996).

This is illustrated in the story of the Hindu god Krishna who was very naughty as a small boy. When he was accused of eating dirt, his foster mother Yasoda ordered him to open his mouth. When he did so, she became terrified at the sight she beheld revealing, as it did, the eternal universe. Krishna understood that such knowledge would be harmful to Yasoda so he erased her memory of all she had witnessed. This tale illustrates how awareness and closeness to the divine can be potentially overpowering or harmful. A sense of connection to the supreme being in religion can be mediated through a connection with nature and the environment. However, if children witness the harm being done to the environment or the threat of war, they can become very anxious. What do children and young people make of the increasing deterioration of their environment and lurid tabloid tales about the greenhouse effect and extreme weather events? Do they see this as the retribution of a powerful god punishing humanity for spoiling a once pristine planet offered to us as a habitat? And, are those teachers and parents lecturing them about the virtues of conservation and recycling instilling a sense of guilt masquerading as virtue?

Children involved in war as victims or combatants are deprived of the enjoyment of spiritual rights. Research demonstrates the severe and enduring mental health problems experienced by refugee and asylum seekers from areas of conflict (Hodes 2000). Psychotherapists and counsellors can utilise spiritual beliefs in helping children recover from dehumanising and traumatising atrocities by enabling the expression of terror and fearfulness through re-connecting them with their prevailing religious constructs that have been abandoned. Some of these children will perhaps have a strong sense of guilt inherited from a religious belief system that blamed humanity for the death of Jesus. The death of parents, siblings or close relatives will probably have resonated with these inherent guilt feelings compounding them into a persecutory frame of mind. Therapists would need to be careful with evoking a religious construct that could inadvertently exaggerate already troubling feelings.

The link between spirituality and cultural competence is emphasised if we enlist an understanding of spirituality that suggests it is the outward expression of the inner workings of the human spirit. In other words it is a personal and social process that refers to the ideas, concepts, attitudes and behaviours that derive from a child or young person's or a community's interpretation of their experiences of the spirit. It is intrapersonal in that it refers to the quest for inner connectivity and it is interpersonal in that it relates to the relationships between people and within communities. And it is transpersonal in so far as it reaches beyond self and others into the transcendent realms of experience that move beyond that which is available at a mundane level (Swinton 2003).

Therapy and cultural belief

Therapeutic work with children and young people whether from a systemic or psychodynamic perspective will amongst other things address the belief system of the individual and/or their family. Belief in this sense usually means exploring the client's beliefs about their problem as the start of establishing a helping relationship. The client may believe that their problem/s are the result of divine intervention – a punishment for a sin or misdemeanour of some kind. Among some cultures, there is a potent belief system that spirits can possess people and make them unwell or be invoked to help them with a problem. In the case of a child or young person who is causing concern among teachers, social workers or health professionals there may be a simple diagnosis or assessment of the cause of the problem but this may not fit with the family's beliefs about the cause. However, belief also relates to religion and spirituality. If the therapist is unable or unwilling to explore this aspect of belief then they may be missing a vital component of the individual or family's overall belief system about how the world works and how problems arise and more importantly what is likely to be effective treatment.

There is the potential for a rich and sophisticated understanding of the interplay between counselling and psychotherapeutic principles and a more explicit acknowledgement of a spiritual dimension to child and adolescent psychological health. Epidemiological studies provide a raft of orthodox explanations for emotional and behavioural problems encountered by children and young people but they neglect the possibility that difficulties may occur from responses to their *spiritual environment*. Recently, the popular diagnostic manual of mental illnesses included the category of spiritual disorder for the first time (DSM IV APA 1994). However, the implication was that this area represented a threat to a young person's psychological health – overlooking the positive effects of spiritual health. In terms of culturally competent practice this ought to provoke our curiosity at the very least.

The notion of a special place that signifies a potent context for reflection has been identified in research with children. It may be a church, mosque, synagogue, temple or even a tree or gang den. The association children and young people have with this special place can be interpreted as an actual or desirable place within themselves seeking peace and contentment. Using this concept therapeutically opens up another avenue for practitioners who seek to explore the inner world of children and young people. It can relate to the notion of the secure attachment base or even a fantasy of returning to the womb and an infantile state. Older children may feel that this concept is beneath them and will be most resistant to exploring this special place but younger children who maintain a more active sense of imagination and magic may be more open to working in this psychic space.

A recurring theme associated with relationship issues as the source of some problems is that of trust. Children learn not only the benefits of developing trusting relationships but also the hurt and pain of a betrayal of trust. These can be related to parental abuse or neglect, or a school friend's disclosure of a promised secret. Thus trust contains an element of hope in something intangible beyond a reassurance or school-yard bargain. If children can connect with a sense of trust in some kind of transcendent benevolent power such as a god then this too can be a fruitful area for exploration of their own vulnerability, limitations and dependence (Crompton 1996).

The importance of spirituality is illustrated when we appreciate, for example, that spirituality is the cornerstone of the aboriginal identity. Australian aboriginal spiritual tradition places the origin of each aboriginal clan in its own land. These clans hold deep spiritual links with their lands which were formed in Dreamtime. The ancestral creative beings that travelled across the continent at the beginning of time established land boundaries between different aboriginal clans and the sacred sites. Ritual obligations and religious ceremonies are carried out at these sites in order to reinforce the bond Aboriginal people feel to their lands. If they move from the land or if it is taken from them, they lose their cultural identity and self-esteem (Yeo 2003). For example, psychological problems have been linked with the Australian government policy of forced removal of people from Aboriginal lands (Human Rights Commission 1997).

A powerful argument is advanced by several authors who recommend incorporating a more explicit acknowledgement of the role that religion and spirituality can play in our work as therapists. The concept of postmodernism and its reductionist thesis for deconstruction of scientific or non-empirical certainties are challenged by an appeal to that which is ignored or rendered silent. In essence it is argued that because postmodernism emphasises separation and groundlessness in a context whereby *every prevailing orthodoxy* is questioned, people are paradoxically developing an appetite for community and connection. Moules (2000) suggests that we exist beyond our cultural creation and interpretations and need to learn from diversity to make connection through variety – to learn from the uncertainty of knowledge but not to deny any knowledge.

In order to respond to this dilemma and enable counsellors and psychotherapists to harness positive aspects of religion and spirituality in their work, a theory of multicultural therapy has been advanced that offers a multidimensional paradigm to guide practice (Raval 1996, Sue et al. 1996). The authors suggest that:

- It is necessary to have a meta-theory of counselling and psychotherapy to allow different theoretical models to be applied and integrated where possible.
- Both counsellor and client identities are formed and embedded in multiple levels of life experiences and contexts, therefore treatment should take greater account of the child or young person's experience in relation to their context.
- The cultural identity development of the counsellor and client and the wider power differentials associated with this play an important role in the therapeutic relationship.
- Multicultural counselling and therapy effectiveness is enhanced when the counsellor uses modalities and defines goals consistent with the life experiences and cultural values of the client.

The theory stresses the importance of multiple helping roles developed by many cultural groups and societies. Apart from the one-to-one encounter aimed at remediation in the individual, those roles often involve larger social units, system intervention and prevention. Multicultural counselling and therapy helps the child or young person develop a greater awareness about themselves in relation to their different contexts. This results in therapy that is contextual in orientation and which is able to respectfully draw on traditional methods of healing with a spiritual or religious dimension from many cultures. Paul Tillich (1963) alluded to this when he described something called *theonomy*, meaning the *pursuit of culture under the impact of spiritual presence* – a liberal humanism with an underlying spiritual depth.

It is perhaps a paradox that the decline of organised religion in white Western societies combined with the consequences of previous imperialist expansion throughout the world has produced a growing culturally diverse population among whom are large numbers of devout religious communities with highly developed spiritual belief systems that organise social behaviour. While pundits, politicians and policy makers observe increases in anti-social behaviour among disaffected and disadvantaged young white people and blame the absence of religious values and thus moral standards, they are at the same time witnessing a growth in ethnic minority religious and spiritual affiliation resulting in social, psychological and educational attainment. Culturally competent practice aspires to understand and support both groups of children and young people to help them make sense of their beliefs or lack of them in terms of vulnerability or resistance to psychological problems.

Summary

The relevance to counselling and psychotherapy of religion and spirituality cannot be underestimated as they form a part of the covert or overt belief systems of children and young people that will to a larger or lesser extent impact on your work. Most cultures can trace deep evidence of their ancestral heritage and the ways early civilisations sought to explain the world around them. These tend to involve the intervention of a supreme being or power with the capacity to control the natural elements vital for the survival of the species.

The history of modern societies has been shaped as much by the religious struggles of previous stages of development as by the economic and political forces motivating people to embark upon social change or revolution. A combination of systemic and psychodynamic theory offers us an interpersonal and intrapsychic therapeutic understanding of these powerfully important contexts within which individual children and young people evolve their own psychic road map.

The Western model of psychological illness tends to ignore the religious or spiritual aspects of the culture in which it is based. However, Eastern, African and Native American cultures tend to integrate them. Spirituality and religion can be critical components of a child and young person's psychological well-being, offering a source of strength and hope in trying circumstances. You need to address this dimension as part of the constellation of factors affecting children and adolescents, bearing in mind the positive and sometimes negative impact spiritual or religious beliefs might have on their mental health.

Four core qualities of spiritual experience have been identified – awareness, mystery, value and meaningfulness/insight. They are often assumed to be consistent with positive life-affirming experiences. However, children who experience wonder, awe and mystery can quickly become distressed and fearful – even terrified if a secure and stable main carer is not available to contain those negative feelings. Many religions contain concepts of hell and punishment which could trigger profound feelings of despair that are experienced as completely physically and psychologically overwhelming.

There is the potential for a rich and sophisticated understanding of the interplay between counselling and psychotherapeutic principles and a more explicit acknowledgement of a spiritual dimension to child and adolescent psychological health. The notion of a special place that signifies a potent context for reflection has been identified in research with children. It may be a church, mosque, synagogue, temple or even a tree or gang den. The association children and young people have with this special place can be interpreted as an actual or desirable place within themselves seeking peace and contentment. Using this concept therapeutically opens up another avenue for practitioners who seek to explore the inner world of children and young people.

7

FAIRY STORIES, MYTHS AND LEGENDS

I don't know why I am so sad; there is an old time fairy tale
that I cannot get out of my mind.

– Heinrich Heine

Introduction

The ancient Greek legend of Oedipus provided Freud with the ideal
vehicle for articulating his theory of infantile sexuality and the death
wish aimed at his father by the son with a sexual desire for his
mother. The legend tells of King Laius of Thebes and Queen Jocasta
who are warned by a prophet that their expected child would grow
up to murder his father and marry his mother. At birth the baby's
feet are pierced and he is left to die in the mountains. The child is
saved by peasants and eventually grows up as the son of a foreign
king and queen. A prophet warns the child that he will murder his
father and marry his mother. Not realising his true origins he decides
to run away from home in order to protect his foster parents. Oedipus
meets a stranger on the road and kills him after an argument – not
realising that this is in fact his real father King Laius.

Oedipus eventually arrives at Thebes to find the city under threat
from a powerful monster called the Sphinx. It can only be van-
quished by whoever answers the riddle: '*Which animal has four feet in
the morning, two at mid-day and three in the evening?*' Oedipus gives the
correct answer: '*Man, who in infancy crawls on all fours, walks upright
on two legs in adulthood, but in old age requires a stick to stay upright.*' As
a reward for saving the city, Oedipus marries Jocasta not realising
she is his mother and reigns as the new king. However, after many
peaceful years a plague threatens to overwhelm Thebes so the
prophets are consulted. They decree that the plague will only end if

the murderer of King Laius is discovered. Oedipus realises that he is indeed the murderer of his own father and in a violent torment blinds himself. Jocasta on learning of the news commits suicide thus completing the tragedy.

The Oedipus legend demonstrates the way that counselling and therapeutic practices can make use of legends, tales, fairy stories and myths. In this example the legend serves to illustrate the unconscious struggles taking place in a child's development. Fairy stories in particular can be used to engage children when conventional ordinary dialogue is inadequate or unsuccessful at promoting therapeutic engagement and process. If we accept that childhood tales form a building block in the construction of the child's fantasy world and therefore their personality development then this offers an opportunity to understand the variety of meanings and influences contained therein at many levels. Myths are poetic tales explaining why the world is the way it is and why people behave the way they do. They usually involve gods and goddesses or spirits. Legends are stories about events that may or may not have taken place a long time ago.

The fairy realm is a central aspect of cultures all over the world yet until very recently the mainstream school and young person's literature reflected a narrow spectrum of examples from a Eurocentric base. Classic tales read in classrooms or appearing in popular culture on television or in annual pantomimes such as 'Jack and the Beanstalk', 'Cinderella' or 'Puss in Boots' neglect the rich diversity of stories from around the world. 'Aladdin', for example, while incorporated into mainstream pantomime is actually one of *The Arabian Nights* stories told over 1001 nights by Scheherezade to King Shahryar as part of a lost collection of Persian tales circa AD 850.

Specific fairies are identified with spiritual qualities of flowers and herbs, echoing back to a time when humans were more connected to the land and nature. In mainly agricultural and developing countries, where industrialisation has not fully trampled over traditional beliefs and practices, the link between the spiritual and earthly realms is closer (Reed 2002). Centuries of traditional practices have been passed on. From a narrow Western perspective this might seem backward, ignorant or downright dangerous if faith is put in spiritual or herbal remedies for the treatment of serious illness. Yet in recent years there has been an explosion of interest in developed countries in natural remedies, herbalism and complementary medicine.

There are studies of folklore contained in holy books such as the Qur'an, Torah and Bible where proverbs, parables and sura are used to convey powerful religious truths (Dundes 2003). There is increasing evidence of the power of faith as an important variable in the prognosis for a variety of medical conditions, and alternative or complementary medicine is increasingly being incorporated in public health provision. Sales of homeopathic or herbal medicines is a huge business and at the very least are testimony to people's appetite for solutions that are unconventional and perhaps more mystical than orthodox scientific cures.

Children and young people have the capacity to conjure feelings of faith and hope when experiencing emotional and psychological distress. Myths, legends and fairy stories as part of their early child development offer a rich source of material to draw from and enlist in the therapeutic endeavour. Fairies often act in a healing capacity in mythology, or they appear as agents between the world of human affairs and the invisible forces of nature (Williams 1997). They also possess powers in advance of mortals, achieving superhuman tasks, but they can also run into trouble and sometimes rely on assistance from humans to succeed.

If we examine a sample of tales from a variety of countries we can discern some common themes as well as unique stories – it is a delicious mixture and reflective of the reservoir of material available to us in our therapeutic work for use with children and young people we are hoping to heal in some way. Harnessing the child's imagination can be a powerful vehicle for a transforming experience at the psychic level (Bettelheim 1991, Crompton 1996). So what better way of accessing their imagination than by exploring memories of fairy stories and using them to address painful or unsettling issues in a non-threatening, playful manner?

These childhood stories are often experienced as bedtime reading or spoken by a parental/carer figure. They are usually extraordinary tales involving fantastical characters and situations where magic is woven in a world outside the physical daily world inhabited during the waking day. Good and evil usually feature in a struggle during trials and tribulations; morality also features and happy endings are the preferred outcome. Before printed books, these myths and legends were part of narrative communication; storytelling was a vital part of entertainment as well as education. For example, the tale of 'Little Red Riding Hood' was a way for parents to warn children not to talk to strangers. A papyrus dated from around 1700 BC revealed that the pharaoh Cheops was fond of fairy tales – many of which bear similarities to modern tales (Philip 1997).

The bedtime context of many fairy tale readings makes the connection between the mythological stories and the dream-world beckoning within sleep. The characters and events within our dreams have the same magical quality possessed by fairy tales. Thus fairy tales resonate with our imaginations and particularly those of children and young people who have not *unlearned* their sense of wonderment and potential. The struggle between good and evil is an obvious theme throughout fairy tales from around the world. In a therapeutic sense we can interpret this as representing internal conflict or the tension between the id and ego, or the Kleinian good and bad breast.

Beneath this classic literary device perhaps lies a desire for a positive outcome, a hopeful belief or a basic trust in such a thing as natural justice. Many of our clients would have struggled so much precisely because these primitive notions have not stood the cruel test of reality. As victims of abuse or neglect they will have experienced the triumph of evil over good rather than the other way round. In addition to the repertoire of helping techniques available within a variety of counselling or therapeutic modes, enabling a young person to identify with a fairy tale or to make their own version up could be a useful means of unlocking feelings of mistrust or guilt.

Towards deeper cultural meaning

Children and young people who are suffering from psychological distress requiring therapeutic help may be either too young or too old to engage in cognitive and verbal communication about their feelings and experiences. The young ones may be more at ease with activities and play materials to aid expression while the older teenagers will often be difficult to engage and open up having learned the basic defence of silence. But they will all know something of fairy tales, myths and legends. Every culture has them and they are usually told during early childhood in a verbal parental or carer ritual as old as time. Earliest school literature incorporates these stories in education curriculum precisely because they are familiar and accessible.

As part of the healing process literature is an often *underrated* asset. Yet it carries information about families, emotions, morality, relationships and so much else in a way that can enable very damaged children to use devices such as fairy stories to help understand themselves at a deeper level. Fairy stories have the capacity to capture the child's imagination because they usually involve fantastical creatures, transformational experiences or complex predicaments in which the child can immerse themselves and relate to their inner world. It is there that a child's repressed feelings and worst fears lurk causing inner conflicts that manifest in acting out behaviour or anxiety states. The fairy story operates at the *overt* level where obvious concepts of right and wrong and other moral dilemmas are struggled with. It also operates at a *covert* level carrying important messages to the conscious, preconscious and unconscious mind that affect the child's sense of culture.

A child needs to understand what is going on within her/his conscious self so that she/he can cope with that which goes on in the unconscious. This will include the psychological problems of growing up such as narcissistic disappointments, Oedipal dilemmas, sibling rivalries, relinquishing childhood dependencies, and gaining a feeling of self-hood and self-worth (Bettelheim 1991). When such unconscious material is brought more into awareness, its potential for being turned into a destructive force is much reduced. This is the therapist dilemma of course because it is this material that parents mostly do not want expressed, discussed or acknowledged, causing the child to be psychologically trapped and allowing the inner chaotic violent feelings and fantasies to grow. Parents often express bewilderment at witnessing the seemingly negative and retrograde behaviour in their child who undergoes therapy only slowly and sometimes never coming to realise that this material is what has been causing the presenting problem of depression, self-harming behaviour or eating disorder. The idea that the child's behaviour must deteriorate before it improves is understandably confusing.

The fairy tale by tackling head on the basic human predicaments of life, death and the meaning of existence is an economic means for children and young people to access these crucial issues and confront them in a *symbolic* form. They are a simplified story reduced to the bare essentials with few details and typical characterisations. For example, many fairy stories begin with the death of a parent figure – thereby capturing instantly the central fear and at times the fantasy wish of every child. Dualities of good and evil are equally the most common theme in fairy stories where the eternal struggle takes place through many trials and tribulations. With the usual triumph of good over evil the child is thereby able to identify with the symbolic figure and absorb the moral message internally.

An example from *The Arabian Nights* tales illustrates one of the central themes in fairy tales that is common to many cultures and relates directly to children's experiences under the power adults hold over them. 'The Fisherman and the Jinny' tells the story of a poor fisherman who hauls in his net four times. The first three times there is no catch but on the fourth occasion he hauls up a copper jar which when opened reveals a huge jinny (genie) that threatens to kill him. Thinking very quickly the fisherman starts to flatter the jinny telling him how powerful and strong and clever he is. The jinny feels good about this. Then the fisherman asks the jinny to demonstrate his powers of transformation by changing into a mouse. This he does and as quick as he can the fisherman grabs the mouse and pushes it into the copper jar which is sealed and thrown back into the sea.

The story illustrates to a child precisely those feelings of power-lessness and awe when faced with an adult figure who can behave in a threatening oppressive manner. The transformative capacity can be seen as representative of adults who can change quickly in their mood but who are also in some way dependent on the child's behaviour. Ultimately it might give a child hope to learn through the story that through persistence and hard work a reward is possible, although the reward (in this example the copper jar) turns out to be tainted. Finally with a sharp wit and quick thinking a child is shown that a powerful threatening figure can be brought down to size and contained safely. This might relate to a parental figure, school bully or a sibling.

Favat (1977) suggests that a child's interest in the fairy tale is at some level a natural search for a world more ordered than their current experience where they are striving for resolution to an internal crisis. It is a salutary utilisation of an implicit cultural device in order to invest the real world with the constructs of the tale. Thus the fairy tale reflects a process of struggle against experiences of suppression and authoritarian control. The more traditional fairy tales represent a regressive notion of family life where arbitrary authority in the form of kings and queens mete out justice. Compared with these classic fairy tale themes, modern authors have actively challenged the fairy tale device and written stories with themes relating to children's liberation, co-operative relationships and even anti-war scenarios (Turn and Selig 1977).

Narrative therapeutic ideas

Narrative therapeutic ideas have developed in recent years among systemic counsellors and psychotherapists captivated by the notion of storytelling as a means to engage children and young people. Perhaps this development is a reaction against the increasingly technocratic age we live in and where children are surrounded and constantly stimulated by largely visual and auditory media or com-munication. Storytelling is advocated by educationalists attempting to reach children in schools, theatres and libraries as a way of preserving some interest in the written word. Ethnic minority communities endeavour to use storytelling in large industrialised countries as a means of recovering their cultural history and maintaining rituals obscured by the homogenised consumer-oriented culture offered by profiteering corporations.

A professor in a major health and social work faculty in England (Ramon 2004) tells the story of how as a child she would listen to and then demand stories from her mother and grandmother about their lives as Jews living in Poland before the Second World War. Her grandmother would tell a favourite story of a grandfather who lived in a kibbutz which he made from chocolate. He would invite his grandchildren and other children to share in the kibbutz but this created a dilemma because if it was eaten then the kibbutz would crumble and be no more. Was this a message about the precious nature of the kibbutz and the perils of taking from it rather than giving to it? There is no answer other than what the individual listener creates for themselves. Her mother's stories were about the tense relationship she had with classmates who were not Jewish and of the very difficult life she had when she immigrated to Israel. The economic hardship was tempered by the enormous sense of freedom she felt in a society where hers was the majority culture.

Narrative therapeutic ideas recognise the ability children and young people have not only to ascribe meaning to events that serve to explain but also to influence choices about the possible courses of action. This capacity to generate and evolve new narratives and stories to make sense of experiences involves the use of culturally shared myths, legends and fairy stories. Thus counselling and therapy are seen as not just offering new perceptions and insights but affecting the very nature of the conversation taking place. Narrative therapists such as White and Epston (1990) suggest that problems are derived and maintained from the *internalisation* of oppressive ways of perceiving the self. These notions can be reinforced by parents who constantly criticise a child or who only respond negatively to behaviours.

Their narrative approach includes the technique of *externalising* the problem whereby the therapist or counsellor encourages the child to objectify or personify the problem outside of themselves. Thus the child can then separate themselves from the problem instead of being seen and related to by others as *the problem*. In the case of anorexia or soiling behaviour, for example, it is then possible to engage the child or young person in a process of exploring and resisting the problem as an unwanted impediment rather than as an integral part of their psychic constitution. Counsellors and psycho-therapists using fairy tales, myths and legends as a means to facilitate the power of narrative can thus enable a troubled young person to begin the process of challenging self-defeating and overwhelming self-concepts.

A tale from Bali in Southeast Asia offers an exquisite example for therapists interested in using narrative techniques to help children and young people who are suffering trauma from broken relationships or fear the threat of a relationship ending (Drury 2003). A traveller was visiting Bali when he noticed that most of the cats he spotted had either broken tails or stumps for tails. Towards the end of his visit he met an older woman to whom he asked about the cats' tails. She explained that it was due to the nature of cats. The older woman went on to explain that Balinese people had a mix of Buddhist and Hindu influences in their culture which results in a widespread belief in reincarnation. This means that you remain on the wheel of Samsara which perpetuates life, death and rebirth until you become perfect. When perfection is achieved you have achieved Buddha nature and then you go to heaven.

The cat has Buddha nature because it has discovered the art of love which is to love without becoming dependent. And we all know how affectionate cats can be when they want to be stroked but how uncooperative they are when they do not want to be stroked. So the Balinese people knowing they are not perfect yet and have more laps to go round the Samsara before they are allowed into heaven think to themselves – 'who on earth wants to go to heaven and find the place full of cats?' So in order to stop heaven being full of cats, they break their tails guaranteeing they will have to keep going round the Samsara for many more laps. This tale might help teenagers trying to make sense of their confusing and intolerable feelings during their early attempts at discovering the meaning of love, affection and the sense of responsibility, guilt and anxiety aroused by issues of dependence and independence.

The third-person narrative voice in Hans Christian Anderson's 'The Tinderbox' is used to define the reader who seeks to challenge a socially imposed identity (Anderson 1913). The story speaks of the social tensions encountered by a young person born into a poor family but who aspires to a higher social station in life. He is hired by a witch to retrieve a fortune but instead of returning it to her he keeps it, kills the witch and assumes enormous power and influence. His money runs out whereupon he learns that new friends quickly disown him and he sinks into social isolation. However, the young man discovers magical properties in a tinderbox which together with three dogs provides him with endless wealth and power. In the end he deposes the ruling monarchs and becomes the head of state. Here the references to mother figures (the witch) and parents embodied in the king and queen represent the adolescent developmental struggle for identity, separation and self-motivation.

Links between dreams/fantasies and legends

Freud discusses the concept of 'uncanny' in terms of one of Hoffman's fairy tales 'The Sandman', where he considers the word *Heimlich* (homely) with its opposite of concealed or hidden *unheimlich* (uncanny) which can be understood in its ambivalent form as touching upon emotional disturbances related to repressed phases in a child's development (Freud 1976). Thus we can see how in the act of reading or listening to a fairy story a child can dislocate themselves from a reality and begin to accept the uncanny as familiar. And in separating in this way the young person can gain access to repressed feelings or in other words allow the unfamiliar to become more familiar.

Freud linked the dream world with popular fairy stories to illustrate how wish-fulfillment can be transformed in a dream into the reverse of a happy ending. In cases where worries and painful reflections are repressed they can either be straightforward dreams of satisfaction, or distressing material can enter the dream content more or less modified. If the gulf between the unconscious and conscious – between the repressed and the ego – is revealed then a situation like the fairy story of the three wishes may unfold (Freud 1953). In this tale a good fairy grants a man three wishes. He and his wife are overjoyed with excitement. However, even after promising to use them carefully and wisely the wife was tempted by the smell of sausages cooking next door and wished for two of them. They duly appeared but the man was furious and in his rage wished that the sausages were hanging from his wife's nose. This happened as well the sausages could not be removed from her nose. His wife was extremely distressed and wished that the sausages were taken away, which of course they were and thus ended the three wishes. This tale illustrates the concept of wish-fulfilment appearing in dreams as both a desire for a happy ending as well as a repudiation or rejection of any pleasure from the wishes.

Others draw a connection between fairy tales and developmental theorists such as Piaget to explain the fascination children have for them. The content and form of some Western fairy tales correspond to the way children at ages 6–8 conceive of their world. During this particular developmental phase the child believes in the magical relationship between thought and things, regards inanimate objects as animate, does not distinguish the self from the external world, and believes that objects can be moved in continual response to their desires. As the child develops towards age 10 and egocentrism gives way to socialisation and more conscious interaction in society, there is a rejection of the fairy tale (Zipes 1983).

Children actually feature in some world myths and legends and offer a fascinating source for exploring fantasies with children and young people who are troubled by difficulties such as low self-esteem (Shepherd 1994). In Russia there is a legend about Gulnara, a young Tartar girl who was strong and brave. She rode off to join the army in defending the country against Mongul invaders. Men in the army laughed at her and ridiculed the idea that she could be of any use in the fighting. Eventually the two armies faced each other across a river but there was no way to cross it and it was deep and treacherous. Gulnara changed herself into a bird in the night and flew across the river to spy on the invading army. When dawn broke she returned to human form and led the Russian army to a hidden rope bridge where they crossed the river and succeeded in routing the invading army.

The Navajos of North America have a story about a boy called Nayenezgani who freed the world from evil. His father was the Sun who gave him magic armour, arrows made from lightning and a stone knife. Nayenezgani then went off to fight the giant monsters who were threatening the people of the world. With the knife he killed the first giant which was drinking up whole rivers to quench its thirst. With the lightning arrows he killed the second giant which took the form of an enormous flesh-eating antelope. Then, using his armour to protect himself Nayenezgani slew the giant who threw people off mountain paths they needed to use to reach better grazing land. However, the boy left four giants unharmed – Old age, Cold, Poverty and Hunger so that people would appreciate the good things in life.

In South America a legend tells of a young boy called Botoque who one day went out hunting but got lost. He became very scared and could find nothing to eat. He took refuge in a cave at night where a jaguar found him and took him back to his lair. Jaguar's wife was cooking meat over a fire. Botoque had never seen fire before and was startled. He tried eating the cooked meat and found it tasted delicious. His tribe, the Kayapo, had not discovered fire and only ate raw meat. However, jaguar's wife became aggressive and scratched the boy with her claws. He shot her with his bow and arrow and fled into the jungle where he was found by people from his tribe. They all returned to the jaguar lair to find jaguar had gone out hunting. The tribe stole some burning embers from the fire to light a fire in their own village. Nowadays the Kayapo have fire and cooked meat thanks to the brave little boy Botoque.

Thematic analysis of myths and legends

Many characters in fairy tales are under a spell of some kind, often transformed into an animal shape. The task of the heroine or hero is to try to spot the genuine person underneath the disguise or spell. This theme occurs across cultures and time in verbal and written renditions. It is not hard to guess that this notion of the genuine person needing to be discovered can serve as a metaphor for the therapeutic process. Did the original storytellers use this concept in a crude yet *elegant* way of helping children and young people understand the role of defences? Although there is more often a 'happy ending' to fairy stories this is not universally the case. For example, in the Cinderella-like tale 'Why the Sea Moans' from Brazil the spell must work itself out for bad or good, and in the amazing Inuit story 'A Whale's Soul and its Burning Heart' the spell that is broken due to constant meddling is life itself.

The use of animals in legends and myths and their connection with feelings and emotions is common across various cultures. They stem from deep history where ancient societies and tribes were beginning to change, develop consciousness and try to make sense of their environment. One way of achieving some level of understanding was to invest animals with powers to be feared, worshipped or eaten. Early humans recognised their dependence on animals just as the child recognises its dependence on their parents, provoking mixed feelings of anger, fear and ambivalence. Aboriginal stories are a particularly rich source of material where the difference between animals and people is blurred and where each can take on the characteristics of the other. The stories and legends date from many centuries before white settlers came to Australia and other countries to colonise and steal land from the native Aboriginal peoples.

The recognition of the importance nowadays of these legends and their role in shaping the culture of the great island continent is slowly being acknowledged. This offers an opportunity to use these stories to simultaneously demonstrate respect for a culture that was for many years denied and deliberately suppressed, and to harness the power of mythology in a therapeutic context with children and young people of various cultural backgrounds. One such legend tells the story of a childless widow who is stricken with grief so much that Nepelle, ruler of the heavens, takes pity and sends her a son named Wyungara. The widow was happy and her foster son grew into a strong healthy young man. One day when he was out hunting in the bush he met a young woman Mar-rallang; a few days later he met her twin sister also called Mar-rallang. Wyungara decided to marry both of them but his uncle objected, so Wyungara and the sisters left to live far away where they thrived and enjoyed total happiness.

But Nepelle disapproved also because Wyungara was a spirit and was not meant to live as a human with wives. Nepelle sent fire to try to separate the three but this only prompted Wyungara to save the sisters from burning to death by casting his spear into heaven with them attached. He prepared to be consumed by the flames but Nepelle recanted in the face of Wyungara's unselfish act and lifted him away from danger to be rejoined with the sisters in heaven where they all were united in everlasting love. This story conveys to a child listening to it the notion that being in foster care can offer hope of knowing happiness while at the same time acknowledging the pain of loss and change in every family. It also illustrates how a person can be looked after while putting the needs of others first and showing how to reciprocate care and protection.

Freud uses the example of a famous legend to interpret a young man's complaint of hysterical vomiting and headaches that would not respond to conventional medicine (Freud 1953). During therapy the young man recalls a dream involving him playing draughts with his uncle. He then saw a dagger lying on the table near the board – this object actually belonged to the young man's father. There was also a sickle and a scythe lying near the draughts board. He then saw a picture of an old peasant mowing grass with the scythe near to his home. Freud's interpretation was that the young man's symptoms had started a few days after his father's second wife came to live in the family home. The young man's father was a violent man who had been unhappily married and who was eventually divorced from his first wife.

The young man's suppressed rage against his father provided the content for the dreams which could be linked to ancient mythology. The sickle was the one with which Zeus castrated his own father; the scythe and the picture of the old peasant represented Kronos, the violent old man who devoured his own children and on whom

Table 7.1   Themes in therapy and tales (Crompton 1996)

Theme	Tale
Stories involving children being cared for by substitute families where the birth mother is involved or where a child is shown to have experienced no disadvantages by such upbringing or where care by non-blood relatives demonstrates the intrinsic worth of all children	*Moses, Muhammad, Esther, Krishna and Guru Nanak*
Stories involving the death of birth parents, or the separation of a child from its family, or where a child dies, encounters dangerous illness or death	*Muhammad, Esther, Krishna, Moses, King Solomon, Buddha, Ismael, Isaac, Ganesha and Jairus's daughter*
Stories involving a child or young person in danger or distress and being helped by people other than own parents, or a child confronting problems and developing strengths	*Pyoli, Buddha, Esther, Menelik, Guru Hargobind, Krishna, Jesus, Maryam, Ganesha and Guru Nanak*
Stories where parents feature as role models or as people imposing their values on a young person or where a child finds their own strengths despite censure or when an adult recognises a young person's latent strengths, or where parental love is unconditional include	*Buddha, Maryam, Ganesha, Muhammad, Menelik, Krishna and Guru Hargobind*

Zeus took murderous vengeance. Thus long-repressed memories and derivatives from them which had remained unconscious slipped into consciousness. Table 7.1 illustrates some themes common to therapeutic work and the sources of stories that contain parallel issues (Crompton 1996).

Engaging children and young people

Counsellors and psychotherapists will understand that storytelling is an important way of communicating with children at many levels. There is the physical sensation of hearing a trusted voice speaking in expressive ways to fire the imagination. There is the story itself which could be full of emotional and cognitive content. Then there is the imagination of the listening child as they interpret the story and then build a mental picture to paint the narrative. The story probably contains a message at an obvious moral level, such as good versus bad, or at an allegorical level. Communication as we know is both ways, so a child can derive immense pleasure from telling an adult stories they have learnt and then watching their reactions. Therapists can harness these valuable and easily accessible narratives as a means of gaining some insight into the child's inner and outer world.

However, the effect of your use of myths and legends with children cannot be predicted or assumed. The significance you attach to a particular story and the assumption that it will have a benign impact on a troubled young person could backfire and provoke a negative result. This could happen when attempting to link a depressive reaction to a family bereavement with stories involving death such as of Jesus or Muhammad. In the case of Jesus and his literal resurrection, a child could become more anxious at the thought of a relative rising from the dead. Legends offer a more fantastical reservoir of material from which to draw extraordinary images that can be employed to start discussion or reflect on situations that parallel their own. Thus the problems they are facing can be considered from a *psychic distance* as it were away from their lived experience. Therapists need to consider whether for some young people this is appropriate, because they may unwittingly be reinforcing a defence system that is working hard to deny the reality of painful feelings and actual experiences.

The Jewish story of Jairus's daughter contains several potential layers of meaning. In it the father pleads with Jesus to help his dying daughter. Although the girl dies before Jesus reaches her he carries on and says the girl is not dead but sleeping. He holds her hand and tells her to rise which she immediately does. Jesus orders food for her and she makes a quick recovery. Crompton (1996) suggests several *layers* of meaning:

- *Female children had little status then,* – yet her father and a male healer come to her aid, providing a message that female children are equally important.
- *Jesus heals the girl, showing diagnostic ability* – children are often labelled as too disturbed, delinquent or beyond help, yet in this story the child was helped.
- *The significance of food could represent an eating disorder* – so the story illustrates how a young woman with this problem can be supported back to health.

- *The girl could have been commencing her period* – Jewish men were not allowed to touch menstruating women, therefore by holding her hand he demonstrates that no child is too unclean or unacceptable to receive care from an adult.

Amoral fairy tales that have no overt theme of good and bad such as 'Puss in Boots' or 'Jack and the Beanstalk' can be used to illustrate that even the meekest can survive in life by using their wits. This contrasts well with stories where the child can choose to be the good person or the hero, even though they may feel inside that this will not make much difference to her/his future chances. Morality is not the central message in these stories, but the assurance that one can succeed thus addresses a fundamental human question. The young person is thus able to reflect on going to deal with adversity believing in the possibility of overcoming it or expecting to be defeated by it. Fairy tales tend to be future-oriented and by using the literary device of the hero figure usually venturing out into the unknown and potentially hostile world, the stories speak to the inner world of the child which is anxious about separation from the parent, struggling to relinquish their infantile dependency and become more independent (Bettelheim 1991).

The story of Hansel and Gretel can be interpreted in several ways, but it seems to fit well with the need of a child embarking on a significant milestone by going to full-time education at about five years of age. This is a time of great change and particularly an important separation from parental control. The story is one of stepping out into a potentially dangerous world where a threatening enemy is symbolised by the witch character. The children triumph of course and in so doing are representing the child reader who can derive reassurance and understanding of separation anxieties. For a female child reading the story it offers a role model of a younger child who becomes less dependent on her brother and eventually actually defeats the witch (Bettelheim 1991).

Movies, television and fairy tales

Cinema cartoon films have been used as a vehicle for mass exposure of some of the more famous fairy tales; yet because of the dominance of one producer the range of material offered is culturally narrow. Various critiques of the organisations that make these cartoons have focused on the ideological nature of the treatment of fairy tales in order to conform to a rigid formula promoting family values, the victory of good over evil and the reinforcement of idealised heterosexual marital relationships. The Hollywood animated cartoon was, it is argued, developed from, expressed and was frequently controlled by a number of shifting and often contradictory discourses about sexuality, race, gender, class, leisure and creativity (Smoodin 1993).

Cartoons were quickly recognised as devices which could be used to capture the interest of children and then expose them to merchandise. Cartoon fairy tales were not produced because of their artistic merit or as contributors to children's cultural development, but because they offered the opportunity to manipulate children's aesthetic interests and consumer tastes. The modern cultural phenomena of mass marketing when a new epic cartoon feature film is premiered is testament to the business skills of the production effort which results in spin-off games, tee-shirts, dolls and a plethora of ephemera designed to maximise profitability. In the last half of the previous century Disney studios produced a formula for each of its fairy tale-based cartoons (Zipes 1997):

- Each film is a musical with catchy lyrics and tunes, background music or special effects that heighten or break the action so that the characters can reveal their innermost thoughts.
- The sequential arrangement of the frames always ensures that the heroine must be rescued by a daring prince. There is no character development because all characters must be recognised as types that remain unchanged throughout the film.
- Since the plot is always the same the danger of provoking boredom is reduced by providing incidental characters with funny, adorable, mischievous antics.
- New concepts are introduced, but only in terms of technical developments, better colour quality and livelier music and lyrics. And they always reinforce the narrow cultural ideology of the studio.
- The success of Disney films lies in their appeal not only to actual children but to the child in all adults. If we can discern an attitude towards children in the cartoons it is that they are to be swept away in a way that involves loss of identity. That is, children as viewers are to lose themselves in the Oedipal wishes that are depicted on the screen in an infantilising process.

In terms of culturally competent practice, counsellors and therapists need to consider the employment of fairy tales, myths and legends as potentially liberating experiences for troubled children and young people. They offer a relatively accessible means to engage children from different cultural backgrounds in a creative and innovative way which challenges assumptions about which stories are privileged and lazily accepted as the only source of inspiration. However, the globalisation of culture and the use made of associated mythological stories and legends in a variety of media by a dominant American global enterprise with a narrow cultural outlook is reinforcing a limited, reduced and essentially Westernised material. We need to acknowledge the risk, in using such widely available material, contributing to a dilution and disappearance of the depth and variety of stories from around the world which are not seen as viable commercial products that can be profitably commodified. The opportunity is there to incorporate in your individual practice a much richer variety of material and thus maintain a culturally competent perspective to your therapeutic endeavour.

Summary

The Oedipus legend demonstrates the way that counselling and therapeutic practices can make use of legends, tales, fairy stories and myths. Fairy stories can be used to engage children when ordinary dialogue is unsuccessful at promoting therapeutic process. Childhood tales form a building block in the construction of the child's fantasy world and personality development, offering an opportunity to understand the variety of meanings and influences contained therein at many levels.

A child needs to understand what is going on within her/his conscious self so that she/he can cope with that which goes on in the unconscious. This will include the psychological problems of growing up such as narcissistic disappointments, Oedipal dilemmas, sibling rivalries, relinquishing childhood dependencies and gaining a feeling of self-hood and self-worth. When such unconscious material is brought more into awareness then its potential for being turned into a destructive force is much reduced.

Many characters in fairy tales are under a spell of some kind, often transformed into an animal shape. This theme occurs across cultures and time in verbal and written renditions. This notion of the genuine person needing to be discovered can serve as a metaphor for the therapeutic process. The original storytellers were probably unaware that use of this concept was an elegant way of helping children and young people understand the role of defences.

Storytelling is an important way of communicating with children at many levels. In addition to the physical sensation of hearing a trusted voice speaking in expressive ways to fire the imagination, the story probably contains a message at an obvious moral level, such as good versus bad, or at an allegorical level. Communication occurs both ways so a child can derive immense pleasure from telling us stories they have learnt and then watching our reactions. Therapists can harness these valuable and easily accessible narratives as a means of gaining some insight into the child's inner and outer world.

The globalisation of culture and the use made of mythological stories and legends in media enterprises with a narrow cultural outlook is reinforcing a limited, reduced and essentially Westernised resource. Using such widely available material contributes to a dilution and disappearance of the depth and variety of stories from around the world which are not seen as viable commercial products that can be profitably commodified. Incorporating in your individual practice a much richer variety of material helps maintain a culturally competent perspective to your therapeutic endeavour.

8

EVALUATING PRACTICE AND THE EVIDENCE BASE

We are often data rich but information poor.

– Cochrane

Introduction

It is not easy trying to define and determine culturally competent practice with children and adolescents by examining the experiences of black and other ethnic minority children and those from less easily designated cultures. However, they all share a similar position in society – they are treated in discriminatory ways in virtually every aspect of their lives and they *feel* different because their minority culture is not validated or respected. In this final chapter we shall consider the research evidence on effectiveness and evaluation in therapeutic work with children and young people. This will help us understand how research methodologies have been influenced and constructed by majority cultures, instinctively starting from a concept of *normality* based on a Western Eurocentric model. Thus we can examine the evidence refracted through our lens of cultural competence with an inquisitive stance and one that seeks to contribute to an evolution in the important area of finding out what works best, for whom, in what circumstances. This process needs to illuminate and question prevailing assumptions about the way data is gathered and interpreted and by what measures effectiveness or improvements are calculated.

Early British and American research in the 1970s on the health and education of black and ethnic minority children, tended to try and find out *why* they were not fitting in. Racist experiences were ascribed to their strangeness, and the solution was thought to be found in the intellectual concept of *assimilation*. This posited that with acculturation and absorption of immigrant families racism would disappear. White researchers offered judgements that we might consider astonishing now but which at the time carried weight. Thus Moynihan (1965) could argue that the personality traits of black boys were inhibited by the 'matriarchal structure of their family'. And Lobo (1978) suggested there was a great lack of understanding among Asian and West Indian parents of the emotional causation of physical symptoms...'they have a fear of mental illness because in their cultures this is ascribed to possession by evil spirits' (p. 55). These stereotypes were only the beginning of course.

As research in this field developed and it became necessary to question the assimilationist assumptions in the light of solid evidence of discrimination and prejudice, the notion of *multiculturalism* was offered as a framework within which to research the experiences of black and ethnic minority children. However, as qualitative data were increasingly made available it was argued that by displaying these families as different or even *exotic*, researchers were unwittingly colluding with racism (Gilroy 1982). The 1980s were a period of intense scrutiny by researchers who debated the merits of adopting a challenge to the perceived cosiness of the multicultural concept because it in effect reinforced racist attitudes and behaviour. It was argued that white researchers were still retaining the power to define reality and to organise their methodologies in ways that merely increased the sophistication of control of knowledge.

Thus it became important to adopt explicitly *anti-racist* methods in research so that a new epistemology could be constructed on the basis of the real life experiences of black people and have relevance and meaning rather than a philosophical discourse that replicated the power imbalance (Fraser et al. 2004). For example, research in Edinburgh into the health of black and ethnic minority children found higher incidences of bed-wetting and sleep disorder – a possible cause for concern in terms of mental health issues. However, after parent interviews it emerged that these children were suffering anxiety, fear and depression due to racist bullying. It is argued that research has tended to ignore such socio-economic and environmental causes of ill-health and concentrated instead on over-generalised and stereotyped socio-ethnic factors (Fraser et al. 2004). Furthermore, by actively seeking the views and perceptions of black and ethnic minority children and adolescents it has been possible recently to begin to reflect something more accurate than that offered by white adult interpretations. For example, a narrative approach using ethnographic methodologies has begun to provide some fascinating and useful data about the experiences of Asian deaf young people and African-Caribbean young males. These indicate that their problems are caused in large part by the inability of society to respect their difference and diversity (Wright et al. 1998, Atkin et al. 2001).

Safeguarding children's culture

The evidence for the need to distinguish the different mental health needs of all children in a culturally diverse society and protect them from indirect or direct racist abuse is strong (Barter 1999, Blackwell and Melzak 2000, Chand 2000, Stanley 2001, Weaver and Burns 2001). For example, refugee and asylum-seeking children, some unaccompanied, many affected by extreme circumstances, might include those witnessing murder of parents or kin, dislocation from school and community, severing of important friendships and extended family support, loss of home and prolonged insecurity. These experiences will likely trigger symptoms consistent with post-traumatic stress syndrome. This is manifested in a variety of ways including shock, grief, depression, anxiety, hyperactivity, self-harming behaviour, anger, aggressive behaviour, fear and guilt. Each individual child or adolescent will react differently according to variables such as

- the context of their departure from the home country;
- the family cohesion and coping capacity;
- the child's own personality and predisposing psychological constitution;
- proximity to extreme acts of murder or violence;
- the child's developmental stage and history of transition.

Recent research is emerging that attempts to identify specific therapeutic orientations with improved outcomes for children and young people (Fonagy and Roth 1997, Carr 2000). A number of studies compared levels of stress in adolescents and family functioning across different national boundaries including Canada, United States, Britain, Malaysia, India, Hong Kong and the Philippines (Bochner 1994, Bagley and Mallick 1995, Martin et al. 1995, Gibson-Cline 1996, Watkins and Gerong 1997). A meta-analysis of these studies found evidence to support the hypothesis that while subjectively perceived levels of stress can vary significantly between cultures, the underlying causes of personal distress could be relatively similar between cultures (Bagley and Mallick 2000). This is useful information to consider when trying to practice in culturally competent ways that avoid racist stereotyping.

The strongest evidence for prediction of mental health problems in children and adolescents across cultures is that of general family stress (Bagley and Mallick 2000). Looked at more closely, this includes the effects of physical, sexual and emotional abuse in the context of a climate of persistent negative family interactions. These findings are supported by other studies, which seek to illuminate and distinguish the particular factors influencing those children likely to develop mental health problems (Bagley and Young 1998, Kashani and Allan 1998, Ackroyd and Pilkington 1999, Vincent and Jouriles 2000). Counsellors and psychotherapists seeking to intervene effectively have to carefully consider the various ways potential mental health problems are thought about, understood and communicated in every family, in every culture.

Family therapy is used in a variety of contexts as we have noted earlier, and is perhaps more commonly associated with child and family problems where concerns have been expressed about the behaviour of an individual child. In therapeutic work it can also feature where a context of abuse, neglect, parental mental ill-health or domestic violence requires an assessment of the impact on the child as well as efforts to promote a more protective environment. These can be addressed in a mixture of specialist resources, primary care interventions or in statutory and voluntary contexts where psychodynamic approaches and systemic skills are used as an aid to decision-making and the preparation of official reports. Counsellors and psychotherapists have the basic skills required to adopt a culturally competent approach in work that can prevent problems deteriorating or in assessment for further intervention by other agencies or social work resources such as fostering or residential care.

As therapeutic practice adjusts to an organisational climate where cost-effectiveness, audit and evaluation are expected to contribute to the growing evidence base, practitioners need to know what works in order to justify their intervention. One of the major problems in attempting to ascertain what works is in distinguishing the impact your particular intervention has had in the context of the multiple cultural influences on a child or young person's existence. They could be receiving a number of interventions from several agencies such as school, health-visiting and youth-offending – each of which, or a combination of all, could be having a significant effect. It is also the case that any or all of these could be contributing to a *deterioration* in the situation. Trying to isolate the particular impact your therapeutic work has had is very difficult, particularly if you avoid seeking feedback from the child or young person. Furthermore, it is argued that counselling or psychotherapeutic work is not even appropriate to evidence-based approaches to practice because unlike medicine and experimental research, therapy is in a dynamic, interconnected relationship with clients – the nature of which cannot be subjected to conventional research methodology examining inputs and outcomes (Webb 2001).

Research into systemic practice can be considered compatible with the process and practice of the model itself. As the modern physical scientists have evolved new ways of thinking about facts and objectivity, so systemic theory in the social sciences can embrace the concepts of progressive hypothesising – formulating ideas about a family, testing them and then reformulating on the basis of feed-back (Dallos and Draper 2000). The use of supervision, videotape recording and family tasks offers a rich source of evidence with which to measure and analyse the impact of the therapy. Systemic theory also sits comfortably within new paradigms in the social sciences which seek to look beyond observed behaviours and recognise the importance of the meanings and beliefs created by families about their problems and attempted solutions. As far as child and adolescent counselling and psychotherapy are concerned, considerable advances have been made in recent years to engage in effectiveness research that identify evidence-based treatments for a range of presenting problems, improve the methodological quality of research studies and to produce clinical practice guidelines to reflect the compelling evidence that some interventions are the treatment of choice for specific child and adolescent problems (Christopherson and Mortweet 2001, Kazdin 2002).

The research evidence

There have been increasing numbers of studies of systemic therapy attempting to measure the effectiveness of this particular therapeutic intervention since it began to be more comprehensively established in the 1970s (Lask 1979, Campbell and Draper 1985, Dallos and Draper 2000). On the whole the evidence is consistent that systemic therapy is a valuable and effective approach to use in a variety of contexts. Before examining some of the studies to gain some detail about how therapy helped, it needs to be acknowledged that most of the studies have been undertaken in 'clinical' settings. There have been relatively few studies of systemic therapy employed in social work agency contexts, for example. However, even within the confines of clinical practice it is clear that systemic therapy has established itself alongside some of the older and more orthodox psychodynamic methods and models of intervention as a reliable and acceptable approach. A meta-analysis of the findings of 163 published and unpublished outcome studies on the efficacy and effectiveness of marital and family therapy concluded that the clients did significantly better than untreated control group clients (Shadish et al. 1995). Based on a substantial literature search of the available research findings recently, some clear findings demonstrate the following (Friedlander 2001, Goldenberg and Goldenberg 2004):

- Compared with no treatment, non-behavioural marital/systemic therapies are effective in two-thirds of all cases.
- The efficacy of systemic, behavioural, emotionally focused and insight-producing therapies is established for marital and adolescent delinquent problems.
- Structural therapy appears to be particularly helpful for certain childhood and adolescent psychosomatic symptoms.
- There is evidence for the efficacy of systemic therapy in treating childhood conduct disorders, phobias, anxieties and especially autism.

A major review of consumer studies of systemic therapy and marital counselling analysed a variety of research including large- and small-scale studies, individual case studies, specific therapeutic methodologies and ethnographic studies (Treacher 1995). These are particularly valuable sources of evidence because whilst they do not have the same methodological rigour as 'clinical' research studies, they nevertheless reflect a more realistic experience of families in front-line working contexts. The review concluded that practitioners who neglected the service user perspective and undervalued the *personal relationship* aspects of their family support work in favour of concentrating on inducing change, ran the risk of creating considerable dissatisfaction among service users. This reinforced findings from an earlier study into the effectiveness of systemic therapy in a social work context that advised that advice and directive work need to be balanced with reflective and general supportive elements (Howe 1989). In particular, the following conclusions are worth highlighting:

- Families needed an explanation of what therapy was about and how it differed from regular social service contact.
- Families felt they were being investigated, judged, manipulated and maligned and were unable to discuss issues they felt were important.

These studies point up the dilemmas faced by practitioners trying to employ therapeutic techniques in the context of a statutory remit which often includes a coercive element to family participation and an inspectorial/monitoring element to the work. Assessment should include a therapeutic element; but in the context of determining whether a child is in need or child protection concerns, it is understandable if both parents and practitioners lose track of the purpose of such assessments. These dilemmas probably also reflect the constraints of time which impose artificial timescales which are inherently anti-therapeutic.

In either perception a number of roles may be prescribed which affect the emotional dynamics between them and the counsellor or psychotherapist. This could range from parents *infantalising* themselves resulting in behaviour that elicits an authoritative/ parental response through to aggressive/hostile behaviour that elicits a compliant or collusive response from the practitioner. These patterns of interaction need to be thoroughly understood in order to figure out the most appropriate way of using a culturally competent approach. Fortunately, as a flexible approach, there are a wide range of options to select from, as we noted earlier. One of the significant conclusions to be drawn from considering the wider role of family support in contemporary therapeutic practice is the impressive amount of activity, the variation in methods of intervention and the worrying lack of systematic review of available research findings on which to build a reliable evidence base (Webb 2001).

The evidence base for individual counselling and psychotherapy for children and young people is growing, but is still relatively sparse. Many of the changes that take place in therapy may just not be outwardly measurable in terms of behaviour or symptomatology (Dogra et al. 2002). Invariably there are pragmatic difficulties in making individual subjective measures of internal change that are not readily compared especially when considering the cultural diversity between and within ethnic minority communities. Choice of outcome measures will affect concepts of effectiveness – for example, a school-refusing Muslim child may be encouraged to attend again after an intervention with that outcome in mind. But the consequence may be the onset of depression as the child is subjected to racist bullying which precipitated their school-refusal in the first place.

It is also important to take account of the natural history and environmental context of children's problems in relation to their developmental stage and acknowledge that there are no useful *standardised* ways of measuring childhood functioning. As discussed earlier, many of these classic measures are based on white Eurocentric models that are not nowadays consistent with culturally competent practice. What is consistent in all the major studies is the general *absence and rarity* of service user evaluation of, and involvement in, the design of child and family research. The implication is that by enlarging the focus of effectiveness measures it is possible to see children as not just with problems but also as having positive and constructive elements in their family lives, and building on these and amplifying them wherever possible. They also have much to tell us about how *they* feel about research into their lives and how methodologies can become more child-centred.

This view is echoed in recommendations based on thorough research into interventions targeted at the child, teacher and parent that demonstrate that the combined effect produces the most sustained reduction in conflict problems, both at home and at school, and in peer relationships (Webster-Stratton 1997). Recognising and building on the children's own perspectives provides new opportunities for therapeutic work with children and families guided by possibilities that adults are not aware of or fail to pay enough attention to. Thus it is possible to adhere to the paramountcy of the child's welfare whilst employing an integrated culturally competent theoretical paradigm that permits an effective analysis of the child's emotional, psychological and environmental family context.

Children in families

Children's perspectives have rarely been explored in relation to the evaluation of help they receive towards their emotional and mental well-being (Gordon and Grant 1997). The prevalence and upward trends of mental health problems in childhood together with findings that young people with such difficulties are reluctant to make use of specialist services or quickly cease contact is worrying (Audit Commission 1999, Mental Health Foundation 1999, Richardson and Joughin 2000). This indicates the importance of developing culturally appropriate sources of help that are experienced as useful and relevant and therefore going to be used effectively.

In order to do that methods of consulting with children and young people need to be developed that are appropriate, effective and methodologically robust. The literature has tended to neglect the individual experience and the voice of the child is unheard in most evaluative studies. Here you have the opportunity of refining your counselling or psychotherapeutic model to include a child's eye perspective. The skill is in having the intellectual agility and confidence to move between the therapeutic dimension and the cultural dimension during the same piece of work.

There is a growing literature on the subject of the rights of children and young people to influence decisions about their own health and healthcare (MacFarlane and McPherson 1995, Treseder 1997, Wilson 1999, Alderson 2000). However, this remains an area of contention for some professionals who believe that the notion that children can think, comment and participate in a meaningful way in evaluations of the help they receive is at best misguided or at worst undermining of parental and/or professional responsibility. There is perhaps added poignancy when this concept is applied to child and family work, where the very emotional and behavioural problems of children give weight to the argument against seeking children's perceptions.

Parents and those with parental responsibility might present powerful arguments for wanting to make exclusive decisions to enable them to cope with and manage sometimes worrying and disturbing behaviour. Equally, where children's difficulties are located in the context of parental discord, abuse, domestic violence or family dynamics it is important to ensure children are not blamed or scapegoated for problems caused by events or actions outside their control (Sutton 1999, Dallos and Draper 2000). Practitioners employing culturally competent approaches need to be sensitive to the power dynamics operating against children in family systems – especially where they are the identified patient/problem.

Research evidence demonstrates the value of consulting children and seeing how much they can achieve with a little help which is appropriate and acceptable (Levine 1993, Griffiths 1998). Children, like adults, have the right, under the terms of the UN Convention, to be consulted with, and to express their views about, services provided for them (UN 1989 Article 12). In some public services in England there is a legal duty to consult them in order to ascertain their wishes and feelings. An examination of some contemporary contributions on the subject of consulting with children and young people reveals a mixed picture in terms of cultural effectiveness, inclusion, methodologies and ethical considerations.

A children's rights perspective

Several studies provide some evidence of the effectiveness of attempts to ascertain the perceptions of children and young people about services they have received. There is, among some practitioners and researchers, a general assumption that seeking the views of children and young people is *of itself* a good thing. Yet the purpose of gaining such perceptions can be varied, the methods employed quite different and the evidence of the impact of seeking their views obscure. Given the power differential between parents and children, combined with the way families can scapegoat individual children, it is very important to consider ways of ascertaining their feelings about work being undertaken. Using an integrated culturally competent approach should not mean abandoning the experience of the individual participants (Walker 2003a).

Hennessey (1999) in a meta-review of a collection of research studies on this subject concluded that with the increasing interest in seeking children's views there need to be better developed instruments for measuring satisfaction and gaining children's evaluation of the services they receive. Research on children's evaluations of education, paediatrics and child mental health services was assessed. Only a minority of studies examined had presented information on the structure, reliability and validity of the instruments they used. Most of the studies concerned education contexts, the paediatric studies treated parents as the sole clients, while in mental health studies the correspondence between children's and parents' evaluations of services seemed to be greater.

The majority of studies used some form of questionnaire to collect information from children. Little information about the administration of these questionnaires was provided in the studies, for instance where they were administered or by whom. Factors that might influence their completion include the gender of the adult involved and whether telephone or postal methods were used. Use of Likert scales revealed little consensus on what were appropriate scales for children of different ages. Only a small number used qualitative methods to gather data.

Hennessey suggests interviews and open-ended questions have the potential to provide valuable information on client evaluations that cannot be tapped by rating scales. Most studies presented limited information on the psychometric properties of the instruments used. Where information was presented it was limited to information on the internal consistency of the instrument used. Only a small number of studies presented any information on re-test reliability. Where the data were qualitative, researchers typically reported inter-rater reliability on the classification of the children's responses. Findings suggest it is possible to develop an instrument with good psychometric properties for use by children aged six plus, there is, however, little evidence on instruments developed for use by younger children.

The extent to which children's evaluations are similar to the evaluations of parents raises important questions about validity. It can be assumed that perceptions should be different, but in the area of child and family practice differences in perception of the help received can indicate that the underlying cause of the difficulty remains untreated. In therapeutic work it is crucial to try to understand everyone's point of view whilst not colluding with the family system producing symptomatic behaviour in an individual. In the case of a child this can result in symptom deterioration, reinforcing parental perceptions that it is the child who has the problem. Or such a consequence can produce a resistance from the child at an older age to engaging with further help, thereby contributing to the development of mental health problems in adulthood.

It is important to explore the extent to which services are meeting the needs of differing groups of children in terms of age, gender, ethnicity, religion and socio-economic status. The research on client satisfaction in mental health services is better developed than in any other service sector. Three types of outcome have been used: client-assessed, parent-assessed and therapist-assessed. There are inconsistent findings reported for the relationship between client satisfaction and therapist evaluation of treatment progress. The problem of practitioner power and status is regarded as influential in determining the ability of children and young people to express discontent with help offered. It is recognised that children and young people feel under pressure to say what they expect the practitioner to hear. In the context of therapeutic work, counsellors and psychotherapists need to recognise that children's views can be obscured or implicitly silenced by a combination of vulnerability due to their ascribed role as 'the problem', a fear of professionals with the power to punish and a therapeutic stance that tries to equalise all members of the family. Enabling children and young people to express themselves in such oppressive environments is crucial.

A few studies have looked at the relationship with personal and/ or family variables. Understanding these relationships is potentially important for understanding the way in which services may or may not be meeting the needs of various clients. The information currently available is limited. There have been relatively small numbers of attempts to do this and those that have, used different measures. It is now acknowledged at central government level that children from different socio-economic backgrounds may have differential access to and/or different expectations from services, but to date these possibilities have not been further explored (Audit Commission 1999).

Age is a particularly important variable because of the different cognitive, social and emotional needs and abilities of children of different ages. Although individual studies differed in whether younger or older clients were more satisfied, a sufficient number of studies reported a moderate or high correlation between age and satisfaction/dissatisfaction (Shapiro et al. 1997). Only a small number of studies explored the relationship between gender and satisfaction, but the evidence suggests no general tendency for greater satisfaction to be associated with either boys or girls. A more useful approach may be to explore the relationship between client/staff gender combinations (Bernzweig et al. 1997). In other words, great care needs to be taken to select the most appropriate form of evidence-gathering that is likely to produce a more valid response from a culturally diverse population of children and young people. What works with a group of teenage clients may not work with a group of under 10s, or it may work but not with mixed gender groups.

There is very little evidence in many studies to demonstrate what impact their findings had on service development or practitioner attitudes and skills. In other words the research must lead to a positive impact on the way help and support are provided. Kalnins et al. (1992) argue that a shift in thinking is required from perceiving children and young people as recipients of health promotion efforts on their behalf, to accepting children and young people as active participants in the whole process. Another gap in the literature is the limited information on how children and young people felt about being asked their views on the service that they had received.

Some children may feel perturbed by this while others are enthusiastic about being given the opportunity to be part of a reflective process. It is a reasonable assumption that in the case of children and young people, those keenest to contribute are likely to reflect a positive perception of the service whereas those least keen reflect a negative experience. It is important for counsellors and psychotherapists to continue to develop creative and flexible methods for enabling representative contributions from all those receiving the same service. It is a truism that we tend to learn more from what went wrong than what went right.

Including children and young people

Few studies have been undertaken with regard to therapeutic interventions with children and young people and whether they found the therapy helpful. Those undertaken have found that generally children speak less than parents when interviewed together. Adolescents express themselves in limited ways tending to agree/disagree, while therapists spoke more often to parents than to children when attempting to evaluate the help and support offered (Friedlander et al. 1985, Mas et al. 1985, Marshal et al. 1989, Cederborg 1997). The question is whether this reflects a generalisable aversion to participating in research of this nature or whether the research design militates against inclusion and active participation. It also highlights the problem in therapeutic work of ensuring that children and young people are able to genuinely participate in expressing views and feelings.

Practitioners have built up a repertoire of therapeutic methods in working with children and young people, engaging with them in areas of great sensitivity such as bereavement, parental separation or sexual abuse. The same repertoire of research techniques is yet to be developed to ensure that children and young people are being given the best possible chance of contributing to service evaluation. Evidence of children's desire to be part of therapy suggests that children's reactions to therapy can be influenced by their attachment style (Smith et al. 1996, Strickland-Clark et al. 2000). In families where there are insecure attachments, for example, children can feel constrained from speaking more freely because of fears of what the consequences might be and the discomfort in exposing painful or difficult feelings. Ways to engage such children have been developed and could be adapted by researchers.

This poses important challenges for practitioners and researchers wanting to research in areas where there are factors likely to inhibit participation. Given the central position that attachment theory occupies in counselling and psychotherapy training, it should not be too difficult for practitioners to incorporate this dimension as we saw in Chapter 5, in evaluating interventions. The alternative is to automatically exclude some children and young people and miss the opportunity to gather valuable evidence to improve service provision rather than designing strategies to overcome these difficulties.

There has been a tendency in approaches to facilitate communication with children to favour those which are standardised and produce quantifiable results (McGurk 1992). Williamson and Butler (1996) note that there is a full literature about observational techniques but little that addresses qualitative approaches. There is, nevertheless, an emerging trend to move towards emphasising children's competencies and strengths in being able to describe their own perceptions (Mayall 1994).

There is little guidance available in the research literature about conversational methods with children. Even child psychology texts concentrate on experimental, observational and standard measurement techniques (Vasta et al. 1993). Children in interview situations are affected by the perceived power and status of adults and by presumptions about what answers are expected. The combination of adult assumptions about children and young people's competence in contributing to service evaluation and children and young people's assumptions about adult power and authority conspire to hinder meaningful developments to improve the situation.

Ethical considerations

In seeking to ascertain the perceptions of children and young people about therapy, the primary ethical consideration is to prevent any harm or wrongdoing during the process of research. While respecting children's competencies, researchers need to also fulfil their responsibilities to protect children and young people. A more social-anthropological approach that allows data to be co-produced in the relationship between researcher and the researched rather than being driven by problem-oriented adult questions is more appropriate because it permits the building-up of information on the general topic over time.

There is considerable uncertainty about the issue of children's consent to participate in research. The issue has yet to be fully tested in court. This is linked to consent for treatment which has been affected by the decision of the House of Lords in 1985 (Gillick 3 All ER) ruling that competent children under 16 years of age can consent. Since then further court cases have modified the Gillick principle so that if either the child or any person with parental responsibility gives consent to treatment, doctors can proceed, even if one or more of these people, including the child, disagree. While these rulings do not strictly apply to research they have implications for children's rights.

Parents may have to sign the research consent form until their child is 16 or 18 for medical research. But non-invasive social and educational research may not require parental consent because of the lack of harm. Social research requiring answers to questions implies consent if the subject co-operates. But is a child co-operating under pressure, afraid to decline or to challenge adult authority figures? It is argued that the onus should be on the adults to prove that the child does not have the capacity to decide, and the safest route is to ask for parental consent as well as the children's when they are able to understand (Alderson 1995). In the context of therapeutic work, the concept of informed consent requires sensitive explanation of the nature and purpose of research clearly and unambiguously. At the very least it should allow for informed dissent from the children and young people themselves (Morrow and Richards 1996).

There is little evidence of researchers *actively involving* children to select topics, plan research or advise on monitoring research. Where this has been done the results demonstrate that young people value being asked to participate in this way, and have much to offer the development of the research process. It has been established that using teenagers as researchers with other young people, for instance, has certain advantages over using adult researchers (Alderson 1995). Properly supported and trained, they can engage with younger children in ways adults are unable to achieve. The timing of research with children and young people, feedback to them and the dissemination of findings are further topics for ethical consideration. Attempting to interview during the course of intervention could be invasive or undermining of the therapeutic or supportive work being undertaken. Gaining access to the children and young people after the problem has resolved could be hampered by a need for the child and family to put their experiences behind them and avoid being reminded of painful issues.

Ethically the findings should be fedback to participants but in practice the time delay between data collection and writing up together with access to children militate against achieving this aim. Dissemination of the findings and the use to which they are put by service managers or government departments presents a clear responsibility to researchers to ensure that the views and perceptions of the children and young people are not misrepresented or distorted. Children as a powerless group in society are not able to challenge the ways in which research findings about them are presented (Thomas and O'Kane 1998, Walker 2003c).

Attempts to gain research evidence from children and young people demonstrate that practitioners and researchers are adopting a wide variety of methods, techniques and approaches to the difficult task of engaging children and young people. The number of studies is relatively small compared with studies of adult populations. This highlights a gap in the evidence base required on which to base judgements about service and practitioner development. Government policy in this area requires high quality research designed to produce more accessible, acceptable and appropriate services (Audit Commission 1999).

It is important to draw attention to the significance of the *emotional impact* such research has and suggest ways of encompassing the effects of research into the research design. The increasing trend towards including children and young people as active, rather than passive, recipients of health and social care means that the task of developing robust methods for obtaining children and young people's perceptions is important. Enabling them to collaborate in the design of research studies and to be consulted fully about the areas they consider important to research can only enrich these studies. The impact such research has in terms of the immediate effect on the child or young person, and on later service and practitioner development, requires attention from researchers involved in this area of work.

Children are not a culturally homogenous group. The age range from childhood to adolescence incorporates several developmental stages which would suggest attention being paid to the design of developmentally appropriate methods. A variety of participatory research methods are being developed including the use of mapping and modelling, diagrams, drawing and collage, drama and puppetry. These methods are designed to empower children and young people by enabling them to represent their own situations, to reflect on their experiences and to influence change (Chambers 1997). Gender differences are considered important in terms of children and young people's perceptions in other areas of life experience, therefore attention needs to be paid to considering the gender dimension in research studies. This means considering the advantages and potential disadvantages of using male or female researchers.

Children and young people from black and other ethnic minorities have experiences conditioned by racism and other social disadvantages, which should be incorporated in research. This might, for instance, mean employing black and other ethnic minority staff to conduct more enabling research. There is growing evidence of the desire from children and young people to be involved in decisions and services affecting their lives. There is equally evidence of a response from a number of researchers and practitioners to incorporate children and young people's perceptions in service evaluation.

Further research is indicated to contribute to the refinement of methodologies, to improve reliability and to increase participation of children and young people as recipients of therapy in order to enhance service quality and development.

Change and the evidence base

Central to an empowering, culturally competent approach in therapeutic work with children and families is finding out whether the work has contributed towards the *process of change*. Change can be considered as something that is endless, constant and inevitable. How it is perceived and experienced by children and adolescents is crucial. Various models of counselling and therapeutic intervention permit change stemming from within the psyche of the person, family or to changes in their environment and abilities.

There are changes imposed on certain children and young people compulsorily and those that are accepted voluntarily – either of which may lead to long-term benefits for them or their kin. Change is often thought of as something initiated by a practitioner in a linear cause-and-effect process. But it can be more useful to think about it in a more circular or reflexive pattern using an integrated psychodynamic and systemic theory as an explanatory model. How much did *you* change during the course of an intervention? What impact did the client have on you and how did this affect your thinking and behaviour? Indeed most of the change may occur within yourself as you find out more over time about a child and their circumstances compared to the first encounter.

Change is connected to difference but every stakeholder in the change process has a unique perception of what counts as difference. Pointing out differences to a family might be experienced as empowering but it might equally provoke feelings of fear or anxiety. A minimum amount of help might produce significant changes and equally a substantial amount of intervention might result in no change or a worsening of circumstances. Where a practitioner chooses to look for change may not be where other professionals or the family is looking. Change can therefore be liberating or constraining; it can generate enlightenment or promote feelings of anger, loss and bereavement. Maintaining a degree of optimism with realism and managing uncertainty with a modest and respectful approach offers you the potential for being a useful resource to your clients.

The need to expand and refine the evidence base of therapeutic practice in order to demonstrate effectiveness is more important than ever, especially in work with children and families (Walker 2003c). The growing problems faced by families require a *concerted* effort from all agencies in contact with children and young people to understand the services they are providing and finding out better ways of measuring success. The drive to encourage a research-minded profession of counsellors and psychotherapists in order to improve practice standards and accountability is, however, in danger of producing a confusion of research studies varying in quality and methodological rigour yet producing potentially useful data hidden within the quantity being produced.

Practitioner research is being encouraged as a means of influencing policy, management and practice, using evaluative concepts moulded by client expectations (Fuller 1996, Walker 2001c). In the context of a range of practice situations, counsellors and psycho-therapists can contribute to good quality effectiveness and evaluation studies by working in partnership and in culturally competent ways with individuals and families to ensure that their perspectives are at the heart of this activity. By taking this broader rather than narrow view of research you can help contribute to social policy changes that will ultimately impact on your services and thus in a benign, continuous, circular process benefit children and young people.

The broader cultural view

There is evidence that research into children's perceptions as recipients of support services that focus on competence and resources, rather than problems or deviance, helps provide a fuller picture of their circumstances and highlights the importance of the personal relation-ship established with their psychotherapist or counsellor (Sandbaek 1999). It is also consistent with the right under the terms of the UN Charter to be consulted with and to express their views about services provided for them (UN 1989). The implications seem to be that by enlarging the focus of effectiveness measures it is possible to see children as not just with problems but also as having positive and constructive elements in their family lives, and building on these and amplifying them wherever possible.

This view is echoed in recommendations based on thorough research into interventions targeted at the child, teacher and parent, which demonstrate that the combined effect produces the most sustained reduction in conflict problems both at home and at school, and in peer relationships (Webster-Stratton 1997). Recognising and building on the children's own perspectives provides new opportunities for work with children and families guided by possibilities that adults are not aware of or fail to pay enough attention to, and thus enriching the cultural perspective.

Creating acceptable, accessible and appropriate support for every family which requires it means acknowledging the poor general health of ethnic minority families attributable to their impoverished socio-economic circumstances and the impact of personal and institutional racism. Clifford offers a useful model for consideration of an anti-oppressive assessment framework which takes into account cultural divisions. Further research with ethnic minority families to investigate culturally competent effectiveness is required to build on the limited work undertaken (Trevino 1999). The needs of gay and lesbian families are virtually absent in the literature on family support, which reflects homophobic and discriminatory practices in health and social care culture. This gap needs to be filled on the grounds of equality and to ensure that appropriate support can be offered to every family – however they are defined, and to enable different parenting practices to be valued and learned from (Eliason 1996, Salmon and Hall 1999).

While we experience the phenomenon of globalisation there is an expectation of the narrowing of the differences that separate countries, cultures and citizens. This is meant to herald a dissolving of the national barriers that have fomented ethnic conflict, religious strife and wasted effort in protectionist economic strategies. The common language of English is meant to facilitate easier communication and the transfer of knowledge, ideas and practices. In the realm of child welfare, international conferences seek to offer *forums* for the exchange of expertise and dissemination of best practice based on valid research. Yet we also know that it is unrealistic if not arrogant for Western professionals to assume that developing nations can simply transplant their models, methods and practices into different social, cultural and ethnic contexts.

There needs to be a genuine exchange of concepts and practices with no assumptions about privileging one perception or cultural interpretation over another in the area of evaluation and effectiveness. By examining children and young people's experiences of counselling and psychotherapy in a wide variety of cultural contexts we can begin to assemble an evidence base that reflects and validates difference and diversity and build towards culturally competent research and practice.

Summary

Research methodologies have been influenced and constructed by majority cultures instinctively starting from a concept of *normality* based on a Western Eurocentric model. We can examine the evidence refracted through our lens of cultural competence with an inquisitive stance and one that seeks to contribute to an evolution in the important area of finding out what works best, for whom, in what circumstances. This process needs to illuminate and question prevailing assumptions about the way data is gathered and interpreted and by what measures effectiveness or improvements are calculated.

Cost-effectiveness, audit and evaluation are expected to contribute to the growing evidence base, requiring us to know what works in order to justify our intervention. It is hard to distinguish the impact your particular intervention has had, considering the multiple cultural influences and influence of other agencies on a child or young person. Choice of outcome measures will affect concepts of effectiveness – for example, a school-refusing black child may return but the consequence may be the onset of depression if the child is subjected to racist bullying which precipitated their school-refusal in the first place.

The evidence base for individual counselling and psychotherapy for children and young people is relatively sparse. Many of the changes that take place in therapy may just not be outwardly measurable in terms of behaviour or symptomatology. There are pragmatic difficulties in making individual subjective measures of internal change that are not readily compared especially when considering the cultural diversity between and within ethnic minority communities.

The problem of practitioner power and status is regarded as influential in determining the ability of children and young people to express discontent with help offered. Children and young people feel under pressure to say what they expect the practitioner to hear. Counsellors and psychotherapists need to recognise that children's views can be obscured or implicitly silenced by a combination of vulnerability due to their ascribed role as 'the problem', a fear of professionals with the power to punish and a therapeutic stance that tries to equalise all members of the family.

There is little evidence of researchers *actively involving* children to select topics, plan research or advise on monitoring research. Where this has been done, the results demonstrate that young people value being asked to participate in this way, and have much to offer the development of the research process. Using teenagers as researchers with other young people, for instance, has certain advantages over using adult researchers. Properly supported and trained, they can engage with younger children in ways adults are unable to achieve.

There is considerable uncertainty about the issue of children's consent to participate in research. In seeking to ascertain the perceptions of children and young people about therapy, the primary ethical consideration is to prevent any harm or wrongdoing during the process of research. While respecting children's competencies, researchers need to also fulfil their responsibilities to protect children and young people. A culturally competent approach that allows data to be co-produced in the relationship between therapist and client rather than being driven by adult questions is more appropriate.

BIBLIOGRAPHY

Ackroyd, J and Pilkington, A (1999) Childhood and the construction of ethnic identities in a global age. *Childhood*, 6(4): 443–454.

Adams, G, Gullotta, T and Montemayor, R (eds) (1992) *Adolescent Identity Formation*. New York, Sage.

Adams, R, Dominelli, L and Payne, M (1998) *Social Work: Themes, Issues and Critical Debates*. Basingstoke, Macmillan.

——(2002) *Critical Practice in Social Work*. Basingstoke, Palgrave.

Aggleton, P, Hurry, J and Warwick, I (eds) (2000) *Young People and Mental Health*. London, Wiley.

Ahmad, B (1990) *Black Perspectives in Social Work*. Birmingham, Venture Press.

Akister, J (1998) Attachment theory and systemic practice: Research update. *Journal of Family Therapy*, 20(4): 353–366.

Alderson, P (1995) *Listening to Children: Children Ethics and Social Research*. Barnardos, London.

——(2000) *Young Children's Rights*. London, Save the Children/Jessica Kingsley.

Alibhai-Brown, Y (1999) *True Colours: Public Attitudes to Multiculturalism and the Role of the Government*. London, IPPR.

American Psychiatric Association (1994) *Diagnostic and Statistical Manual of Mental Disorders (DSM IV)*, 4th edn. Washington, DC, American Psychiatric Association.

Amery, J, Tomkins, A and Victor, C (1995) The prevalence of behavioural problems amongst homeless primary school children in an outer London Borough: A feasibility survey. *Public Health*, 109: 421–424.

Amin, K, Drew, D, Fosam, B, Gillborn, D and Demack, S (1997) *Black and Ethnic Minority Young People and Educational Disadvantage*. London, Runnymede Trust.

Anderson, H and Goolishan, H (1992) The client is the expert: A not knowing approach to therapy. In: S McNamee and KJ Gergen (eds) *Therapy as Social Construction*. London, Sage.

Anderson, HC (1913) *Hans Christian Anderson's Fairy Tales*. London, Constable & Co.

Anderson, K and Anderson, L (eds) (1995) *Mosby's Pocket Dictionary of Nursing, Medicine and Professions Allied to Medicine*. London, Mosby.

Appleby, L, Cooper, J and Amos, T (1999) Psychological autopsy study of suicides by people aged under 35. *British Journal of Psychiatry*, 175: 168–174.

Arcelus, J, Bellerby, T and Vostanis, V (1999) A mental health service for young people in the care of the local authority. *Clinical Child Psychology and Psychiatry*, 4(2): 233–245.

Atkin, K and Rollings, J (1993) *Community Care in a Multi-Racial Britain: A Critical Review of the Literature*. London, HMSO.

Atkin, K, Ahmed, WIU and Jones, L (2001) Young South Asian deaf people and their families: Negotiating relationships and identities. *Sociology of Health and Illness*, 24(1): 21–45.

Audit Commission (1994) *Seen but not Heard*. London, HMSO.

——(1998) *Child and Adolescent Mental Health Services*. London, HMSO.

——(1999) *Children in Mind: Child and Adolescent Mental Health Services*. London, HMSO.

——(2000) *Another Country: Implementing Dispersal under the Immigration and Asylum Act 1999*. London, HMSO.

Australian Institute of Health and Welfare (2001) *Child Protection Australia, 1999–2000*. Canberra, AIHW.

Bagley, C and Mallick, K (1995) Negative self perception and components of stress in Canadian, British and Hong Kong adolescents. *Perceptual Motor Skills*, 81: 123–127.

——(2000) How adolescents perceive their emotional life, behaviour, and self-esteem in relation to family stressors: A six-culture study. In: N Singh, J Leung and A Singh (eds) *International Perspectives on Child and Adolescent Mental Health*. Oxford, Elsevier.

Bagley, C and Young, L (1998) The interactive effects of physical, emotional, and sexual abuse on adjustment in a longtitudinal cohort of 565 children from birth to age 17. In: C Bagley and K Mallick (eds) *Child Sexual Abuse: New Theory and Research*. Aldershot, Ashgate.

Bailey, R and Brake, B (eds) (1980) *Radial Social Work Practice*. London, Edward Arnold.

Bains, R (2001) Psychotherapy with young people from ethnic minority backgrounds in different community based settings. In: G Baruch (ed.) *Community Based Psychotherapy with Young People: Evidence and Innovation in Practice*. Hove, Brunner-Routledge.

Baldwin, M (2000) *Care Management and Community Care*. Aldershot, Ashgate.

Bandura, A (1986) *Social Foundations of Thought and Action: A Social Cognitive Perspective*. New Jersey, Prentice-Hall.

Baradon, T, Sinason, V and Yabsley, S (1999) Assessment of parents and young children – a child psychotherapy point of view. *Child Care Health and Development*, 25(1): 37–53.

Barlow, J (1998) Parent training programmes and behaviour problems – findings from a systematic review. In: A Buchanan and B Hudson (eds) *Parenting, Schooling, and Childrens Behaviour: Interdisciplinary Approaches*. Alton, Ashgate Publishers.

Barnes, C (1991) *Disabled People in Britain and Discrimination*. London, Hurst.

Barnes, C and Mercer, G (1997) *Doing Disability Research*. Leeds, Disability Press.

Barnes, H, Thornton, P and Maynard, S (1998) *Disabled People and Employment: A Review of Research and Development Work*. Bristol, Policy Press.

Barnes, M and Warren, L (1999) *Paths to Empowerment*. Bristol, Policy Press.

Barnes McGuire, J, Stein, A and Rosenberg, W (1997) Evidence based medicine and child mental health services. A broad approach to evaluation is needed. *Children and Society*, 11: 89–96.

Barry, M and Hallett, C (eds) (1998) *Social Exclusion and Social Work*. Lyme Regis, Russell House.

Barter, C (1999) *Protecting Children from Racism and Racist Abuse – A Research Review*. London, NSPCC.

Barter, K (2001) Building community: A conceptual framework for child protection. *Child Abuse Review*, 10: 262–278.

Barton, J (1999) Child and adolescent psychiatry. In: M Hill (ed.) *Effective Ways of Working with Children and their Families*. London, Jessica Kingsley.

BASW (2002) *The Code of Ethics for Social Work*. Birmingham, BASW.

Bateson, G (1973) *Steps to an Ecology of Mind*. St Albans, Paladin.

Baumann, G (1996) *Contesting Culture*. Cambridge, Cambridge University Press.

Bayley, R (1998) *Transforming Children's Lives: The Importance of Early Intervention*. London, Family Policy Studies Centre.

Beatch, R and Stewart, B (2002) Integrating Western and aboriginal healing practices. In: M Nash and B Stewart (eds) *Spirituality and Social Care*. London, Jessica Kingsley.

Beckett, C (2002) *Human Growth and Development*. London, Sage.

Beckett, C and Wrighton, E (2000) What matters to me is not what you're talking about – maintaining the social model of disability in public and private negotiations. *Disability and Society*, 15(7): 991–999.

Beck-Sander, A (1998) Is insight into psychosis meaningful? *Journal of Mental Health*, 7: 25–34.

Belsky, J, Campbell, SB, Cohn, JF and Moore, G (1996) Instability of infant–parent attachment stability. *Developmental Psychology*, 32: 921–924.

Bentovim, A and Bingley Miller, L (2002) *The Family Assessment*. London, DOH/Pavilion.

Beresford, B, Sloper, P, Baldwin, S and Newman, T (1996) *What Works in Services for Families with a Disabled Child?* Barkingside, Barnardos.

Berg, IK and Jaya, A (1993) Different and same: Family therapy with American-Asian families. *Journal of Marital and Family Therapy*, 19(1): 31–39.

Bernzweig, J, Takayama, J, Phibbs, C, Lewis, C and Pantell, RH (1997) Gender differences in physician – patient communication. *Archives of Pediatric Adolescent Medicine*, 151: 586–591.

Berridge, D (1997) *Foster Care: A Research Review*. London, HMSO.

Bettelheim, B (1978) *The Uses of Enchantment: The Meaning and Purpose of Fairy Tales*. London, Penguin.

——(1991) *The Uses of Enchantment – The Meaning and Importance of Fairy Tales*. London, Penguin.

Bhabha, H (1994) *The Location of Culture*. London, Routledge.

——(1997) Cultures in between. In: D Bennett (ed.) *Multicultural Studies – Rethinking Difference and Identity*. London, Routledge.

Bhugra, D (1999) *Mental Health of Ethnic Minorities*. London, Gaskell.

Bhugra, D and Bahl, V (1999) *Ethnicity: An Agenda for Mental Health*. London, Gaskell.

Bhui, K (1997) London's ethnic minorities and the provision of mental health services. In: LK Johnson, R Ramsey, G Thornicroft, L Brooks and P Lelliot (eds) *London's Mental Health*. London, King's Fund Institute.

Bhui, K and Olajide, D (1999) *Mental Health Service Provision for a Multi-cultural Society*. London, Saunders.

Bilton, T, Bonnet, K, Jones, P, Lawson, T, Skinner, D, Stanworth, M and Webster, A (2002) *Introductory Sociology*. Basingstoke, Palgrave Macmillan.

Blackwell, D and Melzak, S (2000) *Far from the Battle but Still at War – Troubled Refugee Children in School*. London, The Child Psychotherapy Trust.

Bochner, S (1994) Cross-cultural differences in the self-concept: A test of Hofstede's individualism/collectivism distinction. *Journal of Cross-Cultural Psychology*, 2: 273–283.

Bollas, C (1987) *The Shadow of the Object: Psychoanalysis of the Unthought Known*. London, Free Association Books.

——(1991) *Forces of Destiny: Psychoanalysis and Human Idiom*. London, Free Association Books.

Bourne, D (1993) Over-chastisement, child non-compliance and parenting skills: A behavioural intervention by a family centre social worker. *British Journal of Social Work*, 5: 481–500.

Bowlby, J ([1969], 1982) *Attachment and Loss*, Vol. 1. New York, Basic Books.

——(1979) *The Making and Breaking of Affectional Bonds*. London, Tavistock Publications.

Boyd-Franklin, N, Steiner, G and Boland, M (1995) *Children, Families and HIV/AIDS*. New York, Guilford Press.

Bradshaw, J (1972) The concept of human need. *New Society*, 30(3): 72.

——(ed.) (2001) *Poverty: The Outcomes for Children*. London, Family Policy Studies Centre/ESRC.

Brammer, A (2003) *Social Work Law*. Harlow, Pearson Education.

Brandon, M, Schofield, G and Trinder, L (1998) *Social Work with Children*. Basingstoke, Macmillan.

Braye, S and Preston-Shoot, M (1995) *Empowering Practice in Social Care*. Buckingham, Open University Press.

——(1997) *Practising Social Work Law*, 2nd edn. London, Macmillan Palgrave.

Brearley, J (1995) *Counselling and Social Work*. Buckingham, Open University Press.

Bretherton, I (1985) Attachment theory: Retrospect and prospect. *Monographs of the Society for Research in Child Development*, 50: 3–35.

Briggs, S (2002) *Working with Adolescents: A Contemporary Psychodynamic Approach*. Basingstoke, Palgrave Macmillan.

Britton, R (1998) *Belief and Imagination: Explorations in Psychoanalysis*. London, Routledge.

Brown, B, Crawford, P and Darongkamas, J (2000) Blurred roles and permeable boundaries: The experience of multidisciplinary working in community mental health. *Health and Social Care in the Community*, 8(6): 425–435.

Burghes, L, Clarke, L and Cronin, N (1997) *Fathers and Fatherhood in Britain*. London, Family Policy Studies Centre.

Burnham, J (1986) *Family Therapy*. London, Tavistock Publications.

Butrym, Z (1976) *The Nature of Social Work*. London, Macmillan.

Byng-Hall, J (1998) *Rewriting Family Scripts – Improvisation and Systems Change*. New York, Guilford Press.

Caan, W and Belleroche, J (2002) *Drink, Drugs and Dependence*. London, Routledge.

Caesar, G, Parchment, M and Berridge, D (1994) *Black Perspectives on Services for Children in Need*. London, Barnardos/NCB.

Cahn, R (1998) The process of becoming a subject in adolescence. In: M Perret-Catipovic and F Ladame (eds) *Adolescence and Psychoanalysis: The Story and the History*. London, Karnac Books.

Calder, M, Peake, A and Rose, K (2001) *Mothers of Sexually Abused Children*. Lyme Regis, Russell House.

Campbell, D and Draper, R (eds) (1985) *Applications of Systemic Family Therapy*. London, Grune and Stratton.

Canino, I and Spurlock, J (2000) *Culturally Diverse Children and Adolescents – Assessment, Diagnosis and Treatment*, 2nd edn. New York, Guilford Press.

Caplan, G (1961) *Principles of Preventive Psychiatry*. London, Basic Books.

Capra, F (1997) *The Web of Life: A New Synthesis of Mind and Matter*. London, Flaming.

Carpenter, J and Sbaraini, S (1997) *Choice, Implementation and Dignity: Involving Users and Carers in Care Management in Mental Health*. Bristol, Policy Press.

Carr, A (ed.) (2000) *What Works for Children and Adolescents? A Critical Review of Psychological Interventions with Children, Adolescents, and their Families*. London, Routledge.

Carroll, M (1998) Social work's conceptualization of spirituality. *Social Thought: Journal of Religion in the Social Sciences*, 18(2): 1–14.

Carter, B and McGoldrick, M (1999) *The Expanded Family Life Cycle: Individual, Family and Social Perspectives*, 3rd edn. Boston, Allyn & Bacon.

Castillo, RJ (1995) *Culture and Mental Illness: A Client Centred Approach*. Thousand Oaks, CA, Brooks/Cole Publishing.

Cederborg, A (1997) Young children's participation in family therapy talk. *The American Journal of Family Therapy*, 25: 28–38.

Central Council for the Education and Training of Social Workers (1989) *Paper 30: Rules and Requirements for the Diploma in Social Work*. London, CCETSW.

Chambers, R (1997) *Whose Reality Counts? Putting the First Last*. London, Intermediate Technology.

Chand, A (2000) The over representation of black children in the child protection system: Possible causes, consequences and solutions. *Child and Family Social Work*, 5: 67–77.

Cheetham, J (1997) The research perspective. In: M Davies (ed.) *The Blackwell Companion to Social Work*. Oxford, Blackwell.

Children's Legal Centre (1994) *Mental Health Handbook: A Guide to the Law Affecting Children and Young People*. London, The Children's Legal Centre.

Christiansen, E and James, G (eds) (2000) *Research with Children, Perspectives and Practices*. London, Falmer Press.

Christopherson, ER and Mortweet, SL (2001) *Treatments that Work with Children: Empirically Supported Strategies for Managing Childhood Problems*. Washington, DC, American Psychological Association.

Clarke, L, Bradshaw, J and Williams, J (2001) *Family Diversity, Poverty and the Mental Well-being of Young People*. London, Health Education Authority.

Clarke, N (2001) The impact of in-service training within social services. *British Journal of Social Work*, 31: 757–774.

Cobb, M and Robshaw, V (1998) *The Spiritual Challenge of Health Care*. Edinburgh, Churchill Livingstone.

Cohn, DA, Silver, DH, Cowan, CP and Cowan, PA (1992) Working models of childhood attachment and couples relationships. *Journal of Family Issues*, 13: 432–449.

Cole, E, Leavey, G and King, M (1995) Pathways to care for patients with first episode of psychosis. A comparison of ethnic groups. *British Journal of Psychiatry*, 167: 770–776.

Coles, R (1990) *The Spiritual Life of Children*. New York, Random House.

Compton, B and Galaway, B (1999) *Social Work Processes*, 6th edn. Pacific Grove, CA, Brooks/Cole Publishing.

Comte, A (1852) *System of Positive Polity*, Vol. 2: *Social Statistics*. London, Longmans Green, p. 3.

Connelly, N and Stubbs, P (1997) *Trends in Social Work and Social Work Education across Europe*. London, NISW.

Cook, WL (2000) Understanding attachment security in family context. *Journal of Personality & Social Psychology*, 78(2): 285–294.

Cooper, P (ed.) (1999) *Understanding and Supporting Children with Emotional and Behavioural Difficulties*. London, Jessica Kingsley.

Copley, B and Forryan, B (1997) *Therapeutic Work with Children and Young People*. London, Cassell.

Corby, B, Millar, M and Pope, A (2002) Out of the frame. *Community Care*, Sept. 2002, pp. 40–41.

Corker, M (1999) New disability discourse, the principle of optimization and social change. In: M Corker and S French (eds) *Disability Discourse*. Buckingham, Open University Press.

Corrigan, P and Leonard, P (1978) *Social Work Practice under Capitalism: A Marxist Approach*. London, Macmillan.

Costner, R, Guttman, H, Sigal, J, Epstein, N and Rakoff, V (1971) Process and outcome in conjoint family therapy. *Family Process*, 10: 451–474.

Cote, GL (1997) Socio-economic attainment, regional disparities, and internal migration. *European Sociological Review*, 13(1): 55–77.

Coulshed, V and Orme, J (1998) *Social Work Practice: An Introduction*, 3rd edn. London, Macmillan/BASW.

Courtney, M, Barth, R, Berrick, J, Brooks, D, Needell, B and Park, L (1996) Race and Child Welfare Services: Past Research and Future Directions. *Child Welfare*, LXXV: 2, March/April.

Cox, A (1994) Diagnostic appraisal. In: M Rutter, L Hersov and E Taylor (eds) *Child and Adolescent Psychiatry*. London, Blackwell.

Crawford, M and Kessel, A (1999) Not listening to patients – the use and misuse of patient satisfaction studies. *International Journal of Social Psychiatry*, 45(1): 1–6.

Crittenden, PM (1999) Danger and development: The organization of self-protective strategies. In: J Vondra and D Barnett (eds) *Monographs for the Society for Research on Child Development*, 64: 145–171.

Crompton, M (1996) *Children, Spirituality and Religion*. London, CCETSW.

Cross, T, Bazron, B, Dennis, K and Isaacs, M (1989) *Toward a Culturally Competent System of Care: A Monograph on Effective Services for Minority Children who are Severely Emotionally Disturbed.* Washington, DC, Georgetown University Child Development Center.

Crutcher, R (1943) Child psychiatry: The history of its development. *Psychiatry,* 6: 191–201.

Currer, C (2001) *Responding to Grief: Dying, Bereavement and Social Care.* Basingstoke, Palgrave.

Daines, R, Lyon, K and Parsloe, P (1990) *Aiming for Partnership.* London, Barkingside, Barnardos.

Dallos, R and Draper, R (2000) *An Introduction to Family Therapy: Systemic Theory and Practice.* London, Open University Press.

Dare, C, Eisler, I, Russell, GFM and Szmukler, G (1990) The clinical and theoretical impact of a controlled trial of family therapy in anorexia nervosa. *Journal of Marital and Family Therapy,* 16(1): 39–57.

David, AS (1998) Commentary on: Is insight into psychosis meaningful? *Journal of Mental Health,* 7: 579–583.

Davies, M (1981) *The Essential Social Worker: A Guide to Positive Practice.* Aldershot, Arena.

——(ed.) (1997) *The Blackwell Companion to Social Work.* London, Oxford: Blackwell.

Davis, A and Ellis, K (1995) Enforced altruism or community care. In: R Hugman and D Smith (eds) *Ethical Issues in Social Work.* London, Routledge.

Davis, A, Ellis, K and Rummery, B (1997) *Access to Assessment: Perspectives of Practitioners, Disabled People, and Carers.* Bristol, Policy Press.

Davis, H and Spurr, P (1998) Parent counselling: Evaluation of a community child mental health service. *Journal of Child Psychology and Psychiatry,* 39: 365–376.

Davis, H, Spurr, P, Cox, A, Lynch, M, Von Roenne, A and Hahn, K (1997) A description and evaluation of a community child mental health service. *Clinical Child Psychology and Psychiatry,* 2(2): 221–238.

Davis, J, Rendell, P and Sims, D (1999) The joint practitioner – a new concept in professional training. *Journal of Interprofessional Care,* 13(4): 395–404.

Daycare Trust (2000) *Ensuring Equality.* London, Daycare Trust.

DeBell, D and Everett, G (1997) *In a Class Apart: A Study of School Nursing.* Norwich, East Norfolk Health Authority.

DeBell, D and Walker, S (2002) *Evaluation of the Family Support Service in Norfolk CAMHS.* Cambridge, Anglia Polytechnic University.

——(2002) *Norfolk Family Support Teams Final Evaluation Report.* Chelmsford, APU Centre for Research in Health and Social Care.

Dennis, J and Smith, T (2002) Nationality, Immigration and Asylum Bill 2002: Its impact on children. *Childright,* 187: 16–17.

Department for Education and Employment (1998) Towards an Interdisciplinary framework for developing work with children and young people. *Childhood Studies Discipline Network,* Conference presentation. Cambridge, Robinson College.

Department of Health (1989) *The Children Act.* London, HMSO.

——(1995) *Child Protection: Messages from Research.* London, HMSO.

——(1995) *A Handbook on Child and Adolescent Mental Health.* London, HMSO.

——(1997) *Developing Partnerships in Mental Health.* London, HMSO.

——(1997) *The New NHS: Modern, Dependable.* London, HMSO.

——(1997) *Innovations Fund. Specific Mental Health Grant.* London, HMSO.

——(1998a) *Disabled Children: Directions for their Future Care.* London, HMSO.

——(1998b) *Partnership in Action.* London, HMSO.

——(1998c) *Modernising Mental Health Services: Safe, Supportive and Sensible.* London, HMSO.

——(1999a) *The Health Act.* London, HMSO.

——(1999b) Lac circular. (99)33. *Quality Protects Programme: Transforming Children's Services 2000–01.* London, HMSO.

——(1999c) *Working Together to Safeguard Children.* London, HMSO.

——(2000) *Framework for the Assessment of Children in Need and their Families.* London, HMSO.

——(2000) *Social Services Inspectorate: Excellence not Excuses – Inspection of Services for Ethnic Minority Children and Families.* London, HMSO.

——(2000) *National Service Framework for Mental Health.* London, HMSO.

——(2001a) *Making it Work: Inspection of Welfare to Work for Disabled People.* London, HMSO.

——(2001b) *Safeguarding Children in Whom Illness is Induced or Fabricated by Carers with Parenting Responsibilities.* London, HMSO.

——(2001c) *Children Looked after in England: 2000/2001.* London, HMSO.

Department of Health/SSI (1991) *Care Management and Assessment: Practitioners' Guide to the NHS and Community Care Act 1990.* London, HMSO.

——(2000) *A Quality Strategy for Social Care.* London, HMSO.

Department of Health and Department for Education and Employment (1996) *Children's Service Planning: Guidance for Inter-agency Working.* London, HMSO.

Department of Health and Social Security (1985) *Social Work Decisions in Child Care.* London, HMSO.

Dimigen, G, Del Priore, C, Butler, S, Evans, S, Ferguson, L and Swan, M (1999) Psychiatric disorder among children at time of entering local authority care. *British Medical Journal,* 319: 675–676.

Dingwall, R (1989) Some problems about predicting child abuse and neglect. In: O Stevenson (ed.) *Child Abuse: Public Policy and Professional Practice.* Hemel Hempstead, Harvester Wheatsheaf.

Doel, M and Marsh, P (1992) *Task-centred Social Work.* Aldershot, Ashgate.

Dogra, N, Parkin, A, Gale, F and Frake, C (2002) *A Multidisciplinary Handbook of Child and Adolescent Mental Health for Front-line Professionals.* London, Jessica Kingsley.

Dominelli, L (1988) *Anti-Racist Social Work.* Basingstoke, Macmillan.

——(1996) Deprofessionalising social work: Equal opportunities, competences, and postmodernism. *British Journal of Social Work,* 26(2): 153–175.

——(1997a) Feminist theory. In: M Davies (ed.) *The Blackwell Companion to Social Work.* Oxford, Blackwell.

——(1997b) *Anti-Racist Social Work,* 2nd edn. London, Macmillan/BASW.

——(1998) Anti-oppressive practice in context. In: R Adams, L Dominelli and M Payne (eds) *Social Work: Themes, Issues and Critical Debates.* Basingstoke, Macmillan.

——(1999) Neo-liberalism, social exclusion and welfare clients in a global economy. *International Journal of Social Welfare,* 8(1): 14–22.

——(2002a) *Anti-Oppressive Social Work Theory and Practice*. Basingstoke, Palgrave Macmillan.

——(2002b) Changing agendas-moving beyond fixed identities in anti-oppressive practice. In: D Tomlinson and W Trew (eds) *Equalising Opportunities, Minimising Oppression*. London, Routledge.

Donnellan, C (2000) *Self Harm and Suicide*. Cambridge, Independence.

Donovan, M (2003) Mind the gap: The need for a generic bridge between psychoanalytic and systemic approaches. *Journal of Family Therapy*, 25: 115–135.

Douglas, T (2000) *Basic Groupwork*, 2nd edn. London, Routledge.

Doyle, C (1997) *Working with Abused Children*. Basingstoke, Macmillan/BASW.

Drury, N (2003) Three stories. *Context Magazine*, 70: 2–6.

Dulmus, C and Rapp-Paglicci, L (2000) The prevention of mental disorders in children and adolescents: Future research and public-policy recommendations. *Families in Society: The Journal of Contemporary Human Services*, 81(3): 294–303.

Dundes, A (2003) *Fables of the Ancients? Folklore in the Qur'an*. New York, Rowman & Littlefield.

Dunn, J (1995) *From One Child to Two*. London, Ballantine Books.

Dunn, S (1999) *Creating Accepting Communities*. London, Mind Publications.

Durlak, J and Wells, A (1997) Primary prevention mental health programs for children and adolescents: A meta-analytic review. *American Journal of Community Psychology*, 25(2): 115–152.

Dwivedi, KN (2002) *Meeting the Needs of Ethnic Minority Children*, 2nd edn. London, Jessica Kingsley.

Eamon, MK (1994). Poverty and placement outcomes of intensive family preservation services. *Child and Adolescent Social Work Journal*, 11(5): 349–361.

Early Childhood Education Forum (1998) *Quality and Diversity in Early Learning*. London, National Children's Bureau.

Eber, L, Osuch, R and Redditt, C (1996) School-based applications of the wraparound process: Early results on service provision and student outcomes. *Journal of Child and Family Studies*, 5: 83–99.

Eisenbruch, M (1990) Cultural bereavement and homesickness. In: S Fisher and CL Cooper (eds) *On the Move: The Psychology of Change and Transition*. Chichester, Wiley.

Eliason, M (1996) Lesbian and gay family Issues. *Journal of Family Nursing*, 2(1): 10–29.

Elliot, A and Frosh, S (eds) (1995) *Psychoanalysis in Contexts*. London, Routledge.

Elliot, R and Shapiro, D (1992) Client and therapists as analysts of significant events. In: SG Tonkmanian and D Rennie (eds) *Psychotherapy Process Research: Paradigmatic Narrative Approaches*. Newbury Park, CA, Sage.

Ely, P and Denney, P (1987) *Social Work in a Multi-Racial Society*. London, Gower.

Erikson, E (1965) *Childhood and Society*. Harmondsworth, Penguin.

Estrada, AV and Pinsoff, WM (1995) The effectiveness of family therapies for selected behavioural disorders in childhood. *Journal of Marital and Family Therapy*, 21: 403–440.

Fagin, CM (1992) Collaboration between nurses and physicians; no longer a choice. *Academic Medicine*, 67(5): 295–303.

Falicov, C (1995) Training to think culturally: A multidimensional comparative framework. *Family Process*, 34: 373–388.

Falloon, I and Fadden, G (1995) *Integrated Mental Health Care – A Comprehensive Community-Based Approach*. Cambridge, Cambridge University Press.

Farrant, F (2001) *Troubled Inside: Responding to the Mental Health Needs of Children and Young People in Prison*. London, Prison Reform Trust.

Farrington, D (1995) The development of offending and antisocial behaviour from childhood: Key findings from the Cambridgeshire study in delinquent development. *Journal of Child Psychology and Psychiatry*, 36: 929–964.

Favat, AF (1977) *Child and Tale: The Origins of Interest*. Urbana, NCTE.

Fawcett, B (2000) Look, listen and learn. *Community Care*, July 27. Surrey, Reed Publications, pp. 24–25.

Feeney, BC and Collins, AR (2001) Predictors of caregiving in adult intimate relationships: An attachment theoretical perspective. *Journal of Personality and Social Psychology*, 80(6): 972–994.

Feeney, JA (2003) The systemic nature of couple relationships: An attachment perspective. In: P Erdman and T Caffery (eds) *Attachment and Family Systems*. New York and Hove, Brunner-Routledge.

Fernando, S (2002) *Mental Health Race and Culture*, 2nd edn. Basingstoke, Palgrave.

Finch, J (1987) The vignette technique in survey research. *Sociology*, 21(1): 105–114.

Firth, M, Dyer, M and Wilkes, J (1999) Reducing the distance: Mental health social work in general practice. *Journal of Interprofessional Care*, 13(4): 335–344.

Fletcher-Campbell, F (2001) Issues of inclusion. *Emotional and Behavioural Difficulties*, 6(2): 69–89.

Fombonne, E (1995) Depressive disorders: Time trends and possible explanatory mechanisms. In: M Rutter and D Smith (eds) *Psychosocial Disorders of Youth*. New York, Wiley.

Fonagy, A and Roth, A (1997) *What Works for Whom? A Critical Review of Psychotherapy Research*. London, Guilford Press.

Fook, J (2002) *Social Work – Critical Theory and Practice*. London, Sage.

Fook, J, Ryan, M and Hawkins, L (1997) Towards a theory of social work expertise. *British Journal of Social Work*, 27: 399–417.

Fowler, J, Nipkow, KE and Schweitzer, F (eds) (1991) *Stages of Faith and Religious Development: Implications for Church, Education and Society*. New York, Crossroads Press.

Franklin, A and Madge, N (2000) *In Our View – Children, Teenagers and Parents Talk about Services for Young People*. London, NCB.

Fraser, S, Lewis, V, Ding, S, Kellett, M and Robinson, C (2004) *Doing Research with Children and Young People*. London, Sage.

Freeman, I, Morrison, A, Lockhart, F and Swanson, M (1996) Consulting service users: The views of young people. In: M Hill and J Aldgate (eds) *Child Welfare Services: Developments in Law, Policy, Practice and Research*. London, Jessica Kingsley, pp. 88–97.

Freeman, J, Epston, D and Lobovits, D (1997) *Playful Approaches to Serious Problems: Narrative Therapy with Children and their Families*. New York, Norton.

Freud, A (1973) *Normality and Pathology in Childhood*. Ringwood, Australia, Penguin.

Freud, S (1905) *Three Essays on the Theory of Sexuality. Standard Edition*, Vol. 6. London, Hogarth Press.

——(1915) The unconscious, *Standard Ed*, 14,161. In: S Freud (ed.) *The Interpretation of Dreams* (1953). London, Allen & Unwin.

——(1953) The interpretation of dreams. In: *The Standard Edition of the Complete Psychological Works of Sigmund Freud, Vols IV and V*. London, Allen & Unwin.

——(1976) Das unhgeimliche. In: *New Literary History*, 619–645. London, Penguin.

Friedlander, ML (2001) Family therapy research: Science into practice, practice into science. In: MP Nichols and RC Schwartz (eds) *Family Therapy: Concepts and Methods*, 5th edn. Boston, Alleyn & Bacon.

Friedlander, M, Highlen, P and Lassiter, W (1985) Content analytic comparison of four expert counsellors approaches to family treatment. *Journal of Counselling Psychology*, 32: 171–180.

Frosh, S (1991) *Identity Crisis: Modernity, Psychoanalysis and the Self*. London, Macmillan.

Fulcher, LC (1999) Cultural origins of the contemporary group conference. *Child Care in Practice*, 6: 328–339.

Fuller, R (1996) Evaluating social work effectiveness: A pragmatic approach. In: P Alderson, S Brill, I Chalmers, R Fuller, P Hinkley-Smith, G Macdonald, T Newman, A Oakley, H Roberts and H Ward (eds) *What Works: Effective Social Interventions in Child Welfare*. Barkingside, Barnardos.

Furedi, F (2003) *Therapy Culture*. London, Routledge.

Furlong, A and Carmel, F (1997) *Young People and Social Change*. Buckingham, Open University Press.

Garbarino, J and Stott, F (1992) *What Children Can Tell Us*. San Francisco, Jossey-Bass.

Gardner, R (1998) *Family Support: A Practitioners Guide*. Birmingham, Venture Press.

Ghate, D and Daniels, A (1997) *Talking about my Generation*. London, NSPCC.

Ghate, D, Shaw, C and Hazel, N (2000) *Fathers and Family Centres*. York, Policy Research Bureau/JRF.

Ghuman, P (2004) *Double Loyalties: South Asian Adolescents in the West*. Swansea, University of Wales Press.

Gibbons, J and Wilding, J (1995) *Needs, Risks and Family Support Plans: Social Services Departments Responses to Neglected Children*. Norwich, University of East Anglia.

Gibson-Cline, J (ed.) (1996) *Adolescence: From Crisis to Coping*. London, Butterworth-Heinemann.

Giddings, FH (1898) *The Elements of Sociology*. New York, Macmillan.

Gilani, NP (1999) Conflict management of mothers and daughters belonging to individualistic and collectivistic cultural backgrounds: A comparative study. *Journal of Adolescence*, 22: 853–865.

Gillick v Wisbech and W Norfolk AHA (1986) AC112.

Gilroy, P (1982) *The Empire Strikes Back*. London, Hutchinson.

Glantz, MD and Johnson, JL (1999) *Resilience and Development: Positive Life Adaptations*. New York, Plenum.

Glaser, D, Prior, V and Lynch, M (2001) *Emotional Abuse and Emotional Neglect: Antecedents, Operational Definitions and Consequences*. York, BASPCAN/DOH.

Goffman, E (1969) *The Presentation of Self in Everyday Life*. Harmondsworth, Penguin.

Goldenberg, I and Goldenberg, H (2004) *Family Therapy – An Overview*. Pacific Grove, CA, Thomson Learning.

Goldner, V (1985) Feminism and family therapy. *Family Process*, 24: 31–47.

——(1991) Sex, power and gender: A feminist analysis of the politics of passion. *Journal of Feminist Family Therapy*, 3: 63–83.

Goodman, R (1997) *Child and Adolescent Mental Health Services: Reasoned Advice to Commissioners and Providers*. Discussion Paper no. 4. London, Maudsley Hospital.

——(1997) The strengths and difficulties questionnaire: A research note. *Journal of Child Psychology and Psychiatry*, 38(5): 581–586.

Goodman, R and Scott, S (1997) *Child Psychiatry*. London, Sage.

Gordon, G and Grant, R (1997) *How We Feel: An Insight into the Emotional World of Teenagers*. London, Jessica Kingsley.

Gorell Barnes, G (1998) *Family Therapy in Changing Times*. Basingstoke, Macmillan.

Gowers, S, Harrington, R, Whitton, A, Lelliot, P, Beevor, A, Wing, J and Jezzard, R (1999) Brief scale for measuring the outcomes of emotional and behavioural disorders in children. *British Journal of Psychiatry*, 174: 413–416.

Gowers, S, Bailey-Rogers, S, Shore, A and Levine, W (2000) The health of the nation outcome scales for child and adolescent mental health (HoNOSCA). *Child Psychology and Psychiatry Review*, 5(2): 50–56.

Graham, P (1992) *Child Psychiatry: A Developmental Approach*. New York, Oxford University Press.

——(1996) The thirty year contribution of research in child mental health to clinical practice and public policy in the UK. In: B Bernstein and J Brannen (eds) *Children Research and Policy*. London, Taylor & Francis.

Greenbaum, T (1987) *The Practical Handbook and Guide to Focus Group Research*. Lexington, USA, Lexington Books.

Grey, M (1993) Stressors and children's health. *Journal of Pediatric Nursing*, 8(2): 85–91.

Griffiths, R (1998) *Educational Citizenship and Independent Learning*. London, Jessica Kingsley.

Gross, D, Fogg, L and Tucker, S (1995) The efficacy of parent training for promoting positive parent–toddler relationships. *Research in Nursing and Health*, 18: 489–499.

Guerin, S (2002) *Aggression and Bullying*. Leicester, UK, British Psychological Society.

Gunnell, D, Wehner, H and Frankel, S (1999) Sex differences in suicide trends in England and Wales. *Lancet*, 353: 556–557.

Hacking, I (1999) *The Social Construction of What?* London, Harvard University Press.

Hague, G and Malos, E (1993) *Domestic Violence: Action for Change*. Cheltenham, New Clarion Press.

Haley, J (1976) *Problem Solving Therapy*. San Francisco, Jossey-Bass.

Hall, S (1993) Culture, community, nation. *Cultural Studies*, 7(3): 16–29.

Hampson, S (1995) The construction of personality. In: SE Hampson and AM Coleman (eds) *Individual Differences and Personality*. London, Longman.

Haralambos, M (1988) *Sociology – Theses and Perspectives*. London, Unwin Hyman.

Hardiker, P (1995) *The Social Policy Contexts of Services to Prevent Unstable Family Life*. York, Joseph Rowntree Foundation.

Hare-Mustin, R (1991) Sex, lies and headaches: The problem is power. *Journal of Feminist Family Therapy*, 3: 39–61.

Harrington, R (1997) The role of the child and adolescent mental health service in preventing later depressive disorder: Problems and prospects. *Child Psychology and Psychiatry Review*, 2(2): 46–57.

Hartley, J (2003) *A Short History of Cultural Studies*. London, Sage.

Hawton, K, Arensman, E and Townsend, E (1998) Deliberate self harm: Systematic review of efficacy of psychosocial and pharmacological treatments in preventing repetition. *British Medical Journal*, 317: 441–447.

Hay, D (1990) *Religious Experience Today: Studying the Facts*. London, Mowbray/Cassell.

Hazan, C and Shaver, PR (1987) Romantic love conceptualised as an attachment process. *Journal of Personality & Social Psychology*, 52(3): 511–524.

Hazel, N (1995) Seen and heard: An examination of methods for collecting data from young people. *Social Research Update*. Guildford, England, University of Surrey.

Health Advisory Service (1995) *Together We Stand: Thematic Review on the Commissioning, Role and Management of Child and Adolescent Mental Health Services*. London, HMSO.

Healy, K (2002) *Social Work Practices – Contemporary Perspectives on Change*. London, Sage.

Heath, I (1994) The poor man at his gate: Homelessness is an avoidable cause of ill health. *British Medical Journal*, 309: 1675–1676.

Hellinckx, W, Colton, M and Williams, M (1997) *International Perspectives on Family Support*. Aldershot, Ashgate Publishing.

Henderson, P and Thomas, D (1987) *Skills in Neighbourhood Work*. London, Allen & Unwin.

Hendrick, H (1997) Constructions and reconstructions of British childhood: An interpretive survey 1800 to the present. In: A James and A Prout (eds) *Constructing and Reconstructing Childhood: Contemporary Issues of the Sociology of Childhood*. London, Falmer Press.

Hennessey, E (1999) Children as service evaluators. *Child Psychology & Psychiatry Review*, 4(4): 153–161.

Hester, M, Pearson, C and Harwin, N (2000) *Making an Impact: Children and Domestic Violence*. London, Jessica Kingsley.

Hetherington, J and Baistow, R (2001) Supporting families with a mentally ill parent: European perspectives on interagency cooperation. *Child Abuse Review*, 10: 351–365.

Heyman, I, Fombonne, E, Simmons, H, Ford, T, Meltzer, H and Goodman, R (2001) Prevalence of obsessive-compulsive disorder in the British nationwide survey of child mental health. *British Journal of Psychiatry*, 179: 324–329.

Higgins, K, Pinkerton, J and Devine, P (1997) *Family Support in Northern Ireland: Pespectives from Practice*. Belfast, Centre for Child Care Research.

Hill, J, Fonagy, P, Safier, E and Sargent, J (In Press) The ecology of attachment in the family: The theoretical basis for the development of a measure. *Family Process*.

Hill, M (ed.) (1999) *Effective Ways of Working with Children and their Families*. London, Jessica Kingsley.

Hill, M, Laybourn, A and Borland, M (1996) Engaging with primary aged children about their emotions and well being: Methodological considerations. *Children and Society*, 10: 129–144.

HMSO (1968) *Local Authority and Allied Personal Social Services* (Cmnd 3703). London, HMSO.

——(2000) *Social Inequalities in the United Kingdom*. London, Office for National Statistics.

Hodes, M (1998) Refugee children may need a lot of psychiatric help. *British Medical Journal*, 316: 793–794.

——(2000) Psychologically distressed refugee children in the United Kingdom. *Child Psychology and Psychiatry Review*, 5(2): 57–67.

Hogg, MA and Abrams, D (1988) *Social Identification: A Social Psychology of Intergroup Relations and Group Processes*. London, Routledge.

Holland, S (1990) Psychotherapy, oppression and social action: Gender, race, and class in black women's depression. In: RJ Perelberg and A Miller (eds) *Gender and Power in Families*. London, Routledge.

Holliday, A (1999) Small cultures. *Applied Linguistics*, 20(2): 237–264.

Holman, B (1983) *Resourceful Friends: Skills in Community Social Work*. London, Children's Society.

Holt, C (1998) Working with fathers of children in need. In: R Bayley (ed.) *Transforming Childrens Lives: The Importance of Early Intervention*. London, Family Policy Studies Centre.

Holterman, S (1995) *All Our Futures: The Impact of Public Expenditure and Fiscal Policies on Britain's Children and Young People*. Barkingside, Barnardos.

Horwath, J and Calder, M (1998) Working together to protect children on the child protection register: Myth or reality. *British Journal of Social Work*, 28: 879–895.

House of Commons (1997) *Child and Adolescent Mental Health Services*. Health Committee. London, HMSO.

Howarth, J (2002) Maintaining a focus on the child? *Child Abuse Review*, 11: 195–213.

Howe, D (1987) *An Introduction to Social Work Theory*. Aldershot, Gower.

——(1989) *The Consumers View of Family Therapy*. London, Gower.

——(ed.) (1999) *Attachment and Loss in Child and Family Social Work*. Aldershot, Ashgate.

Howe, D, Brandon, M, Hinings, D and Schofield, G (1999) *Attachment Theory, Child Maltreatment and Family Support*. Basingstoke, Macmillan.

Howe, G (1999) *Mental Health Assessments*. London, Jessica Kingsley.

Hughes, P (1999) *Dynamic Psychotherapy Explained*. London, Radcliffe.

Human Rights Commission (1997) Bringing them home. *Report of the Inquiry into the Separation of Aboriginal and Torres Strait Islander Children from their Families*. Sydney, HR & EOC.

Hunter, J, Higginson, I and Garralda, E (1996) Systematic literature review: Outcome measures for child and adolescent mental health services. *Journal of Public Health Medicine*, 18: 197–206.

Hutchings, J, Nash, S, Smith, M and Parry, G (1998) *Long-term Outcome for Pre-school Children Referred to CAMH Team for Behaviour Management Problems*. Bangor: School of Psychology, University of Wales.

Imam, U (1994) Asian children and domestic violence. In: A Mullender and R Morley (eds) *Children Living with Domestic Violence*. London, Whiting and Birch.

Issit, M (1995) Competence, professionalism and equal opportunities. In: P Hodgkinson and M Issit (eds) *The Challenge of Competence*. London, Cassell.

Iwaniec, D (1995) *The Emotionally Abused and Neglected Child: Identification, Assessment and Intervention*. Chichester, Wiley.

Jackson, R (ed.) (2003) *International Perspectives on Citizenship, Education and Religious Diversity*. London, Routledge Falmer.

——(2004) Intercultural education and recent European pedagogies of religious education. *Intercultural Education*, 15(1): 3–14.

James, A and Prout, A (eds) (1990) *Constructing and Reconstructing Childhood*. Basingstoke, Falmer.

JCWI (2002) *Joint Council for the Welfare of Immigrants Response to the White Paper Secure Borders, Safe Haven: Integration with Diversity in Modern Britain*. London, JCWI.

Jenkins, R (2002) *Foundations of Sociology – Towards a Better Understanding of the Human World*. Basingstoke, Palgrave Macmillan.

Jenks, C (1996) *Childhood*. London, Routledge.

Johnson, S and Orrell, M (1996) Insight, psychosis and ethnicity: A case note study. *Psychological Medicine*, 26: 1081–1084.

Johnson, SM and Best, M (2003) A systemic approach to restructuring adult attachment: The EFT model of couples therapy. In: P Erdman and T Caffery (eds) *Attachment and Family Systems*. New York and Hove, Brunner-Routledge.

Johnson, SM, Makinen, JA and Millikin, JW (2001) Attachment injuries in couple relationships: A new perspective on impasse in couples therapy. *Journal of Marital & Family Therapy*, 27(2): 145–155.

Jones, C (1997) Poverty. In: M Davies (ed.) *The Blackwell Companion to Social Work*. Oxford, Blackwell.

Jones, D and Jones, M (1999) The assessment of children with emotional and behavioural difficulties – psychometrics and beyond. In: C Cooper (ed.) *Understanding and Supporting Children with Emotional and Behavioural Difficulties*. London, Jessica Kingsley.

Jones, T (1996) *Britain's Ethnic Minorities: An Analysis of the Labour Force Survey*. London, Policy Studies Institute.

Jordan, B (1990) *Social Work in an Unjust Society*. Hemel Hempstead, Harvester Wheatsheaf.

Jung, CG (1978) *Psychological Reflections*. Princeton, Bollingen.

Kalnins, I, McQueen, D, Backett, K, Curtice, L and Currie, C (1992) Children empowerment and health promotion: Some new directions in research and practice. *Health Promotion International*, 7(1): 53–59.

Kashani, J and Allan, W (1998) *The Impact of Family Violence on Children and Adolescents*. London, Sage.

Kay-Shuttleworth, J (1832) *The Moral and Physical Condition of the Working Classes Employed in the Cotton Manufacture in Manchester*. Ridgway (1987) reprint ed. E.L. Burney, Liverpool, Acorn Press.

Kazdin, AE (2002) The state of child and adolescent psychotherapy. *Child and Adolescent Mental Health*, 7(2): 53–59.

Kehily, J and Swann, J (2003) *Children's Cultural Worlds*. London, Wiley/OUP.

Kelson, M (1997) *Consumer Involvement Initiatives in Clinical Audit and Outcomes*. London, College of Health.

Kemps, C (1997) Approaches to working with ethnicity and cultural issues. In: K Dwivedi (ed.) *Enhancing Parenting Skills*. London, Wiley, pp. 59–77.

Kemshall, H (1993) Assessing competence: Process or subjective inference? Do we really see It? *Social Work Education*, 12(1): 36–45.

Kenny, DA and LaVoie, L (1984) The social relations model. In: L Berkowitz (ed.) *Advances in Experimental Social Psychology*. Orlando, Fl, Academic Press.

Kent, H and Read, J (1998) Measuring consumer participation in mental health services: Are attitudes related to professional orientation? *International Journal of Social Psychiatry*, 44(4): 295–310.

Kiddle, C (1999) *Traveller Children: A Voice for Themselves*. London, Jessica Kingsley.

Kim, WJ (1995) A training guideline of cultural competence for child and adolescent psychiatric residencies. *Child Psychiatry and Human Development*, 26(2): 125–136.

Kitzinger, J (1994) The methodology of focus groups: The importance of interaction between research participants. *Sociology of Health and Fitness*, 16(1): 103–120.

Klineberg, O (1971) Race and IQ. *Courier*, 24: 10.

Klusmeyer, D (2001) A guiding culture for immigrants? Integration and diversity in Germany. *Journal of Ethnic and Migration Studies*, 27(3): 519–532.

Knapp, M and Scott, S (1998) *Lifetime Costs of Conduct Disorder* (mind). Sternfels, Wissenschaft and Praxis.

Kohn, M (1995) *The Race Gallery*. London, Jonathan Cape.

Kolbo, J, Blakley, E and Engelman, D (1996) Children who witness domestic violence: A review of empirical literature. *Journal of Interpersonal Violence*, 11(2): 281–293.

Kozlowska, K and Hanney, L (2002) The network perspective: An integration of attachment and family systems theories. *Family Process*, 43(3): 285–312.

Kraemer, S (1995) What are fathers for? In: C Burcke and B Speed (eds) *Gender, Power and Relationships*. London, Routledge.

Kurtz, Z (ed.) (1992) *With Health in Mind Quality Review Series on Mental Health Care for Children and Young People*. London, Action for Sick Children, SW Thames Regional Health Authority.

——(1996) *Treating Children Well: A Guide to Using the Evidence Base in Commissioning and Managing Services for the Mental Health of Children and Young People*. London, Mental Health Foundation.

——(2001) *Report on Evaluation of CAMHS Innovation Projects* (unpublished). London, Young Minds.

Kurtz, Z, Thornes, R and Wolkind, S (1994) *Services for the Mental Health of Children and Young People in England*. London, Maudsley Hospital, SW Thames Regional Health Authority and Dept of Health.

——(1995) *Services for the Mental Health of Children and Young People in England: Assessment of Needs and Unmet Need*. London, HMSO.

Lader, D, Singleton, N and Meltzer, H (1997) *Psychiatric Morbidity Among Young Offenders in England and Wales*. London, HMSO.

Laing, RD (1969) Interventions in social situations. Philadelphia Association. Cited in *Context* 60, pp. 2–7, April 2002, Association for family therapy and systemic practice, Warrington.

——(1976) *Facts of Life*. London, Allen Lane.

Lane, M (1997) Community work, social work: Green and postmodern? *British Journal of Social Work*, 27: 319–341.

Lansdowne, G (1995) *Taking Part: Children's Participation in Decision-Making*. London, IPPR.

Larner, G (2000) Towards a common ground in psychoanalysis and family therapy: On knowing not to know. *Journal of Family Therapy*, 22: 61–82.

Larsen, L and Plesner, IT (eds) (2002) *Teaching for Tolerance and Freedom of Religion and Belief*. Oslo, Oslo Coalition on Freedom of Religion and Belief, University of Oslo.

Lask, B (1979) Family therapy outcome research. *Journal of Family Therapy*, 1(4): 87–91.

Lask, J and Lask, B (1981) *Child Psychiatry and Social Work*. London, Tavistock.

Lau, A (1995) Ethnocultural and religious issues. In: C Burck and B Speed (eds) *Gender Power and Relationships*. London, Routledge.

Laufer, M (ed.) (1985) *The Suicidal Adolescent*. London, Karnac Books.

Lawrence, M (2001) Loving them to death: The anorexic and her objects. *International Journal of Psychoanalysis*, 82: 43–55.

Laws, S, Armitt, D, Metzendorf, W, Percival, P and Reisel, J (1999) *Time to Listen – Young People's Experiences of Mental Health Services*. London, Save the Children.

Le Grange, D (1999) Family therapy for anorexia nervosa. *Journal of Clinical Psychology*, 55: 727–739.

Leathard, A (1994) *Going Inter-professional*. London, Routledge.

Lefley, HP (1990) Culture and chronic mental illness. *Hospital & Community Psychiatry*, 41: 277–286.

Leganger-Krongstad, H (2000) Developing a contextual theory and practice of religious education, Panorama. *International Journal of Comparative Religious Education and Values*, 12(1): 94–104.

Leighton, AH (1981) Culture and psychiatry. *Canadian Journal of Psychiatry*, 26(8): 522–529.

Leonard, P (1994) Knowledge/Power and postmodernism-implications for the practice of a critical social work education. *Canadian Social Work Review*, 11(1): 11–26.

——(1997) *Postmodern Welfare: Reconstructing an Emancipatory Project*. London, Sage.

Levine, H (1993) Context and scaffolding in developmental studies of mother–child problem-solving dyads. In: S Chaiklin and J Lave (eds) *Understanding Practice*. Cambridge, Cambridge University Press.

Lidchi, VG (2003) Cross cultural transferability in child protection: Challenges and opportunities. *Child Abuse Review*, 12: 238–250.

Little, M and Mount, K (1999) *Prevention and Early Intervention with Children in Need*. Aldershot, Ashgate.

Llewelyn, S (1988) Psychological therapy as viewed by clients and therapists. *British Journal of Clinical Psychology*, 27: 223–237.

Lloyd, E (ed.) (1999) *Parenting Matters: What Works in Parenting Education?* London, Barnardos.

Lobo, E (1978) *The Children of Immigrants to Britain: Their Health and Social Problems*. London, Allen & Unwin.

Lutz, CA (1990) Engendered emotion: Gender, power and the rhetoric of emotional control in American discourse. In: CA Lutz and L Abu-Lughood (eds) *Studies in Emotion and Social Interaction*. Cambridge, Cambridge University Press.

Lyon, J, Dennison, C and Wilson, A (2000) *Tell Them so they Listen: Messages from Young People in Custody*. Home Office Research Study 201. London, HMSO.

Lyons, P, Doueck, H and Wodarski, J (1996) Risk assessment for child protective services: A review of the empirical literature on instrument performance. *Social Work Research*, 20(3): 143–155.

Ma, JLC, Chow, MYM, Lee, S and Lau, K (2002) Family meaning of self-starvation: Themes discerned in family treatment in Hong Kong. *Journal of Family Therapy*, 24: 57–71.

McCabe, M and Ricciardelli, L (2001) Body image and body change techniques among young adolescent boys. *European Eating Disorders Review*, 9: 335–347.

McCann, J, James, A, Wilson, S and Dunn, G (1996) Prevalence of psychiatric disorders in young people in the care system. *British Medical Journal*, 313: 1529–1530.

McClelland, M and Sands, R (2002) *Interprofessional and Family Discourses*. New Jersey, Hampton Press.

McClure, G (2001) Suicide in children and adolescents in England and Wales 1970–1998. *British Journal of Psychiatry*, 178: 469–474.

McConville, B (2001) *Saving Young Lives: Calls to Childline about Suicide*. London, Childline.

Macdonald, G (1999) Social work and its evaluation: A methodological dilemma? In: F Williams, J Popay and A Oakley (eds) *Welfare Research: A Critical Review*. London, UCL Press.

Macdonald, G and Roberts, H (1995) *What Works in the Early Years? Effective Interventions for Children and their Families*. Barkingside, Barnardos.

MacFarlane, A and McPherson, A (1995) Primary healthcare and adolescence. *British Medical Journal*, 311: 825–826.

McGill, DW (1992) The cultural story in multicultural family therapy. *Families in Society, The Journal of Contemporary Human Services*, 73: 339–349.

McGlone, F, Park, A and Smith, K (1998) *Families and Kinship*. London, Family Policy Studies Centre.

McGuire, JB, Stein, A and Rosenberry, W (1997) Evidence-based medicine and child mental health services. *Children and Society*, 11(2): 89–96.

McGurk, H (ed.) (1992) *Childhood and Social Development*. London, Lawrence Earlbaum.

McLennan, G (1996) Post-Marxism and the four sins of modernist theorizing. *New Left Review*, 218: 53–75.

McLuhan, M (1964) *Understanding Media*. London, Routledge.

MacNeil, G, Dressler, WW and Kaufman, AV (2000) Ethnic differences in risk factors associated with substance use in adolescence. In: NN Singh, JP Leung and AN Singh (eds) *International Perspectives on Child and Adolescent Mental Health*. London, Elsevier.

Madge, N (2001) *Understanding Difference – The Meaning of Ethnicity for Young Lives*. London, National Children's Bureau.

Magrab, P, Evans, P and Hurrell, P (1997) Integrated services for children and youth at risk: An international study of multidisciplinary training. *Journal of Interprofessional Care*, 11(1): 99–108.

Main, M, Kaplan, N and Cassidy, J (1985) Security in infancy, childhood and adulthood: A move to the level of representations. *Monographs of the Society for Research in Child Development*, 50: 66–104.

Malek, M (1993) *Passing the Buck: Institutional Responses to Children with Difficult Behaviour*. London, Children's Society.

Marcia, J (1980) Identity in adolescence. In: J Adelson (ed.) *Handbook of Adolescent Psychology*. New York, Wiley.

Marsh, P (1997) Task-centred work. In: M Davies (ed.) *The Blackwell Companion to Social Work*. Oxford, Blackwell.

Marshal, M, Feldman, R and Sigal, J (1989) The unravelling of a treatment paradigm: A follow-up study of the Milan approach to family therapy. *Family Process*, 28: 457–470.

Martin, G, Rozanes, P, Pearce, C and Alison, S (1995) Adolescent suicide, depression and family dysfunction. *Acta Psychiatrica Scandinavica*, 92: 336–344.

Martslof, DS and Mickley, JR (1998) The concept of spirituality in nursing theories: Differing world-views and extent focus. *Journal of Advanced Nursing*, 27: 294–303.

Marvin, RS and Stewart, RB (1990) A family systems framework for the study of attachment. In: MT Greenberg, D Cicchetti and EM Cummings (eds) *Attachment in the Pre-school Years*. Chicago, III, University of Chicago Press.

Mas, C, Alexander, J and Barton, C (1985) Modes of expression in family therapy: A process study of roles and gender. *Journal of Family and Marital Therapy*, 11: 411–415.

Masson, J (1988) *Against Therapy*. London, Collins.

May, T (ed.) 2002 *Qualitative Research in Action*. London, Sage.

Mayall, B (1994) *Children's Childhoods Observed and Experienced*. Lewes, England, Falmer Press.

Meltzer, H, Gatward, R, Goodman, R and Ford, T (2000) *Mental Health of Children and Adolescents in Great Britain*. London, HMSO.

Mental Health Foundation (1993) *Mental Illness: The Fundamental Facts*. London, Mental Health Foundation.

——(1999) *The Big Picture: A National Survey of Child Mental Health in Britain*. London, Mental Health Foundation.

——(2001) *Turned Upside Down*. London, Mental Health Foundation.

——(2002) *The Mental Health Needs of Young Offenders*. London, Mental Health Foundation.

Micklewright, J and Stewart, K (2000) Well being of children in the European Union. *New Economy*. London, Institute for Public Policy Research.

Middleton, L (1997) *The Art of Assessment*. Birmingham, Venture Press.

Midgley, J (2001) Issues in international social work – resolving critical debates in the profession. *Journal of Social Work*, 1(1): 21–35.

Mikulincer, M and Florian, V (1999) The association between spouses' self-reports of attachment styles and representations of family dynamics. *Family Process*, 38(1): 69–83.

——(1999) The association between parental reports of attachment style and family dynamics, and offspring's report of adult attachment style. *Family Process*, 38(2): 243–257.

Mikulincer, M, Florian, V, Cowan, PA and Cowan, CP (2002) Attachment security in couple relationships: A systemic model and its implications for family dynamics. *Family Process*, 43(3): 405–434.

Miller, G and Prinz, R (1990) Enhancement of social learning family interventions for childhood conduct disorders. *Psychological Bulletin*, 108: 291–307.

Mills, R and Duck, S (2000) *The Developmental Psychology of Personal Relationships*. Chichester, Wiley.

Milner, D (1983) *Children and Race Ten Years On*. London, Ward Lock Educational.

Milner, J and O'Byrne, P (1998) *Assessment in Social Work*. Basingstoke, Macmillan.

Minuchin, S (1974) *Families and Family Therapy*. London, Tavistock Publications.

——(1984) *Family Kaleidoscope*. Cambridge and London, Harvard University Press.

Mishra, R (1999) *Globalization and the Welfare State*. Northampton MA, Edward Elgar.

Modood, T and Berthoud, R (1997) *Ethnic Minorities in Britain*. London, Policy Studies Institute.

Moffic, H and Kinzie, J (1996) The history and future of cross-cultural psychiatric services. *Community Mental Health Journal*, 32(6): 581–592.

Morris, J (1998) *Accessing Human Rights: Disabled Children and the Children Act*. Barkingside, Barnardos.

Morris, K and Tunnard, J (1996) *Family Group Conferences: Messages from UK Practice and Research*. London, Family Rights Group.

Morrison, L and L'Heureux, J (2001) Suicide and gay/lesbian/bisexual youth: Implications for clinicians. *Journal of Adolescence*, 24: 39–49.

Morrison, TL, Urquiza, AJ and Goodlin-Jones, BL (1997) Attachment and the representation of intimate relationships in adulthood. *Journal of Psychology*, 131(1): 57–71.

Morrissey, J, Johnsen, M and Calloway, M (1997) Evaluating performance and change in mental health systems serving children and youth: An interorganizational network approach. *The Journal of Mental Health Administration*, 24(1): 4–22.

Morrow, V (1998) *Understanding Families: Children's Perspectives*. London, National Children's Bureau.

Morrow, V and Richards, M (1996) The ethics of social research with children: An overview. *Children and Society*, 10: 90–105.

Moules, N (2000) Postmodernism and the sacred: Reclaiming connection in or greater-than-human worlds. *Journal of Marital and Family Therapy*, 26: 229–240.

Moynihan, B (1965) *The Negro Family: The Case for National Action*. Washington, DC, University of Chicago.

Mullender, A and Ward, D (1991) *Self Directed Groupwork: Users Take Action for Empowerment*. London, Whiting and Birch.

Mullender, A, Burton, S, Hague, G, Malos, E and Imam, U (2000) *Children's Needs, Coping Strategies and Understanding of Woman Abuse*. Coventry, Warwick University.

Mun, E, Fitzgerald, H, Von Eye, A, Puttler, L and Zucker, R (2001) Temperamental characteristics as predictors of externalising and internalising child behaviour problems in the contexts of high and low parental psychopathology. *Infant Mental Health Journal*, 22(3): 393–415.

Munley, A, Powers, CS and Williamson, JB (1982) Humanising nursing home environments: The relevance of hospice principles. *International Journal of Ageing and Human Development*, 15: 263–284.

Murdock, G (1949) *Social Structure*. New York, Macmillan.

Nakagawa, M, Lamb, ME and Kazuo, M (1992) Antecedents and correlates of the strange situation behaviour of Japanese infants. *Journal of Cross-Cultural Psychology*, 23: 300–310.

Nash, M and Stewart, B (2002) *Spirituality and Social Care: Contributing to Personal and Community Well-being*. London, Jessica Kingsley.

Nathanson, V (2001) Health and children's rights: Inequality, autonomy and consent to treatment. *Childright*, 161: 11–13.

NCH Action for Children (2000) *Fact File*. London, NCH.

Newbigging, K (2001) Promoting social inclusion. *The Mental Health Review*, 6(3): 5–12.

Newman, T (2002) *Promoting Resilience: A Review of Effective Strategies for Child Care Services*. Barkingside, Barnardos.

Newnes, C, Holmes, G and Dunn, C (eds) (1999) *This is Madness – A Critical Look at Psychiatry and the Future of Mental Health Services*. Herefordshire, PCCS Books.

NHS Health Advisory Service (1995) *Together We Stand: Child and Adolescent Mental Health Services*. London, HMSO.

NISW/DOH Barclay Report (1982) *Social Workers: Their Role and Task*. London, Bedford Square Press.

Nixon, C and Northrup, D (1997) *Evaluating Mental Health Services: How Do Programmes for Children Work in the Real World?* Thousand Oaks, CA, Sage.

Noam, G (1999) The psychology of belonging: Reformulating adolescent development. In: A Esman and L Flaherty (eds) *Adolescent Psychiatry Development and Clinical Studies*, Vol. 24. Hillsdale NJ, The Analytic Press.

Nolan, M and Caldock, K (1996) Assessment: Identifying the barriers to good practice. *Health and Social Care in the Community*, 4(2): 77–85.

Oberhuemer, P (1998) A European perspective on early years training. In: L Abbott and G Pugh (eds) *Training to Work in the Early Years: Developing the Climbing Frame*. Buckingham, Open University Press.

Oberklaid, F, Sanson, A, Pedlow, R and Prior, M (1993) Predicting pre school behaviour problems from temperament and other variables in infancy. *Pediatrics*, 91(1): 113–120.

O'Connor, P and Neugebauer, R (1992) The contribution of maternal depressive symptoms and life events to child behaviour problems. *Paediatric and Perinatal Epidemiology*, 6: 254–264.

O'Donnell, G (2002) *Mastering Sociology*. London, Palgrave.

Office for National Statistics (2001) *Child and Adolescent Mental Health Statistics*. London, HMSO.

——(2002) *Social Trends 32*. London, HMSO.

OFSTED (1996) *Exclusions from Secondary Schools 1995–96*. London, HMSO.

O'Hagan, K (ed.) (1996) *Competence in Social Work Practice: A Practical Guide for Professionals*. London, Jessica Kingsley.

O'Sullivan, T (1999) *Decision Making in Social Work*. London, Macmillan.

Oldman, C and Beresford, B (1998) *Disabled Children and their Families*. York, Joseph Rowntree Foundation.

Oliver, M (1996) *Understanding Disability; from Theory to Practice*. London, Macmillan.

Oliver, M and Sapey, B (1999) *Social Work with Disabled People*. Basingstoke, Macmillan.

Olsen, DH, Porter, J and Lavee, Y (1985) *Faces III*. St Paul MN, University of Minnesota.

Onyet, S, Heppleston, T and Bushnell, N (1994) *A National Survey of Community Mental Health Teams: Team Structure*. London, Sainsbury Centre for Mental Health.

Oosterhorn, R and Kendrick, A (2001) No sign of harm: Issues for disabled children communicating about abuse. *Child Abuse Review*, 10: 243–253.

Otikikpi, T (1999) Educational needs of black children in care. In: R Barn (ed.) *Working With Black Children and Adolescents in Need*. London, BAAF.

Oullette, P, Lazear, K and Chambers, K (1999) Action leadership: The development of an approach to leadership enhancement for grassroots community leaders in children's mental health. *The Journal of Behavioural Health Services and Research*, 26(2): 171–185.

Ovretveit, J (1996) Five ways to describe a multidisciplinary team. *Journal of Interprofessional Care*, 10(2): 163–171.

Owen, D (1992–1995) *1991 Census Statistical Papers 1–9*, Centre for Research in Ethnic Relations. University of Warwick, London, Commission for Racial Equality.

Paloutzian, RF (1996) *Invitation to the Psychology of Religion*, 2nd edn. London, Allyn & Bacon.

Parekh, B (2000) *Rethinking Multiculturalism: Cultural Diversity and Political Theory*. Basingstoke, Palgrave.

Parsloe, P (ed.) (1999) *Risk Assessment in Social Care and Social Work*. London, Jessica Kingsley.

Parton, N (1994) The nature of social work under conditions of (post) modernity. *Social Work and Social Sciences Review*, 5(2): 93–112.

——(1999) Reconfiguring child welfare practices: Risk, advanced liberalism and the government of freedom. In: AS Chambon, A Irving and L Epstein (eds) *Reading Foucault for Social Work*. Chichester, Columbia Press.

Parton, N and O'Byrne, P (2000) *Constructive Social Work*. London, Macmillan.

Patmore, C and Weaver, T (1991) Community mental health teams: Lessons for planners and managers. *Good Practices in Mental Health*. London, Harrow.

Payne, M (1997) *Modern Social Work Theory*. London, Macmillan.

Peacock, B, Qureshi, T, Berridge, D and Wenman, H (2000) *Where to Turn? Family Support for South Asian Communities – A Case Study*. London, National Children's Bureau/JRF.

Pearce, JB (1999) Collaboration between the NHS and social services in the provision of child and adolescent mental health services: A personal view. *Child Psychology and Psychiatry Review*, 4(4): 150–152.

Pearson, G, Teseder, J and Yelloly, M (eds) (1988) *Social Work and the Legacy of Freud: Psychoanalysis and its Uses*. London, Macmillan.

Pearson, V and Leung, BKP (1995) Introduction: Perspectives on women's issues in Hong Kong. In: V Pearson and KPL Leung (eds) *Women in Hong Kong*. Hong Kong, Oxford University Press.

Pease, B and Fook, J (eds) (1999) *Transforming Social Work Practice: The Challenge of Postmodernism*. London, Routledge.

Pentini-Aluffi, A and Lorenz, W (1996) *Anti Racist Work with Young People*. Lyme Regis, Russell House.

Perelberg, RJ and Miller, AC (eds) (1990) *Gender and Power in Families*. London, Routledge.

Perret-Catipovic, M and Ladame, F (1998) *Adolescence and Psychoanalysis: The Story and the History*. London, Karnac Books.

Philip, N (1997) *The Illustrated Book of Fairy Tales*. London, Dorling Kindersley.

Phillipson, J (1993) *Practising Equality: Women, Men and Social Work*. London, CCETSW.

Piaget, J (1953) *The Origin of Intelligence in the Child*. London, Routledge & Kegan Paul.

Pickering, W (1979) *Durkheim: Essays on Morals and Education*. London, Routledge.

Pickles, A, Rowe, R, Simonoff, E, Foley, D, Rutter, M and Silberg, J (2001) Child psychiatric symptoms and psychosocial impairment: Relationship and prognostic significance. *British Journal of Psychiatry*, 179: 230–235.

Pierson, J (2002) *Tackling Social Exclusion*. London, Routledge.

Pieterse, JN (2004) *Globalization and Culture*. Oxford, Rowman & Littlefield.

Pincus, A and Minahan, A (1973) *Social Work Practice: Model and Method*. London, Ithaca, IL, Peacock.

Pinkerton, J, Higgins, K and Devine, P (2000) *Family Support – Linking Project Evaluation to Policy Analysis*. Aldershot, Ashgate.

Platt, D and Edwards, A (1996) Planning a comprehensive family assessment. *Practice*, 9(2): 14–21.

Plummer, DC (2001) The quest for modern manhood: Masculine stereotypes, peer culture and the social significance of homophobia. *Journal of Adolescence*, 24: 15–23.

Pocock, D (1997) Feeling understood in family therapy. *Journal of Family Therapy*, 19: 279–298.

Pollard, A (1987) Studying children's perspectives: A collaborative approach. In: G Walford (ed.) *Doing Sociology of Education*. Lewes, England, Falmer Press.

Pollock, S and Boland, M (1990) Children and HIV infection. *New Jersey Psychologist*, 40(3): 17–21.

Polowczyk, D (1993) Comparison of patient and staff surveys of consumer satisfaction. *Hospital and Community Psychiatry*, 14(4): 88–95.

Pote, H and Orrell, MW (2002) Perceptions of schizophrenia in multi-cultural Britain. *Ethnicity & Health*, 7(1): 7–20.

Powell, F (2001) *The Politics of Social Work*. London, Sage.

Powell, J and Lovelock, R (1992) *Changing Patterns of Mental Health Care*. London, Avebury.

Priestly, M (1999) *Disability Politics and Community Care*. London, Jessica Kingsley.

——(2001) *Disability and the Life Course: Global Perspectives*. Cambridge, Cambridge University Press.

Pringle, N and Thompson, P (1999) *Social Work, Psychiatry and the Law*. Aldershot, Ashgate.

Pugh, G and Smith, C (1996) *Learning to be a Parent*. London, Family Policy Studies Centre.

Qureshi, T, Berridge, D and Wenman, H (2000) *Where to Turn? Family Support for South Asian communities – A Case Study*. London, National Children's Bureau/JRF.

Ramon, S (1999) Social work. In: K Bhui and D Olajide (eds) *Mental Health Service Provision for a Multi-cultural Society*. London, Saunders.

——(2004) *Personal Communication*. Cambridge, Anglia Polytechnic University.

Ranger, T, Samad, S and Stuart, O (eds) (1996) *Culture Identity and Politics*. Aldershot, Avebury.

Rank, MR (2000) Socialisation of socioeconomic status. In: WC Nichols, MA Pace-Nichols, DS Becvar, AY Napier (eds) *Handbook of Family Development and Intervention*. New York, Wiley.

Raval, H (1996) A systemic perspective on working with interpreters. *Child Clinical Psychology and Psychiatry*, 1: 29–43.

Ravazzola, MC (1997) Historia infames: Los malatros en las relaciones, *Paidos Terapia Familiar*. Buenos Aires, Argentina, Libreria Paidos Psicologico.

Rawlinson, S and Williams, R (2000) The primary/secondary care interface in child and adolescent mental health services: The relevance of burden. *Current Opinion in Psychiatry*, 13: 389–395.

Rawson, D (1994) Models of interprofessional work: Likely theories and possibilities. In: A Leathard (ed.) *Going Interprofessional: Working Together for Health and Welfare*. London, Routledge.

Read, J and Barker, S (1996) Not just sticks and stones. *A Survey of the Stigma, Taboo and Discrimination Experienced by People with Mental Health Problems*. London, MIND.

Reed, AW (2002) *Aboriginal Stories*. Sydney, New Holland Publishers.

Remschmidt, H (ed.) (2001) *Schizophrenia in Children and Adolescents*. Cambridge, Cambridge University Press.

Repper, J, Sayce, L, Strong, S, Wilmot, J and Haines, M (1997) *Tall Stories from the Back Yard*. London, MIND.

Resnik, MD, Harris, LJ and Blum, RW (1993) The impact of caring and connectedness on adolescent health and wellbeing. *Journal of Paediatrics and Child Health*, 14: 254–269.

Reynolds, AJ (1998) Resilience among black urban youth: Intervention effects and mechanisms of influence. *American Journal of Orthopsychiatry*, 68(1): 84–100.

Richardson, J and Joughin, C (2000) *The Mental Health Needs of Looked After Children*. London, Gaskell.

Richmond, M (1922) *What is Social Casework?* New York, Russell Sage.

Robbins, D (1998) The refocusing children's initiative: An overview of practice. In: R Bayley (ed.) *Transforming Children's Lives: The Importance of Early Intervention*. London, Family Policy Studies Centre, pp. 86–90.

Robinson, L (1995) *Psychology for Social Workers: Black Perspectives*. London, Routledge.

——(2001) A conceptual framework for social work practice with black children and adolescents in the United Kingdom. *Journal of Social Work*, 1(2): 165–185.

Rodney, C (2000) Pathways: A model service delivery system. In: NN Singh, JP Leung and AN Singh (eds) (2000) *International Perspectives on Child and Adolescent Mental Health*. London, Elsevier, pp. 421–430.

Rodriguez, J, Cauce, AM and Wilson, L (2002) A conceptual framework of identity formation in a society of multiple cultures. In: KN Dwivedi (ed.) *Meeting the Needs of Ethnic Minority Children*. London, Jessica Kingsley.

Rogers, A, Pilgrim, D and Lacey, R (1993) *Experiencing Psychiatry: Users' Views of Services*. London, Macmillan/Mind.

Rogers, C (1942) *Counselling and Psychotherapy*. Boston MA, Houghton Mifflin.

——(1951) *Client-centred Therapy*. Boston, MA, Houghton Mifflin.

——(1957) The necessary and sufficient conditions of therapeutic personality change. *Journal of Consulting Psychology*, 21: 95–103.

——(1975) Empathic: An unappreciated way of being. *Counselling Psychologist*, 5: 2–10.

Romero, AJ and Roberts, RE (1998) Perception of discrimination and ethnocultural variables in a diverse group of adolescents. *Journal of Adolescence*, 21: 641–656.

Rossi, PH (1992) Assessing family preservation programmes. *Children and Youth Services Review*, 14: 77–97.

Roth, A and Fonagy, P (1996) *What Works for Whom? A Critical Review of Psychotherapy Research*. London, Guilford Press.

Royal College of Psychiatrists (2002) Parent-training programmes for the management of young children with conduct disorders. *Findings from Research*. London, RCP.

Russell, M (1990) *Clinical Social Work: Research and Practice*. Newbury Park, Sage.

Rustin, ME and Quagliata, E (eds) (2000) *Assessment in Child Psychotherapy*. London, Duckworth.

Rutter, M (1985) Resiliance in the face of adversity. *British Journal of Psychiatry*, 147: 598–611.

——(1991) Services for children with emotional disorders. *Young Minds Newsletter*, 9: 1–5.

——(ed.) (1995) *Psychosocial Disturbances in Young People: Challenges for Prevention*. Cambridge: Cambridge University Press.

——(1999a) Preventing anti-social behaviour in young people: The contribution of early intervention. In: R Bayley (ed.) *Transforming Children's Lives: The Importance of Early Intervention*. London, Family Policy Studies Centre.

——(1999b) Resilience concepts and findings: Implications for family therapy. *Journal of Family Therapy*, 21: 119–144.

Rutter, M and Smith, D (1995) *Psychosocial Disorders in Young People*. London, Wiley.

Rutter, M, Hersov, L and Taylor, E (1994) *Child and Adolescent Psychiatry*. Oxford, Blackwell Scientific.

Ryan, M (1999) *The Children Act 1989: Putting it into Practice*. Aldershot, Ashgate.

Saint-Exupery, A (1943) *The Little Prince*. London, Heinemann.

Salmon, D and Hall, C (1999) Working with lesbian mothers: Their healthcare experiences. *Community Practitioner*, 72(12): 396–397.

Saltzberger-Wittenberg, I (1981) *Psycho-Analytic Insight and Relationships: A Kleinian Approach*. London, Routledge.

Sandbaek, M (1999) Children with problems: Focusing on everyday life. *Children and Society*, 13: 106–118.

Sanderson, H (1997) *Peoples Plans and Possibilities: Exploring Person Centred Planning*. Edinburgh, Scottish Health Services.

Sanford, M, Offord, D, Boyle, M, Pearce, A and Racine, Y (1992) Ontario child health study: Social and school impairments in children aged 6–16 years. *Journal of the American Academy of Child and Adolescent Psychiatry*, 31(1): 66–175.

Saravanan, B, Jacob, KS, Prince, M, Bhugra, D and David, AS (2004) Culture and insight revisited. *British Journal of Psychiatry*, 184: 107–109.

Sataro, J, Mullen, PE, Burgess, PM, Wells, DL and Moss, DJ (2004) Impact of child sexual abuse on mental health: Prospective study in males and females. *British Journal of Psychiatry*, 184: 416–421.

Save the Children (2001) *Denied a Future? The Right to Education of Roma/Gypsy Traveller Children in Europe*. London, Save the Children.

Save the Children Fund (1995) *Towards a Children's Agenda*. London, Save the Children.

Savin-Williams, R (2001) A critique of research on sexual minority youth. *Journal of Adolescence*, 24: 5–13.

Sayce, L and Measey, I (1999) Strategies to reduce social exclusion for people with mental health problems. *Psychiatric Bulletin*, 23: 65–67.

Scott, RL and Cordova, JV (2002) The Influence of adult attachment styles on the association between marital adjustment and depressive symptoms. *Journal of Family Psychology*, 16(2): 199–208.

Sebuliba, D and Vostanis, P (2001) Child and adolescent mental health training for primary care staff. *Clinical Child Psychology and Psychiatry*, 6(2): 191–204.

Segal, H (1975) *An Introduction to the Work of Melanie Klein*. London, Hogarth Press.

Shadish, WR, Ragsdale, K, Glaser, RR and Montgomery, LM (1995) The efficacy and effectiveness of marital and family therapy: A perspective from meta-analysis. *Journal of Marital and Family Therapy*, 21: 345–360.

Shah, R (1992) *The Silent Minority – Children with Disabilities in Asian Families*. London, National Children's Bureau.

——(1994) Practice with attitude: Questions on cultural awareness training. *Child Health*. April/May. Ilford, UK, Barnardos.

Shapiro, JP, Welker, CJ and Jacobson, BJ (1997) The youth client satisfaction questionnaire: Development, construct, validation, and factor structure. *Journal of Child Clinical Psychology*, 26: 87–98.

Shardlow, S and Payne, M (1998) *Contemporary Issues in Social Work: Western Europe*. Aldershot, Arena.

Sharkey, P (2000) *The Essentials of Community Care: A Guide for Practitioners*. London, Macmillan.

Sharman, W (1997) *Children and Adolescents with Mental Health Problems*. London, Bailliere Tindall.

Sharpsteen, DJ and Kirkpatrick, LA (1997) Romantic jealousy and adult romantic attachment. *Journal of Personal & Social Psychology*, 72(3): 627–640.

Shaw, I (1996) *Evaluating in Practice*. Aldershot, Arena.

——(1999) *Qualitative Evaluation*. London, Sage.

Sheldon, B and Chilvers, R (2000) *Evidence-based Social Care*. Lyme Regis, Russell House.

Shepherd, S (1994) *Myths and Legends from Around the World*. London, Marshall Editions.

Silberg, J (2001) Child psychiatric symptoms and psychosocial impairment: Relationship and prognostic significance. *British Journal of Psychiatry*, 179: 230–235.

Simonian, SJ, Tarowski, K, Park, A and Bekney, P (1993) Child, parent, and physician perceived satisfaction with pediatric outpatient visits. *Developmental and Behavioral Pediatrics*, 14: 8–12.

Sinclair, R, Garnett, L and Berridge, D (1995) *Social Work and Assessment with Adolescents*. London, National Children's Bureau.

Singh, N, Leung, J and Singh, A (2000) *International Perspectives on Child and Adolescent Mental Health*. Oxford, Elsevier.

Sinha, C (1988) *Language and Representation: A Socio-naturalistic Approach to Human Development*. London, Harvester Wheatsheaf.

Skerrett, D (2000) Social work – a shifting paradigm. *Journal of Social Work Practice*, 14(1): 63–73.

Skinner, B (1953) *Science and Human Behaviour*. New York, Macmillan.

Sluzki, CE (1979) Migration and family conflict. *Family Process*, 18(4): 379–390.

Smaje, C (1995) *Health, Race and Ethnicity: Making Sense of the Evidence*. London, Kings Fund Institute.

Smale, G, Tunson, G, Biehal, N and Marsh, P (1993) *Empowerment Assessment, Care Management and the Skilled Worker*. London, HMSO.

Smale, G, Tuson, G and Statham, D (2000) *Social Work and Social Problems*. Basingstoke, Palgrave.

Smith, S, Rosen, K, McCollum, E, Coleman, J and Herman S (1996) The voices of children: Pre-adolescent children's experiences in family therapy. *Journal of Marital and Family Therapy*, 22: 69–86.

Smith, D, McAra, L and McVie, S (2001) *The Edinburgh Study of Youth Transitions*. Edinburgh, Edinburgh University.

Smoodin, EL (1993) *Animating Culture: Hollywood Cartoons from the Sound Era*. New Brunswick, Rutgers State University.

Snelgrove, S and Hughes, D (2000) Interprofessional relations between doctors and nurses: Perspectives from South Wales. *Journal of Advanced Nursing*, 31(3): 661–667.

Social Exclusion Unit (2002) *Reducing Re-Offending by Ex-Offenders*. London, HMSO.

Social Services Inspectorate (1998) *Partners in Planning: Approaches to Planning Services for Children and their Families*. London, HMSO.

——(2000) *Excellence not Excuses: Inspection of Services for Ethnic Minority Children and Families*. London, HMSO.

Solomos, J (1989) *Race and Racism in Contemporary Britain*. Basingstoke, Macmillan.

Sontag, S (1979) *Illness as Metaphor*. New York, Random House.

Speak, S, Cameron, S, Woods, R and Gilroy, R (1995) *Young Single Mothers: Barriers to Independent Living*. London, Family Policy Studies Centre.

Spencer, MB (1999) Social and cultural influences on school adjustment: The application of an identity-focused cultural ecological perspective. *Educational Psychologist*, 34(1): 43–57.

Spencer, N (1996) Race and ethnicity as determinants of child health: A personal view. *Child Health and Development*, 22(5): 327–345.

SSI (2000) *Excellence not Excuses: Inspection of Services for Ethnic Minority Children and Families*. London, HMSO.

Stahmann, R (2000) Premarital counselling: A focus for family therapy. *Journal of Family Therapy*, 22: 104–116.

Stanley, K (2001) *Cold Comfort: Young Separated Refugees in England*. London, Save the Children.

Stanton, M and Shadish, W (1997) Outcome, attrition and family-couples treatment for drug abuse: A meta-analysis and review of the controlled comparative studies. *Psychological Bulletin*, 122: 170–191.

Statham, J (2000) *Outomes and Effectiveness of Family Support Services: A Research Review*. London, Institute for Education, University of London.

Stephens, J (2002) *The Mental Health Needs of Homeless Young People*. London, Mental Health Foundation.

Stephens, S (ed.) (1995) *Children and the Politics of Culture*. Princeton NJ, Princeton University Press.

Stepney, R and Ford, S (2000) *Social Work Models, Methods, and Theories*. Lyme Regis, Russell House.

Stewart, M and Roter, D (1989) *Communicating with Medical Patients*. London, Sage.

Strickland-Clark, L, Campbell, D and Dallos, R (2000) Children's and adolescent's views on family therapy. *Journal of Family Therapy*, 22: 324–341.

Stuntzer-Gibson, D, Koren, P and DeChillo, N (1995) The youth satisfaction questionnaire: What kids think of services. *Families in Society*, 76: 616–624.

Sue, D, Ivey, A and Penderson, P (1996) *A Theory of Multicultural Counselling and Therapy*. New York, Brooks/Cole Publishing.

Sutton, C (1999) *Helping Families with Troubled Children*. London, Wiley.

——(2000) *Child and Adolescent Behaviour Problems*. Leicester, BPS.

Sveaass, N and Reichelt, S (2001) Refugee families in therapy: From referrals to therapeutic conversations. *Journal of Family Therapy*, 23(2): 119–136.

Swinton, J (2003) *Spirituality and Mental Health Care*. London, Jessica Kingsley.

Sylva, K (1994) School influences on children's development. *Journal of Child Psychology and Psychiatry*, 35(1): 135–170.

Talbani, A and Hasanali, P (2000) Adolescent females between tradition and modernity: Gender role socialization in South Asian immigrant culture. *Journal of Adolescence*, 23: 615–627.

Target, M and Fonagy, P (1996) The psychological treatment of child and adolescent psychiatric disorders. In: A Roth and P Fonagy (eds) *What Works for Whom? A Critical Review of Psychotherapy Research*. New York, The Guilford Press.

Taylor, B and Devine, D (1993) *Assessing Needs and Planning Care in Social Work*. London, Arena.

Taylor, C and White, S (2000) *Practising Reflexivity in Health and Welfare*. Buckingham, Open University Press.

Thoburn, J, Wilding, J and Watson, J (1998) *Children in Need: A Review of Family Support Work in Three Local Authorities*. Norwich, University of East Anglia/Dept of Health.

Thomas, N and O'Kane, C (1998) The ethics of participatory research with children. *Children and Society*, 12: 82–96.

Thompson, N (1995) *Theory and Practice in Health and Social Welfare*. Buckingham, Open University Press.

——(2001) *Anti-discriminatory Practice*. London, Palgrave.

——(2001) *Understanding Social Work*. Basingstoke, Palgrave.

——(2002) *Building the Future: Social Work with Children, Young People and their Families*. Lyme Regis, Russell House Publishing.

Thompson, N and Thompson, S (2002) *Understanding Social Care*. Lyme Regis, Russell House.

Tiller, P (1988) Barn Som sakkyndige informanter (Children as reliable sources of information). In: MK Jensen (ed.) *Interview Med Born* (Interviews with Children). Copenhagen, National Institute of Social Research.

Tillich, P (1963) *Christianity and the Encounter of the World Religions.* Washington, DC, Columbia University Press.

Titmuss, RM (1958) *Essays on the Welfare State.* London, George, Allen & Unwin.

Tomlinson, D and Trew, W (2002) *Equalising Opportunities, Minimising Oppression.* London, Routledge.

TOPPS (2000) *National Occupational Standards for Child Care at Post Qualifying Level.* London, TOPPS.

Townsend, P (1993) *The International Analysis of Poverty.* Hemel Hempstead, Harvester Wheatsheaf.

Treacher, A (1995) Reviewing consumer studies of therapy. In: A Treacher and S Reimers (eds) *Introducing User-Friendly Family Therapy.* London, Routledge, pp. 128–149.

Treseder, P (1997) *Empowering Children and Young People: A Training Manual for Promoting Involvement in Decision-Making.* London, Save the Children.

Trevino, F (1999) Quality of health care for ethnic/racial minority populations. *Ethnicity and Health,* 4(3): 153–164.

Trevithick, P (2000) *Social Work Skills.* Buckingham, Open University Press.

Triseliotis, J (1995) *Teenagers and the Social Work Services.* London, HMSO.

Trotter, J (2000) Lesbian and gay issues in social work with young people: Resilience and success through confronting, conforming and escaping. *British Journal of Social Work,* 30(1): 115–123.

Trowell, J and Bower, M (1995) *The Emotional Needs of Children and their Families.* London, Routledge.

Tseng Yueh-Hung (2002) A lesson in culture. *ELT Journal,* 56(1): 11–21.

Tucker, N and Gamble, N (eds) (2001) *Family Fictions.* London, Continuum.

Tucker, S, Strange, C, Cordeaux, C, Moules, T and Torrance, N (1999) Developing an interdisciplinary framework for the education and training of those working with children and young people. *Journal of Interprofessional Care,* 13(3): 261–270.

Tunstill, J (1996) Family support: Past, present and future challenges. *Child and Family Social Work,* 1: 151–158.

Turn, D and Selig, T (1977) *Of Caterpillars and Cannons.* London, Writers and Readers Publishing Cooperative.

UNICEF (2000) *Child Poverty in Rich Nations.* New York, UNICEF, Innocenti Research Centre.

United Nations (1989) *UN Convention on the Rights of the Child.* New York, United Nations.

Utting, D (1995) *Family and Parenthood: Supporting Families, Preventing Breakdown.* York, Joseph Rowntree Foundation.

Valentine, CA (1976) Poverty and culture. In: P Worsley (ed.) *Problems of Modern Society.* London, Penguin.

Valentine, L and Feinauer, LL (1993) Resilience factors associated with female survivors of childhood sexual abuse. *American Journal of Family Therapy,* 21(3): 216–224.

VanDenBerg, J and Grealish, M (1996) Individualized services and supports through the wraparound process: Philosophy and procedures. *Journal of Child and Family Studies,* 5: 7–21.

Van Ijzendoorn, MH and Sagi, A (1997) Cross-cultural patterns of attachment: Universal and contextual dimensions. In: J Cassidy and PR Shaver (eds) *Handbook of Attachment Theory, Research and Clinical Applications*. Guilford Press, New York.

Vasta, R, Haith, R and Miller, S (1993) *Child Psychology*. New York, John Wiley.

Vicary, D and Andrews, H (2000) Developing a culturally appropriate psychotherapeutic approach with indigenous Australians. *Australian Psychologist*, 35: 181–185.

Vincent, J and Jouriles, E (eds) (2000) *Domestic Violence: Guidelines for Research Informed Practice*. London, Jessica Kingsley.

Von Bertalanffy, L (1968) *General Systems Theory: Foundation, Development, Application*. New York, Brazillier.

Vostanis, P and Cumella, S (1999) *Homeless Children: Problems and Needs*. London, Jessica Kingsley.

Waddell, M (1998) *Inside Lives: Psychoanalysis and the Growth of the Personality*. London, Duckworth.

Walker, S (1995) Family therapy: Concepts, models and applications. *Nursing Times*, 91(38): 36–37.

——(1997) In confidence. *Journal of Community Nursing*, 11(7): 42–44.

——(1999) Child mental health – promoting prevention. *Journal of Child Health Care*, 3(4): 12–16.

——(2001a) Tracing the contours of postmodern social work. *British Journal of Social Work*, 31: 29–39.

——(2001b) Developing child and adolescent mental health services. *Journal of Child Health Care*, 5(2): 71–76.

——(2001c) Consulting with children and young people. *The International Journal of Children's Rights*, 9: 45–56.

——(2001d) Domestic violence – analysis of a community safety alarm system. *Child Abuse Review*, 10: 170–182.

——(2001e) Family support and social work practice: Opportunities for child mental health work. *Social Work and Social Sciences Review*, 9(2): 25–40.

——(2002) Family support and social work practice: Renaissance or retrenchment? *European Journal of Social Work*, 5(1): 43–54.

——(2003a) Interprofessional work in child and adolescent mental health services. *Emotional and Behavioural Difficulties*, 8(3): 189–204.

——(2003b) *Social Work and Child and Adolescent Mental Health*. Lyme Regis, Russell House Publishers.

——(2003c) Social work and child mental health-psychosocial principles in community practice. *British Journal of Social Work*, 33: 673–687.

——(2004) Community work and psychosocial practice – chalk and cheese or birds of a feather? *Journal of Social Work Practice*, 18(2): 161–175.

Walker, S and Akister, J (2004) *Applying Family Therapy – A Guide for Caring Professionals in the Community*. Lyme Regis, Russell House Publishers.

Walker, S and Beckett, C (2004) *Social Work Assessment and Intervention*. Lyme Regis, Russell House Publishers.

Wallace, S, Crown, J, Cox, A and Berger, M (1995) *Epidemiologically Based Needs Assessment: Child and Adolescent Mental Health*. London, Wessex Institute of Public Health.

Watkins, D and Gerong, A (1997) Culture and spontaneous self-concepts among Filipino college students. *Journal of Social Psychology*, 137: 480–488.

Weaver, H and Burns, B (2001) I shout with fear at night – understanding the traumatic experiences of refugee and asylum seekers. *Journal of Social Work*, 1(2): 147–164.

Webb, S (2001) Some considerations on the validity of evidence-based practice in social work. *British Journal of Social Work*, 31: 57–79.

Webster-Stratton, C (1997) Treating children with early-onset conduct problems: A comparison of child and parent training interventions. *Journal of Consulting and Clinical Psychology*, 65(1): 93–109.

Welldon, EV (1988) *Mother, Madonna, Whore: The Idealization and Denigration of Motherhood*. London, Free Association Books.

Westermeyer, J (1995) Cultural aspects of substance abuse and alcoholism. *Psychiatric Clinics of North America*, 18: 589–605.

White, K (ed.) (1999) *Children and Social Exclusion*. London, NCVCCO.

White, M and Epston, D (1990) *Narrative Means to Therapeutic Ends*. New York, W.W. Norton.

Whiting, L (1999) Caring for children of differing cultures. *Journal of Child Health Care*, 3(4): 33–38.

Williams, B, Catell, D, Greenwood, M, LeFevre, S, Murray, I and Thomas, P (1999) Exploring person centredness: User perspectives on a model of social psychiatry. *Health and Social Care in the Community*, 7(6): 475–482.

Williams, R (1997) *The Barefoot Book of Fairies*. Bath, Barefoot Books.

Williams, S and Bendelow, G (1998) *The Lived Body: Sociological Themes, Embodied Issues*. London, Routledge.

Williamson, H and Butler, I (1996) No one ever listens to us. In: C Cloke and M Davies (eds) *Participation and Empowerment in Child Protection*. London, Pitman.

Wilson, J (1999) *Child Focused Practice*. London, Karnac Books.

Winkley, L (1996) *Emotional Problems in Children and Young People*. London, Cassell.

Winnicot, D (1971) *Playing and Reality*. Harmondsworth, Penguin.

Wiseman, RI (1995) *Intercultural Communication Theory*. London, Sage.

Wolbring, G (2001) Surviving eugenics. In: M Priestly (ed.) *Disability and the Life Course*. Cambridge, Cambridge University Press.

Woodcock, J (2001) Threads from the labyrinth. *Journal of Family Therapy*, 23(2): 136–155.

Woodhead, M (1997) Psychology and the cultural construction of children's needs. In: A James and A Prout (eds) *Constructing and Reconstructing Childhood*. London, Falmer Press.

——(1998) Understanding child development in the context of children's rights. In: C Cunninghame (ed.) *Realising Children's Rights*. London, Save the Children.

Woods, M and Hollis, F (1990) *Casework: A Psychological Process*, 2nd edn. New York, Random House.

World Health Organisation (1992) *International Classification of Diseases (ICD 10)*. New York, World Health Organisation.

——(2001) World Health Day. *Mental Health: Stop Exclusion-Dare to Care*. Geneva, WHO.

Wright, C, Weekes, D, McGlaughlin, A and Webb, D (1998) Masculine discourses enter education and the construction of black male identities amongst African Caribbean youth. *British Journal of Sociology*, 49(2): 241–260.

Yelloly, M (1980) *Social Work Theory and Psychoanalysis*. New York, Van Nostrand.

Yeo, SS (2003) Bonding and attachment of Australian Aboriginal children. *Child Abuse Review*, 12: 292–304.

Young, K and Haynes, R (1993) Assessing population needs in primary health care: The problem of GOP attachments. *Journal of Interprofessional Care*, 7(1): 15–27.

Young, M and Wilmott, P (1957) *Family and Kinship in East London*. London, Routledge & Kegan Paul.

Young Minds (2001) *Briefing on the NSF for Mental Health*. London, Young Minds.

Youth Justice Board (2002) *Building on Success – YJB Annual Review*. London, HMSO.

Zavirsek, D (1995) Social innovations: A new paradigm in Central European Social Work. *International Perspectives in Social Work*. University of Ljubljana, 1: 106–121.

Zipes, J (1983) *Fairy Tales and the Art of Subversion*. London, Heinemann.

——(1997) *Happily Ever After: Fairy Tales, Children and the Culture Industry*. New York, Routledge.

INDEX

Aboriginal, 110
  children, 130
  communities, 149
  stories, 149
Abuse, 1
  human rights, 11, 33
  emotional, 57
  double, 85
  drug, 121
  sexual, 142
  and neglect, 159
  racist, 63, 88, 159
adolescent, 12, 14–16, 33, 41, 53, 69, 92, 99, 147
Africa, 11, 13, 78
African–American, 79, 93, 99, 130, 137
African-Caribbean, 8, 22, 123, 159
alcohol, 11, 42, 66
ambivalent, 11, 73, 87, 147
American, 20, 27, 42, 46, 66, 79, 93, 97, 99, 123, 130, 131, 137, 155, 157
analytical, 44, 63, 87, 104
anorexia, 71–3, 75, 128, 145
anti-discriminatory, 3, 4, 26, 61, 62, 78, 85, 99, 117
anthropological, 5, 9, 170
anxiety, 3, 8, 18, 27, 30, 44, 59, 64, 65, 82, 83, 98, 100, 105, 119, 126, 128, 143, 146, 158, 159, 173
Arabian, 140, 143
Asian, 22, 42, 60, 82, 92, 99, 100, 158, 159
Assessment, 4, 5, 10, 15, 16, 24, 26, 28, 31, 33, 34, 35, 39, 57, 58, 60, 62, 82, 85, 88, 92, 93, 96–106, 109–111, 117, 118, 134, 160, 163, 175
assimilationist, 158
asylum, 2, 10, 12, 22, 27, 34, 53, 59, 81, 82, 88, 89, 95, 133, 159

attachment, 18, 57, 68, 69, 71, 85, 95, 101, 105, 109–18, 130, 131, 135, 169
attitudes, 7, 10, 12, 28, 40, 44, 63, 68, 69, 72, 74, 79, 80, 98, 105, 119, 133, 154, 158, 168
Australia, 110, 149
authentic, 2, 61, 67, 91, 105

backgrounds, 3, 7, 10–12, 26, 31, 32, 39, 40, 87, 93, 99, 130, 150, 154, 168
Bali, 146
Bangladeshi, 8, 13, 82, 86, 92
behaviour, 7, 9, 10, 12, 14, 15, 18, 20, 21, 25, 27–9, 34, 36, 37, 40, 43–8, 53, 56–7, 60, 62–4, 66, 74, 80, 89, 91, 93, 95–100, 102, 105–7, 110, 112, 114, 117, 125, 127, 128, 133, 134, 137, 143–5, 158–63, 165, 167, 173, 176
beliefs, 2, 7, 14, 23, 26, 28, 32, 39, 42, 43, 46, 51, 52, 57, 58, 60, 61, 63, 64, 66, 72, 74, 78, 79, 85, 86, 93, 94, 98, 99, 105, 119, 120, 121–2, 125–31, 133, 134, 137, 140, 142, 146, 161
biological, 12, 39, 110, 112, 120
birthplace, 11
black, 2, 5, 8, 10–12, 22, 25, 38–43, 64, 69, 79–83, 85–8, 93, 94, 97–100, 112, 131, 157–9, 172, 176
Brazil, 149
Britain, 11, 13, 34, 78, 82, 85, 89, 159
Buddhist, 146
Bulimia, 73

Canada, 13, 34, 69, 92, 159
categorisation, 9, 111
certainty, 20, 33, 36, 52, 53, 108, 120, 122, 125, 127, 136, 170, 173, 177
child, 99, 127, 132

children, 35, 62, 99–101, 129, 151, 154, 159, 164, 165, 169
child abuse, 11, 34, 63
Chinese, 71, 72, 98
Christian, 30, 122–4, 131, 146
citizen, 11, 62, 78, 81–4, 109, 117, 175
class, 12, 27, 47, 61, 71, 78, 79, 86, 94, 154
collective, 6, 12, 60, 80, 84, 86
colonialism, 3, 9
community, 3, 5, 6, 8, 9, 12, 23, 24, 29, 30, 39, 41, 43, 49, 72, 73, 78, 82–4, 88, 92, 93, 95, 103, 130, 133, 136, 159
competent, 23, 115
confusion, 10, 11, 17, 61, 78, 85, 174
consciousness, 9, 12, 20, 30, 51, 54, 80, 81, 124, 149, 151
construction, 6, 14, 35, 51, 52, 60–2, 109, 140, 155
contain, 58–60, 68, 71, 73, 87, 90, 102, 104, 119, 132, 135, 138, 140, 144, 151, 152, 155, 156
context, 47, 80, 113
counter-transference, 105
Cree, 69
cultural, 7, 23, 80, 83, 89, 115, 134, 142, 174
culture, 2, 5, 7–9, 10–11, 12, 20, 41, 108, 125, 159
customs, 3, 7, 12, 25, 39, 57, 66, 67, 74, 90, 122

defence, 42, 44, 53, 61, 70, 73, 91, 105, 121, 128, 142, 149, 152, 155
depression, 44, 59, 66, 97, 106, 126, 130, 132, 143, 158, 159, 163, 176
development, 14, 17–19, 50, 83, 127, 129
difference, 20, 32
discriminatory, 5, 12, 38, 63, 74, 83, 103, 157, 175
diversity, 9, 10, 13, 20, 23, 25, 29, 36, 51, 53, 55, 69, 82, 88, 93, 99–101, 109, 117, 119, 126, 136, 140, 159, 163, 175, 176
divorce, 11, 49, 57, 72, 77, 108, 150
domestic violence, 47, 50, 54, 63, 92, 100, 131, 160, 165
drugs, 10, 11, 42, 66, 74, 85, 97, 106
dual, 11, 12, 81

Eastern, 27, 61, 89, 93, 99, 124, 130, 137
eating disorder, 71, 73, 74, 143, 152
economically, 9, 13, 78

emigration, 10
emotional, 3, 4, 8, 10, 14, 15–18, 23, 26, 28, 30, 31, 33, 34, 36, 43, 48, 50, 60, 69, 73, 82, 93, 95–8, 102, 125, 134, 141, 147, 151, 158, 160, 162–5, 168, 172
empowerment, 26, 61, 86, 131
engage, 3, 7, 14, 20, 28, 32, 36, 51, 53, 62–5, 70, 84, 85, 87–9, 92–4, 98, 105, 117, 126, 140, 142, 144, 145, 154, 155, 161, 169, 171, 177
environment, 6, 8, 12, 14, 17, 28, 29, 33, 37, 39, 42, 55, 56, 62, 66, 68, 73, 92, 99, 100–2, 111, 117, 118, 120, 129, 130, 132, 133, 134, 149, 158, 160, 163–4, 167, 173
evidence, 157, 173
ethnic, 6, 11, 12, 25
eugenics, 12
Eurocentric, 16, 26, 31, 61, 90, 105, 140, 157, 164, 176
Europe, 12, 13, 21, 30, 40, 69, 78, 79, 89
exploitation, 6, 10, 21, 24, 97, 109, 117
extroversion, 16

fairy tales, 5, 59, 139, 141–4, 146–9, 153–5
faith, 99, 120, 121, 125, 128–30, 140, 141
family, 6, 45, 112, 127
female, 12, 41, 49, 152, 172
feminist, 50, 51, 54, 55, 63, 90, 92, 109
folklore, 140
France, 13, 78, 126

gay, 8, 57, 90, 175
gender, 12, 35, 41, 50, 51, 54, 56, 63, 71, 73, 74, 78, 90, 92, 97, 115, 154, 166–8, 172
genetic, 11, 12, 14, 37, 66, 97, 101, 120
globalisation, 9, 21, 22, 30, 80, 94, 109, 155, 156, 175
Greek, 124, 139
grief, 27, 150, 159

heritage, 8, 11, 12, 49, 81, 122, 137
Hindu, 30, 124, 133, 146
Homophobia, 8, 30, 62
Hong Kong, 34, 71, 159
hysteria, 13

identification, 4, 90, 98
identity, 21, 36
immigration, 13, 22, 40, 81, 82, 126
imperial, 3, 5, 9, 80, 136

inclusion, 2, 24, 31, 78, 83, 94, 165, 169
Indian, 20, 66, 69, 82, 92, 98, 158
indigenous, 6, 7, 22, 26, 31, 80, 86, 94, 127, 130
inequalities, 9, 12, 14, 76, 109
innate, 12, 112
insight, 40, 43, 49, 60–2, 71, 97, 102, 105, 132, 137, 145, 152, 156, 162
internal, 6, 11, 14, 20, 29, 30, 37, 38, 42–4, 53, 59–61, 69, 71, 73, 74, 77, 80, 84–6, 90, 94, 95, 99, 121, 142–5, 163, 166, 176
internally, 11, 73, 143
international, 9, 21–3, 29, 175
interpersonal, 23, 24, 31, 42, 44, 56, 57, 114, 133, 137
interplay, 15, 110, 117, 134, 138
interpretation, 6, 8, 15, 20, 28, 32, 38, 40, 50–2, 60–2, 69, 92, 93, 107, 109, 117, 126, 131, 133, 136, 150, 158, 175
intrinsic, 70, 99, 126, 128, 131, 151
Iraqi, 27
Islam, 119, 122, 124
Israel, 69, 145

Japan, 69
jewish, 145, 152, 153

language, 9, 12, 19, 25, 28, 43, 52, 60, 65, 68, 78, 90, 107, 109, 120, 128, 175
lesbian, 8, 57, 90, 175
legends, 5, 121, 139, 140–3, 145–6, 147–8, 149–50, 152, 154, 155, 156
linguistic, 11, 87, 88
loss, 59, 61, 68–73, 84, 88, 89, 95, 105, 112, 130, 150, 154, 159, 173

Malaysia, 34, 159
Male, 12, 49, 50, 51, 61, 63, 105, 152, 172
Maori, 127
marginalised, 10, 91, 109, 117
masculine, 63, 73, 74
mental health, 11, 12, 14–16, 21, 23, 24, 26, 30, 33–6, 41–3, 45, 53, 59–61, 72, 82, 84, 87, 88, 90, 93–5, 97–100, 106–8, 110, 116, 118, 121, 127, 128, 130, 132–3, 137, 158–60, 164, 166, 167
mentally ill, 11
methods, 3, 5, 7, 8, 10, 11, 15, 26, 42, 45, 46, 57, 62, 76, 79, 122, 136, 158, 162–4, 166, 168–2, 175

migration, 2, 8, 30, 40, 79, 89
minority, 2, 8, 12, 22, 25, 26, 30, 31, 34, 36–8, 40, 41, 42, 53, 56, 60, 74, 80, 82, 85, 86, 88, 93, 95, 97, 98, 100, 101, 105, 112, 117, 122, 137, 145, 157, 158, 163, 166, 172, 175, 176
mixed, 11, 12, 43, 81, 89, 122, 149, 165, 168
monoculture, 13
monotherapeutic, 7
Muslim, 29, 30, 86, 120, 163
multi-cultural, 2, 4, 10, 15, 25, 30, 40, 41, 42, 53, 55, 86, 97, 136, 158, 160, 176
myths, 5, 46, 121, 129, 139–42, 145, 146, 148, 149, 150, 152, 154–6

nationality, 25, 81, 82
native, 9, 122, 149
Native American, 66, 93, 99, 130, 137
nature, 7, 9, 14, 33, 38, 49, 52, 68, 73, 81, 93, 97, 107, 114, 118, 119, 121, 123, 126, 128, 133, 140, 141, 145, 146, 153, 161, 169, 171
Navajos, 148
Neglected, 3, 5, 10, 51, 98, 102, 107, 162
neurosis, 128
neuroticism, 16
New Zealand, 127
normative, 14, 16, 29, 45, 46, 103, 112
nurture, 14, 89

orthodox, 10, 14, 15, 23, 29, 30, 35, 36, 44–6, 50, 51, 55, 71, 81, 108, 120, 122–7, 134, 136, 141, 162
other, 13, 29, 64, 98, 125

Pakistani, 30, 70, 82, 92
para-suicide, 8
parents, 6, 11, 17, 21, 26, 36, 38, 45, 57, 62, 64, 78, 83, 86, 88, 92, 95, 106, 111, 127, 133, 139, 141, 143, 151, 158, 163, 165, 169, 170
perception, 14, 15, 16, 17, 25, 27, 29, 43, 45, 46, 62, 63, 67, 68, 89, 97, 99, 103, 106, 107, 116, 145, 158, 163, 165–8, 170–5, 177
personal, 5, 11, 14, 17, 22, 24, 29, 34, 36, 41–3, 47, 49, 53, 58, 63, 65, 69, 84, 89–92, 104, 105, 109, 117, 119, 129, 132, 133, 159, 162, 167, 174, 175
Philippines, 34, 159

political, 3, 9, 63, 64, 74, 78, 80, 86, 94, 123, 137
poverty, 2, 10, 11, 38, 41, 66, 78, 79, 82, 91, 94, 131, 148
power, 7, 12, 21, 26, 30, 36, 37, 38, 41, 47, 50, 53, 54, 59, 61–3, 74, 87, 90, 104, 108, 109, 117, 120, 122, 123, 135–7, 141, 143, 146–7, 150, 158, 165–7, 170, 176
projection, 41, 80
psyche, 58, 71, 120, 121, 173
psychodynamic, 3, 4, 5, 15, 24, 26, 30, 32–4, 37–9, 43, 44, 46, 47, 50–2, 54–60, 62–3, 67, 70, 73, 74, 77, 83, 84, 86, 87, 91, 92, 94, 95, 101, 105, 106, 115, 116, 123, 134, 137, 160, 162, 173
psychological, 3, 6–10, 12, 15, 21, 26, 29, 30, 33, 34, 38, 39, 42–4, 53, 55, 58, 60, 61, 70, 71, 73, 76, 79, 82, 83, 88, 89, 93, 95, 96, 97, 99, 117, 119, 120–2, 126, 130, 132, 134, 135, 137, 138, 141, 142, 143, 155, 159, 164
psychosocial, 17, 26, 31, 36, 38, 97, 101, 116, 117, 119, 126

racial, 9, 11, 12, 14, 40, 81, 86, 87
racism, 2, 5, 8, 11, 12, 22, 26, 30, 41, 62, 63, 64, 66, 79, 80, 82, 86, 87, 97, 98, 100, 110, 117, 158, 172, 175
Rastafarianism, 22, 125
reflection, 20, 32, 55, 87, 91, 120, 131, 134, 138, 147
reflective, 5, 15, 24, 31, 62, 90, 141, 162, 168
refugee, 2, 10, 12, 22, 34, 53, 59, 70, 81, 88, 89, 95, 133, 159
relationships, 4, 9, 17, 18, 20, 35, 50, 58, 64, 89, 95, 101, 109, 114, 120, 134, 162, 167, 170, 177
religion, 119, 121, 123, 130
research, 161
resilience, 8, 33, 53, 88, 101, 102
resistance, 20, 37, 46, 65, 93, 95, 137, 167
rights, 70, 80, 81, 82, 86, 87, 91, 94, 96, 103, 108, 120, 133, 135, 165, 170
risk, 4, 10, 11, 12, 33, 36, 41–3, 53, 59, 73, 84, 89, 91–3, 100, 102, 106, 107, 120, 128, 155, 162
Russia, 124, 148

safety, 10, 11, 84, 112, 114, 119
security, 11, 17, 100, 111
sexual, 18, 23, 33, 39, 71, 90, 91, 121, 139, 160, 169
Sikh, 30
Sioux, 20
social, 51, 78, 80, 91, 113
social exclusion, 78, 79, 83, 89, 128
society, 3, 9, 38, 52, 54, 63, 71, 92, 97, 117, 122, 124, 126, 148, 157, 159, 171
sociological, 2, 3, 35, 44
South America, 131, 148
South East Asia, 13, 146
spirituality, 5, 93, 99, 119–22, 125–9, 130–1, 132–3, 134–7
status, 2, 12, 39, 70, 104, 128, 152, 167, 170, 176
stereotyping, 12, 63, 80, 93, 159
strength, 5, 14, 37, 58, 62, 79, 81, 93, 96, 99, 100, 112, 122, 130, 137, 151, 170
stress, 5, 9, 11, 25, 28, 33, 34, 38–42, 48, 56, 64, 65, 68, 70, 72, 74, 88, 93, 95, 97, 98, 101, 102, 104, 108, 132, 136, 159, 160
subculture, 29
substance misuse, 66, 74
suicide, 8, 90, 127, 140
supervision, 15, 32, 46, 47, 77, 104, 105, 161
support, 5, 8, 11, 23, 33, 39, 40, 46, 70, 72, 73, 77, 82, 83, 84, 86, 88, 90, 92–5, 101, 106, 107, 116, 118, 128, 137, 159, 162, 163, 168, 169, 171, 174, 175
symbolic, 59, 73, 143
synchronise, 3, 52, 54, 62
synthesis, 26, 56, 59, 60, 67, 74, 104, 130
systemic, 44, 46, 111
systems, 9, 21, 26, 28, 39, 43–5, 51, 86, 93, 112–13, 116, 118, 120, 121, 130, 137, 165

tales, 5, 133, 140, 141–4, 146–7, 149, 151, 153–5
therapeutic, 64, 144
therapy, 6, 8, 45, 52, 83, 108, 134, 151
transcendent, 58, 121, 134, 135
transference, 68, 87, 105

UK, 11, 13, 44, 78, 81, 82, 88, 98, 126, 127, 131
USA, 8, 13, 34, 44, 124, 159
understanding, 2, 8, 9, 16, 20, 23, 25, 27, 30, 32, 33, 48, 55, 69, 71, 73, 83, 86, 89, 93, 95, 97, 99, 103, 109, 111, 122, 133, 134, 167
unemployment, 8, 38, 41, 66, 85, 89
universal, 10, 14, 23, 25, 33, 34, 35, 40, 53, 76, 103, 124, 126, 149

welfare, 10, 21, 22, 26, 31, 70, 83, 91, 109, 127, 164, 175

Western, 4, 7–10, 20–2, 55, 56, 60–1, 64, 68–72, 74, 75, 80, 93, 95, 98, 99, 120, 125–7, 130, 136, 137, 140, 147, 155–7, 175, 176
White, 2, 5, 11, 12, 16, 20, 22–4, 38–42, 55, 61, 64, 80–2, 86, 87, 97, 98, 136, 137, 145, 149, 158, 164

xenophobia, 13

young people, 20, 151, 169